THE LEGAL MIND AND THE PRESIDENCY

by
Albert Lebowitz

© 2012 Albert Lebowitz
All Rights Reserved.

No part of this publication may be reproduced, stored in a retrieval system, or transmitted, in any form or by any means, electronic, mechanical, photocopying, recording, or otherwise, without the written permission of the author.

First published by Dog Ear Publishing
4010 W. 86th Street, Ste H
Indianapolis, IN 46268
www.dogearpublishing.net

ISBN: 978-1-4575-1798-3

This book is printed on acid-free paper.

Printed in the United States of America

For Nay, Joel, Judith, Drew, Julie,
Josh, Graham, Mouse, Rosie
– what a lovely crew without a lawyer among them.

CONTENTS

INTRODUCTION 1

PART ONE—LAWYER RULE - SKEPTICISM IN THE PRESIDENCY

1. A Bird's Eye View of Lawyer Rule-Skeptical Presidents 12

2. Father and Son: John and Quincy Adams 14

3. Self-Inflicted War with Mexico: James K. Polk 26

4. A Great Life and Death: Abraham Lincoln 34

5. An American Tragedy: Richard Milhaus Nixon 47

PART TWO—LAWYER MORALISM IN THE PRESIDENCY

6. A Bird's Eye View of Lawyer Moralist Presidents.....................66

7. Words Speak Louder Than Actions: Thomas Jefferson 68

8. The Bank is Trying to Kill Me, But I Will Kill It:
   Andrew Jackson...75

9. The Man Who Would Save the World: Woodrow Wilson 82

10. The Fox and the Lion: Franklin Delano Roosevelt..................92

PART THREE—LAWYER FORMALISM IN THE PRESIDENCY

11. A Birdseye View of Lawyer Formalist Presidents.....................114

12. Founding Fathers: James Madison and James Monroe 117

13. The Little Magician: Martin Van Buren 123

14. The Dough-Faces: Fillmore, Pierce, Buchanan 127

15. The Golden Age: Hayes, Arthur, Cleveland,
B. Harrison, McKinley...132

16. The Golden Age's MVP: Grover Cleveland 135

17. Twentieth-Century Formalists: Taft, Coolidge, Ford.............138

18. Anti-Intellectualism and the Popular Distaste for Lawyers ...148

19. The Ivy Leaguers: Bill Clinton and Barack Obama 155

20. The Comeback Kid: Bill Clinton 157

    I.   Of Birth and Death—Bill and Daddy...........................158

    II.   The Economy, Stupid 163

    III.   Foreign Affairs...166

21. The Spirit of 1787: Barack Obama

    I.   The Year is 1787...170

    II.   The Year is 2012 176

Notes 183

INTRODUCTION

As if afraid to look directly at the sun, Americans, on the whole, have consistently faced away from a recognition of what their revered Rule of Law, their Constitution, entails. This has led to the Janus-faced picture which not only they, but the rest of the world, have of the American and his self-congratulatory way of life. This dualism consists of constant overt claims of liberty, equality, and democracy, cradled in moral rhetoric, poised against a fierce, largely unspoken commitment to the burdensome rule of lawyers and their perpetuation of the Rule of Reason, deified and made sacrosanct in the name of the untouchable: no American, president, or jobless, is 'above the law.' The genius of America is a paradox; it is not only a democracy (political equality), but a judicial supremacy, administered and tended by lawyers; reason guides entry into an eminent class prescribed by a democratic society.

One of the many strange fallouts of the dualism is that while American intellectuals consider much of de Tocqueville's early nineteenth century observations in Democracy in America unerring and applicable even today, they, especially after Watergate, tend to join the bulk of their countrymen in neglecting the truth of his observation that the rule of lawyerdom is indispensable to the survival of democracy in America: "When the American people are intoxicated by passion or carried away by the impetuosity of their ideas, they are checked and stopped by the almost invisible influence of their legal counselors."

The virulence of the storm generated by Watergate cannot be explained simply by a general dislike of Nixon and his lack of charm—a desire to 'get' him, as by an irresistible urge to wipe the smile off Reagan's magic-lantern face or to darken Clinton's 'bubba' image. It is not enough, either, to deal in sweeping moralistic outrage at men in high political places committing crimes or engaging in extra-marital sex. A great deal has been made of the qualitative distinction between the primitive venality of prior public scandals and, compounding the burglaries, Watergate's sophisticated invasions of privacy and obstructions of justice; and, of course, these actions are particularly indefensible when they are committed by presidents. It is not even enough, although it approaches the key to the violence of the reaction, to condemn the Watergate crowd for having, perhaps permanently, corroded the faith of the American people in their ability to elect honorable men to the presidency—which implies the deterioration of their faith in the democratic process itself.

It should be remembered, too, that the dismay at the cluster of crimes and abuse of presidential power that became identified as Watergate did not become pervasive among the American people until they had been led, through televised Congressional hearings and intensive newspaper and news magazine coverage, to accept the 'horror' of a president's obstruction of justice. For, until they were so educated, to most Americans, forced to accept among them the possibility of monsters like Manson or Calley, of wholesale practices of murder and rape from sea to shining sea, the obstruction of justice in punishing burglars of then unoccupied premises, seemed as unreal and nominal a crime against society as insider trading.

There is little question that the central force of the fury evoked by Nixon in Watergate was generated by the idea that he might think he was above the law, and there is even less question that the fury originated with, and was propagated by, Nixon's fellow lawyers in the Senate, the House, on the Supreme Court, in the Special Prosecutor's office—by lawyers everywhere. Lawyers were genuinely horrified at the idea, not that a president, a human being after all, might commit a crime, but that Nixon, a lawyer, might presume he could be above other lawyers (the law), and, even worse, that he employed mostly lawyers to enforce this idea.

The drama of Watergate is, of course, a legal drama, and it was played out by lawyers operating in courtrooms and in congressional hearings that were converted into courtrooms. Lawyers like Sam Ervin, masquerading as senators and congressmen, along with their hired guns, such as Chief Counsel Sam Dash, controlled the hearings as effectively as Chief Judge Sirica and Special Prosecutor Jaworski in the courtroom. The constant thread tying together the unrelenting accusations of constitutional violations and abuse of presidential authority is that Nixon, by merciless exposure of a lawyer gone wrong, was threatening the ultimate American rule, not of the military-industrial complex, but of the lawyer clan. And this was a threat to the existence of America as we know it, as de Tocqueville, Madison, Lincoln, Coolidge, Franklin Roosevelt, and, sadly, Richard Nixon, knew it. What had to be done immediately was done: the lawyers cleaned up their act by replacing a discredited lawyer with one who 'could not be bought' — Gerald A. Ford.

It is the lawyer rule that has insisted upon, and kept inviolate, individual rights against the, at times, terrible pressure of moral impulses, equally necessary to the American way of life, toward political liberty and equality. Lawyer rule, navigating the course, takes the majority of the American people where it wants to go—but only so long as the destination is not too astray from reason—and this distinguishes the successful United States experience from the disasters of the French Revolution and experiments in Latin America. Nixon, a man later accused of dictatorial propensities, in a discussion with Fidel Castro early in both men's careers, points up the vital tension between democracy's 'voice of the people' and rights enforced by the lawyer society of advocates and judges: "(Castro) went into considerable detail...with regard to the reasons for not holding elections, emphasizing particularly that "the people did not want elections because the elections in the past had produced bad government... (Castro) used the same argument that he was simply reflecting the will of the people in justifying the executions of war criminals and his overruling the acquittal of Batista's aviators. In fact he seemed to be obsessed with the idea that it was his responsibility to carry out the will of the people whatever it might appear to be at a particular time... I tried to impress upon him the fact that while we believe in majority rule that even a majority can be tyrannous and that there are certain individual rights which a majority should never have the power to destroy."

What Nixon failed to do in his argument with Castro illustrates what America has consistently failed to do in its foreign policy; he conjoined, instead of contrasted, the American employment of free elections and lawyer rule. "I used the same argument," says Nixon, "with regard to freedom of the press, the right to a fair trial before an impartial judge and jury..." This same confusion led Nixon toward blind devotion to Woodrow Wilson and his quixotic insistence on 'self-determination' of nations too weak or muddled to determine much of anything. It led him into embracing the will of a majority of the people while twisting and turning in agony to escape its stranglehold on his reason.

I chanced, some years ago, to be at dinner with a Mexican diplomat. During the dinner conversation, he commented upon an American State Department official's typical impatience with a Mexican civil servant's emphasis on what the American called 'legalisms.' I ventured to suggest that this consistent depreciation of law in American foreign policy has invariably created suspicion and scorn in other countries: we have, with a great deal of self-deception, been trying to 'sell' the world a Jeffersonian vision of 'liberty, equality, and fraternity' instead of the actuality of an American democracy governed by the law. Upon more serious reflection, I have not abandoned the notion.

What America really has to 'sell' is not equality—a rhetorical ideal unfortunately projected much more persuasively by the French Revolutionists and their successors, the Russians and Chinese, who can proudly point to the overthrow of their existing upper classes, and conveniently ignore the creation of a new upper class of bureaucrats—but its reverence for a judicial system, reasonably fair and impartial in the enforcement of that Bill of Rights which, as Madison long ago understood, would otherwise be only a 'parchment barrier.' It is vital to a true understanding of the American system, that this judicial law revered by Americans not be confused, as it so often is by Europeans and South Americans, with their concept of the law, an amalgam of arbitrary, discriminatory, and unappealable legislative statutes, executive decrees, and bureaucratic regulations—tyrannies of the one (Hitler), the few (the *Politboro*), or even the majority (the French Revolutionists). The ultimate American product is a rights-oriented legal caste entrusted by the American people with enforcement of the judicial last word.

Along with de Tocqueville, one comes to the inescapable conclusion that democracy, the American form as a constitutional republic at any rate, cannot exist successfully for very long without an enlightened and educated lawyer group to fuel its checks, to provide its balances. The true checks and balances are not between the executive, legislative, and judicial branches—these are largely managed by fellow-travelling lawyers reaching out for reason, or at least reasonableness, among the many moralities poked at them—but between those in government who are attuned to the people's 'voice' and those, mainly legal-minded, who hold out for exercises of a counter-ing reason. This, then, is a book about the American legal mind and the presidency and what, when they are conjoined, makes them tick. Two of the last three presidents are lawyers. Twenty-seven of forty-four presidents have been legal-minded.

The legal mind cannot be viewed simply as a logic-powered vessel moving along inexorably in a single, deep channel. From the outside looking in, the polemics, depending on the concerns of the viewer, have been characterized in various other ways, usually as one of two extremes. Legal minded presidents have been labeled radical or conservative, political or apolitical, moral or amoral, strict or liberal construers of the Constitution, of presidential powers, of Congressional powers, of Supreme Court powers, of aggregated Federal powers, of states' powers, idealist or pragmatist, activist or pacifist, protector of property rights or personal rights, party man or political maverick, and on and on. The problem with these characterizations is that they cloud rather than clarify any attempt at understanding a president's form of legal mindedness and the resulting impact on the presidency.

The consistency with which moral, political, economic, or social expectations of a legal minded president's behavior are frustrated leads to the conclusion that it is usually not so much a president's politics, but the way he thinks that resists fluctuation and shapes a harmonious pattern of his career. And, as H.L.A. Hart, in The Concept of Law, graphically and succinctly indicates, the legal mind operates between polarities of formalism and rule-skepticism (with, I suggest, an aberrant excursion into moralism): "Legal theory as formalism or conceptualism consists in an attitude to verbally formulate rules which both seeks to disguise and to minimize the need for such choice, once the general rule has been laid down. One way of doing this is to freeze the meaning of the rule so that its general terms must have the same meaning in every case where its application is in question. To secure this we may fasten on certain features present in the plain case and insist that these are both necessary and sufficient to bring anything which has them within the scope of the rule, whatever other features it may have or lack, and whatever may be the social consequence of applying the rule in this way."... "The rule-sceptic is sometimes a disappointed absolutist; he has found that rules are not all they would be in a formalist's heaven, or in a world where men

5

were like gods and could anticipate all possible combinations of fact, so that open-texture was not a necessary feature of rules. The sceptic's conception of what it is for a rule to exist, may thus be an unattainable ideal, and when he discovers that it is not attained by what are called rules, he expresses his disappointment by the denial that there are, or can be, any rules."

The rule of lawyers, to which I refer, has not, of course, gone unchallenged. The United States is a democracy and anyone—haberdashers, tailors, businessmen, peanut farmers, engineers, actors, generals—can be, and has been, increasingly in the twentieth century, elected to the presidency. These challenges, however, have generally been diverted from the central core of control lodged in the judiciary and its power, without reprisal, to void the acts and actions of the other two branches. The presidents, lawyers all, of course, ironically most united in their distaste for lawyer rule—such as Jefferson, Jackson, Wilson, Franklin Roosevelt—as lawyer moralists, knew that it was the judiciary they must dominate if their brand of democracy, in all its idealized perfectibility, was to reign.

It is arguable that lawyers are miscast as legislators in the American Federal government, at least if they are present in considerable numbers. The natural tendency of any large, democratic, political body is to slow down decision-making processes and, certainly, the leisurely, meandering, cautious pace of much Congressional debate and decision making emphasizes this quality. Lawyers, particularly formalists as Congressmen, may very well be instrumental in further slowing Congress down, to the point of ineffectiveness.

Congress, given a strong and stable caste of lawyers in the judiciary and presidency, consisting of elected officials, serves a democracy well as a non-legal-minded crucible in which the American people can test their passions and prejudices, in which conflicting, impetuous moralities can hammer out compromises as Acts of Congress. Lawyers and the exercise of reason would seem to get in the way of this self-regulating process of moralities cutting each other down to size. They seem to function much better in their natural role of weighing the consequences of congressional action, after the fact, by way of presidential veto or Supreme Court decision.

It is in the presidency, where lawyers tended to fade in the twentieth-century stretch, that their value to the American system has been seriously questioned. Arguments can be mounted against them: the presidency should be a 'jolly pulpit' where the president can speak in moral terms to all the people; the president should be capable of making bold and quick decisions, and lawyers are painfully slow in coming to decisions; there are enough officious legal intermeddlers on the Supreme Court—the people need someone to speak out in a different, more dramatic, and dashing voice, someone, perhaps, like Teddy Roosevelt or Jack Kennedy.

These criticisms hit the mark, certainly, and yet I believe that even the criticisms can be turned into virtues; far from being dubious presidential fare, the presidents trained in the law, particularly the formalists, have fitted the role of the presidency. Any executive placement agency seeking required presidential skills of negotiation, bargaining, diplomacy, verbal skills, reasoning powers, and knowledge of governmental and political processes, complemented by a series of ethical commandments, such as promise-keeping, honoring confidential communications, and cautiously and painstakingly seeking the best interests of the client (the American people), would on the whole agree.

Jimmy Carter's reaction to Menachem Begin's delay in signing the Camp David accords, at least as reported by Victor Lasky, is markedly different: "Carter insisted on a peace settlement ... by December 17, 1978. But it was not to be. And Carter was described by aides as 'livid' at Begin for being 'intransigent.' All Begin (a lawyer) wanted was to make certain that his ... nation's security would not be threatened by hastily signed agreements. Carter called this 'quibbling' over 'technicalities' and 'legalisms.'"

Historians tend to deprecate the 'caretaker' president, but this, either on logical grounds or the more emotional one of devotion to democratic principles, is difficult to understand. The lawyer formalist is the typical caretaker—Cleveland, Hayes, Taft, Arthur, Buchanan, Pierce, Fillmore, Clinton, Obama—he is passionate about individual rights, he resists controversy, and especially war, he is devoted to the Constitution and intent upon not exceeding its bounds as president. Democracy is safe with him even though he is a member of de Tocqueville's lawyer ruling caste. He should be a shoo-in for greatness in the presidency by these criteria, but instead, he is delegated to mediocrity, or worse, by most historians. Aggressiveness in the presidential personality, the burning drive for greatness in the Roosevelts, Wilson, Kennedy, Lincoln, strikes a responsive chord, not only in the historians, but in each American who would be aristocratic— if it were not forbidden.

The perpetuation of slavery is unthinkable, but so is the killing of 600,000 Civil War soldiers. Two unthinkables do not make for rational thought, but at least disprized formalists Fillmore, Pierce and Buchanan tried awfully hard to ride it through on rationality and formalism—at least there was no war in their time. It remained for Lincoln, the rule-skeptic, to provoke the war simply by his election, and to ride it through to greatness.

It should be faced that the 'select' groups, from whom historians recruit our 'greatest' presidents, the rule-skeptics such as Lincoln and Polk, (and Nixon, perhaps, without Watergate, which relegated him to the failure group reserved for the scandalous like Harding and Grant), and the lawyer moralists such as Jefferson, Wilson, and Franklin Roosevelt, are often frightening in the critical areas of war and civil liberties. A constitutional republic, just as it cannot afford to rely much longer upon the inexperience, naiveté, and unadulterated morality of a non-lawyer, has little margin of error in entrusting to 'great' lawyers the nation's peace and a citizen's individual rights—the two most precious things for a president to protect and preserve. Formalists such as Fillmore, Pierce, and Buchanan can often be accused of that particular form of leadership cowardice known as peace at any price, but, as with Buchanan preparing, if it came to that, for war if it meant preventing secession of the Southern states, it is rather peace at almost any price—an extenuating difference. And supposing a contemporary Hitler, armed with an arsenal of nuclear weapons, whom do we want in the presidency to sell us a used car?

Allowing for the risks of electing a rule-skeptic or lawyer moralist, it seems to me, for several reasons, as desirable for a president to be a lawyer, or at least have had legal training, as a Supreme Court Justice. Not only is a non-lawyer more prone to cling to intuitive, impulsive, simplistic, 'moral' decisions based upon a mystic sense of right or wrong, but he seems terribly susceptible to that siren call of an intuitive, impulsive, sense of 'honor,' of being a Teddy Roosevelt or Kennedy or Lyndon Johnson. An America in a world of suicide bombers can hardly afford to charge up Kettle Hill or to remember the Alamo. The impossible dream is impossible. The 'big stick' is much too big. .

Then there is the question of a non-lawyer's exaggerated deference toward the law, exemplified by Congress and the Supreme Court, that a non-lawyer is compelled to exhibit. Americans are brought up to bow down to the law—no American, they are taught, is above it. A young Lincoln exhorted them to let reverence for the law become "the political religion of the nation," and they did. But a president is not, after all, supposed to lie down and roll over before the law; he is supposed to share in its formulation. The lawyer presidents have all seemed to know this; whether they attacked the other lawyers in the other branches or courted them, they knew this—and in the American system, this is of vital importance.

In foreign policy, particularly with the one-on-one type of diplomacy introduced so effectively by Nixon, the lawyer's experience would appear to be invaluable: his whole career consists of cases in which he is one-on-one with another lawyer, testing strengths and weaknesses of the adversary's case, fighting him tooth and nail, haranguing, criticizing, even condemning him, and yet being able to walk away with an amiable hand on his shoulder. Nixon, a sad, discredited example of a lawyer defending himself (who has, traditionally, a fool for a client), was, nevertheless, one of the finest examples of legal advocacy applied to international confrontations. He has provided a shining example of what other lawyer presidents, if there should be any, should consult in foreign affairs: their legal experience and expertise.

Would a lawyer president have dropped the bombs on Hiroshima and Nagasaki? Jefferson preached that the tree of liberty should be refreshed from time to time with the blood of patriots, but practiced with the hateful embargo acts to obtain peace at any price. John Adams lost his party by winning his peace. Franklin Roosevelt, rather than, as he has been so often accused, provoking a war, delayed as long as possible and almost lost Great Britain and, very nearly, America as well. Wilson's war was so far delayed that he was accused of being pro-German; when the point of no return to peace was reached, and only then, did he ask for a declaration of war.

It is, of course, clear that Polk's war with Mexico was self-induced, but it posed only a problem of morality and not of national survival. It was, then, a mini-war involving a minimum of risk, and promising enormous booty in the form of California and New Mexico. Wars do not have the same flavor to a man of much reason and very little conscience when national survival is not at stake. Nixon felt that it took a war to cause a great leader to surface, but it seems clear that 'small' wars project 'small' leaders, and that even great wars do not make great presidents unless the war is won. It is an exhilarating feeling for a nation to overcome a serious threat to its survival; the feeling slops over into its regard for the incumbent president.

The United States is a nation that particularly idolizes stars—they substitute for publicly disavowed aristocracy. But America cannot afford stars in the presidency. I read of the glories of an 'imperial presidency,' a la Franklin Roosevelt, and I conclude, the place for imperialism, or whatever is to pass for it in America, must finally be lodged where Madison conceived it to be, in Congress, that polyglot of ideology, that place where every morality is absorbed, chewed, and mostly spit out.

PART ONE

LAWYER RULE-SKEPTICISM IN THE PRESIDENCY

1

A Bird's Eye View of Rule-Skeptical Presidents

EXPLORERS OF AMERICAN intellectual history have largely been more or less content to assume the homogeneity of the legal mind, which, to the contrary, is often occupied with drastic civil wars that pit, against each other, formalism (adherence to precedent legal rules), rule-skepticism (the indifference to, and denial of, precedent rules), and lawyer moralism (adherence to natural law or other 'higher' rules). This triggers the intriguing question as to which form or forms of legal mind we might regard favorably or unfavorably in the American lawyer presidents.

The distance between lawyer formalists and lawyer moralists, while significant, is not as great as it might be. Both at least depend upon certain premises which shape their minds and motivate their behavior. They diverge mainly in the formalist's steady devotion to legal precedents while the lawyer moralist expands his givens into concerns with more generalized virtues. It is with rule-skeptics that a gulf created by disbelief occurs, where nothing is granted or conceded, where the rule is always in the process of coming into being, and, once having been created, immediately itself becomes an object of suspicion. Even a rule-skeptic's exaggerated show of patriotism is designed to occupy his vulnerable internal spaces by default. Finally, it comes back to the rule-skeptic's confession that to embrace 'all' is to hold on to very little, and he remains true to his sense that nothing may be true. The rule-skeptics are, consequently, on the whole, among the most troubled and troublesome of the presidents, and among the most unpredictable.

It is in the complicated area of rule-skepticism that such lawyer presidents as Abraham Lincoln and Richard Milhaus Nixon function. It helps to explain the eternal fascination with Lincoln—why more words have been written and said about him than perhaps any other American, why he battles it out with George Washington and Franklin Roosevelt as our greatest president, not only in the opinion of the general public, but of historians, why myths swirl around this political mystery man who had so much to say and revealed so little of himself. It helps to explain why, even as we may recoil from the idea, Lincoln so often reminds us of Nixon.

It is relatively easy to see that Lincoln supplied fuel for some of our most cherished faiths—that of the possibility of a rise from humble origins, of a president's willingness, if need be, to fall for us into martyrdom—but a less obvious, highly significant impact was to incorporate within himself, and to balance, in an highly dramatic fashion, the American's reverence toward the judicial law with his criticism of it. He metaphorizes the tension between this branch of law, the lawyers who service it, and statutory and administrative law which express the so-called 'voice of the people.' It is, of course, in the area of deference to judicial common law and judicial supremacy that the American's love of law and order differs from, say, the Napoleonic Code or the breakdown of Mexican law into legalisms more easily served by bribes than reason or fairness.

A distinguishing physical rule for lawyer rule-skeptics is the law of inertia, which dictates that a motionless body will not move unless acted upon by a force, and that a body once in motion will continue in the original motion unless acted upon by another force. This would seem to describe not only Abraham Lincoln and Richard Nixon, but such other presidential rule-skeptics as John Adams, John Quincy Adams, and James K. Polk in their actions and reactions in the world.

2

Father and Son: John and Quincy Adams

JOHN ADAMS REFUSED to move even when his cabinet threatened to destroy him, and an essential part of him must have known the degree of its antagonism and scorn. A basic ingredient in the characters of rule-skeptics is fear of exploding at the sight of the 'void', which is to say that, although trained in reason, they will resist accepting anyone's reason but their own— who refuse to believe that a precedent rule has any binding element that demands respect, much less obedience. It is no wonder that John Adams would observe, "Experience is the crutch men hobble on in the course of reasoning." Rule-skepticism, like all failures of belief, involves a great deal of cynicism and despair, and other rule-skeptical presidents besides Lincoln and Nixon shared these characteristics. They went so far with John Adams as to occasion severe breakdowns. Adams' most severe episode is recorded in his letter of October 9, 1781, to his wife, Abigail: "This is the first Time I have been able to write you, since my Sickness. Soon after my Return from Paris, I was seized with ... a nervous Fever, of a dangerous kind, bordering upon putrid. It seized upon my head in such a manner that for five or six days I was lost, and so insensible to the Operations of the Physicians ... as to have lost the memory of them." On his part, John Quincy Adams suffered from "an exaggerated awareness of his own failings" and an "uncontrollable dejection of spirits."

Having lost faith in the rules, above all in the general application of the rule of reason, the rule-skeptic, isolated in an almost mystic belief in the unique quality of his own logical processes, invites and is extremely vulnerable to criticism and self-doubt. The rule-skeptic has supreme confidence in his own reason and opinions at the same time that he needs constant assurance from others (whose ideas on any subject other than the rule-skeptic himself, or his production, he barely endures) that his superior talents, character, and intelligence do in fact exist. The resulting paradox arises from the abiding dread of the rule-skeptic, not that he doesn't really have such talents and intelligence (although he may pretend a disavowing humility), but that they won't be sufficiently admired by others. Self-awareness of his talents, integrity, and intelligence cannot sustain a rule-skeptic who considers himself unappreciated. The consequence is depression mixed with anger, a dangerous combination. He lives by the most simple of adages: he will like those who admire him, and scorn, often even hate, those who do not. "Man's heart," John Adams professed, "is deceitful above all things, and desperately wicked."

Gilbert Chinard posits John Adams as a prime example of "The New England tradition (which) developed out of near poverty, artisanship, and self-help coupled with a reverence for intellectual culture that reminds one strongly of the attitude of later waves of immigrants, particularly the Jews." I find this analogy apt, not necessarily as an inevitable equation between the early New Englanders and the Jews, but for inviting a particular comparison between John Adams and Felix Frankfurter, a classic rule-skeptic on the Supreme Court.

Felix Frankfurter came to America as a twelve-year-old Jewish immigrant from Vienna in 1890. Through the use of his intelligence, which permitted him to rank third in his class at City College of New York and to make the Law Review at Harvard Law School, he became a Harvard law professor, and ultimately a U.S. Supreme Court Justice. John Adams, the intellectually ambitious son of a hard-working farmer of modest means, reincarnated in the twentieth century, might well have had a similar career. Frankfurter, indeed, like Adams, was "full of energy and charm ... (with) a seeming abundance of self-confidence (and) felt) ... anointed, the man of destiny; ... (he could) ... even stand jokes about himself ... (but) must never be questioned seriously. His being at the bottom unrelated to others (was) bound to show in close relations."

The basic strand that ties Adams and Frankfurter ineluctably together, and for that matter, John's son, John Quincy, is their rule-skeptical way of thinking, not their psychological gears. John Adams,

John Quincy Adams, and Felix Frankfurter emerge as highly volatile, highly prickly, highly self-centered, highly demanding, and highly argumentative human beings. If they were enigmatic and puzzling, it is because, as paradoxical as all rule-skeptics, they were skeptical of the ultimate efficacy of the rule of reason, and yet they believed completely in the effectiveness of their applications of the rule of reason; they were skeptical of the power of reason to rule passions, yet they believed fiercely in the power of their reason to rule their passions; they were intellectually arrogant and snobbish, yet regarded public service as the highest of all activities; they did not believe in being bound by rules, and yet they believed fiercely in being bound by the rules of patriotism. John Quincy Adams confesses, "I disclaim as unsound all patriotism incompatible with the principles of eternal. But the truth is that the American union, while united, may be certain of success in every rightful cause ... They are at this moment the strongest nation upon the globe for every purpose of justice." His father was equally chauvinistic: "I have great reason to rejoice in the happiness of my country, which has fully equaled ... the sanguine anticipation of my youth. God prosper long our glorious country, and make it a pattern to the rest of the world!"

Not to be overlooked, Frankfurter, according to Liva Baker, "possessed almost childlike patriotism. He could be aggressive about it, even arrogant, sometimes self-righteous." To be a rule-skeptic is, perhaps, to be a neurotic in much the same way as a writer of fiction. For taking on the world one on one, which is what rule-skeptics and creative writers tend to do, involves stress, anxiety and guilt— hardly that far away from neurosis. Yet neurosis suggests and predicts forms of behavior while rule-skepticism identifies and predicts modes of thought.

Frankfurter wasted no love on the 'common man.' At Harvard Law School, he "had time and patience only for the brilliant and the boys of old and wealthy families." Frankfurter was, above all, a snob. The Harvard Law School was the best law school; his friends were the wisest men, the best lawyers, and the most charming people. Among the elitists he counted as friends were Franklin D. Roosevelt, Oliver Wendell Holmes, Jr., Henry L. Stimson, and Dean G. Acheson. The image of a liberal can be alarming (as an articulate conservative such as John Adams, or Edmund Burke, or even William Buckley might point out) if Frankfurter can be so defined for passionately defending the 'aristocratic' legal system he adored, and, only incidentally, Saccho and Vanzetti. If Frankfurter believed in anything beyond the pre-eminence of his own reasoning powers and his power to influence, it would have to be the law. To revere the law is to be a conservative even when protection of the law happens to coincide with those civil liberties contemporaneously embraced by liberals (such as personal freedoms [liberal] versus property freedoms [reactionary]). Unfortunately for such a conservative, he is in great danger of being confused with the liberals—enter Felix Frankfurter. Frankfurter, to give him his credit, never asked or expected to be considered a liberal; having cast his lot with Stimson, he asked only to be the impossible—a Brahmin, or, failing that, a pre-eminent lawyer and mover of law and lawmakers . If we ask as Yeats, 'how can you tell the dancer from the dance?' it is easy today, in the era of instant replay, to refuse to be distracted by the chorus line of social reformers.

Adams had a similar disdain for the 'common man', and a similar passion for the law's majesty, yet no one thought to call him a liberal when he defended Captain Preston and the other unfortunate British soldiers caught in the historical cul-de-sac known as the Boston Massacre. His account of his reactions on the night of the "Massacre", March 5, 1770, when he stayed at home with "nothing but (his) reflections to interrupt (his) repose," is highly revelatory of his antagonism to civil disorder, however commendable the motivation (Samuel Adams was successfully agitating for a removal of British soldiers from Boston proper to a fort in the harbor): "Endeavors had been systematically pursued for many months, by certain busy characters, to excite quarrels... and combats, single or compound, in the night, between the inhabitants of the lower class and the soldiers, and at all risks to enkindle an immortal hatred between them. I suspected that this was the explosion which had been intentionally wrought up by designing men, who knew what they were aiming at better than the instruments employed. If these poor tools should be prosecuted for any of their illegal conduct, they must be punished. If the soldiers in self-defence should kill any of them, they must be tried, and if truth was respected and the law prevailed, must be acquitted. To depend upon the perversion of law, and the corruption or partiality of juries, would insensibly disgrace the jurisprudence of the country and corrupt the morals of the people."

Adams' defense was of the law, and Captain Preston and his men were the benefactors, much as civil liberty lawyers would defend the right of American Nazi party members to march through the streets of Skokie, Illinois. "Mobs," declared Adams years later, "will never do to govern States or command armies. I was as sensible of it in 1770 as I am in 1787. To talk of liberty in such a state of things! Is not a Shattuck or a Shays as great a tyrant, when he would pluck up law and justice by the roots, as a Bernard or a Hutchinson, when he would overturn them partially?"

Adams played up his self-sacrifice in defending such unpopular defendants: "Before or after the trial, Preston sent me ten guineas, and at the trial of the (British) soldiers afterwards, eight guineas more, which were all the fees I ever received ...This was all the pecuniary reward I ever had for fourteen or fifteen days labor in the most exhausting and fatiguing causes I ever tried, for hazarding a popularity very general and very hardly earned, and for incurring a clamor, popular suspicions and prejudices, which are not yet worn out, and will never be forgotten as long as the history of this period is read." However, Chinard feels that not only did he remain in the good graces of his radical cousin, Samuel, but his "reaffirmation of the principles of law and order had placed him in good stead with the rich merchants of the town." There is no reason to doubt either that this was so, or that Adams' self-congratulations were hypocritical.

John Adams, both in his time and ours, has been accused of having 'aristocratic propensities,' a very serious accusation indeed in a country that takes its rhetoric of democracy and equality so seriously. Any definition of him, and his relationships with such men as Jefferson and Franklin, must consider his involvement, personally and philosophically, with his sense of the inequalities among people.

To begin with, Adams was not a social snob nor, unlike Frankfurter in his less attractive moments, did he want or try to be. Furthermore, neither Adams nor Frankfurter had any interest in proving his worth through the making or amassing of money. Like Frankfurter, Adams identified intellectual superiority as his cutting edge of success, which, however much qualified by puritanical self-castigation, he nevertheless equated with public recognition of his 'greatness' of intellect and character: "We are now explicitly agreed, in one important respect, viz. that there is a natural Aristocracy among men; the grounds of which are Virtue and Talents." For a man of his intelligence, Adams

THE LEGAL MIND AND THE PRESIDENCY

had a psychological obtuseness that inevitably caused him great difficulties. He could not, for example, as Jefferson was able to do so easily, disentangle his philosophical system of thought from the daily ideas required for immediate action. The scornful label, 'His Rotundity', arose in this fashion, during Adams's unsuccessful campaign to 'dignify' the virgin government with some European pomp and circumstance. Senator William Maclay records a caustic version: "The Vice-President rose in the chair and repeated twice, with more joy in his face than I had ever seen him assume before, he hoped the Government would be supported with dignity and splendor... Mr. Izard and sundry gentlemen of the Senate (were) dissatisfied with our Vice-President. He takes on him to school the members from the chair. His grasping after titles has been observed by everybody. Mr. Izard, after describing his air, manner, deportment, and personal figure in the chair, concluded with applying the title of Rotundity to him."

While there is irony in the contemplation of Adams as a snob about money or family, yet his condescension to those of inferior intelligence validates the accusations of his "aristocratic propensities." For, ultimately, what difference does it make if one condescends here over money or family, or there over talent or intelligence? Adams, himself, considered it all of a piece: "Fashion has introduced an indeterminate Use of the Word 'Talents.' Education, Wealth, Strength, Beauty, Stature, Birth, Marriage, graceful Attitudes and Motions, Gait, Air, Complexion, Physiognomy, are Talents, as well as Genius and Science and learning."

Any thoughtful assessment of John Quincy Adams's character and mental attitudes also inevitably poses contradictions. Consider for example: "He (Everett) also asked me if I was determined to do nothing ... to promote my future election to the Presidency ... I told him I should do absolutely nothing. He said that as others would not be so scrupulous, I should not stand upon equal footing with them. I told him that was not my fault— my business was to serve the public to the best of my abilities ... and not to intrigue for further advancement... The principle of my life had been never to ask the suffrage of my country, and never to shrink from its call... I shall adhere to the principle upon which I have always acted ... (I) am conscious of my inability to make interest by caballing, bargaining, place-giving, or tampering with members of Congress...Upon the foundation of public service must I stand."

Credited, as the son of John Adams, with an unimpeachable, albeit self-congratulatory, integrity, moral courage, and lack of hypocrisy, Quincy Adams's career was marked with equivocal acts that in another, so-called 'political' president, such as Van Buren, would have unhesitatingly been labeled as contemptible. He was inexplicably reticent in an otherwise exhaustively detailed diary, in his utter refusal to lash out against the accusations of 'corrupt bargain' leveled against him by the Jacksonians, other than recording in his diary in 1831, almost two years after he left the presidency, a tangential diatribe positing Jackson and Buchanan as the 'corrupt bargainers' rather than himself.

Quincy Adams records his dislike and lack of respect for Clay. He was "essentially a gamester... with a mind very defective in elementary knowledge, and a very undigested system of ethics. In 1821, he was only half educated and his morals, public and private, are loose. And by 1824 he was so 'ardent, dogmatical', and overbearing, that it is extremely difficult to preserve the temper of friendly society with him." Yet a year later, Clay became Adams's Secretary of State.

The famed integrity of the Adamses, father and son, however, on the whole well-deserved, amounted to intellectual snobbery. They were inordinately proud of their ideas and would not easily betray them. They were, probably, of the relatively few intellectuals who occupied the White House, the most obvious ones to exemplify the worst and the best in them: on the one hand, their arrogance, their self-doubts, their scorn of intellectual mediocrity, their dogmatism; and on the other, their deference to intellectual worth, their fierce desire to serve the 'truth', their energy and enthusiasm on the trail of, and their love for ideas.

The Adamses, as their contemporaries, rather uneasily, knew at the time, were improbable presidents even when no one had the slightest idea, other than George Washington, of what a probable president might be. John Quincy Adams was a 'minority' president, elected by the House of Representatives despite Jackson's popular vote majority and fifteen more electoral votes, and John Adams squeaked into the White House by getting three more electoral votes than Thomas Jefferson. John Adams' lack of discernible support from the 'liberal' party forming under Jefferson was more than matched by his alienation from the ultra-conservative 'right wing' of the Federalist party headed by Hamilton. He was not a political being, which

THE LEGAL MIND AND THE PRESIDENCY

would have made his election to the presidency impossible if the idea of parties involving partisanship had attained respectability before Andrew Jackson. It was probably Jefferson's soon-to-fade detachment—an attitude based upon the idealized view, shared by Adams, that the election of a president was a pure and virtuous act—which handed Adams the presidency.

The vital difference between the Adamses and Jefferson is revealed by their subsequent behavior during their presidencies. Adams continued to equate the presidential role with virtuous character while Jefferson settled for rhetorical virtue and real *politik* inc practice. Adams had "the rule-skeptic's idealized passion for self-improvement arising out of a nagging fear that nothing would be quite good enough to satisfy 'the people.' This was far removed from Jefferson's uncomplicated confidence in his own merit, and in that of a generalized mankind. Jefferson, of course, thought very little of specific individuals such as Marshall, Burr, and Hamilton.

Quincy Adams's presidency was largely a carbon copy of his father's: "(He) had demonstrated a reckless independence of outlook, an appeal to reason in defense of his views, a restraint toward those who opposed him, and a proud withdrawal in the face of defeat. In the presidency he pursued much the same course." The Adamses were hardly Marxist in the sense of creating a new territory for political ideas, or even a Jefferson, who by devising an exciting rhetoric (new wine in old bottles), triggered the creation of ideologues. It was in this sense that they differed so drastically from Jefferson; they were simply not capable of recruiting an army of followers interested in either their ideas or their rhetoric, and in their self-recognition of this incapability, they fashioned lives based upon independence from, and scorn of, others. Suitable as it may have been for Daniel Webster, commemorating the deaths of Adams and Jefferson on the same July 4, 1816, to have claimed that "No two men now live...perhaps,...ever lived, in one age, who (have) given a more lasting direction to the current of human thought," it seems that history, partial to Jefferson's, has been relatively indifferent to Adams's opinions.

The French Revolution was, of course, an event of tremendous significance to a country which had just won its independence and was struggling to insure domestic tranquility and provide for the common defense, while at the same time securing liberty. It was comforting and euphoric to Americans, at first, to imagine that they had led the way to a more equitably handled world. The ensuing Reign of Terror, however, was bound to disenchant and horrify such a fierce devotee of legal supremacy as John Adams.

If Adams can be said to be a political intellectual, or, if you will, an ideologue, his commitment would be to the preservation at all costs of the law's dominance, and it was over his cherishing of this value that the great split from Jefferson was ultimately bound to occur.

The reconciliation between Adams and Jefferson after an extended severance makes their relationship rare in American political history. The grounds for the breach were vital to both men and yet, although it took some eleven years, they managed, not without self-consciousness, to connect once again with each other in an extended correspondence. As with many writers, this was their best chance for intimacy. It seems fairly evident, as when they were flung together officially during Washington's presidency, that they had relatively little to say to each other in person and made no particular effort to seek each other out.

The earlier letters, before the break in 1801, concerned with whale oil and tobacco contracts, are pedestrian when compared with the later ones that begin in 1812. However, interestingly enough, they reveal the tentative and public nature of the relationship in the early period. Further, they are marked by deference on the part of Jefferson, and a certain patronization by Adams. Uncharacteristically, it is Adams, rather than Jefferson, who seems to be in control of his feelings. In line with this emphasis, (at least of those currently verified), prior to the break, Jefferson sent 91 letters to Adams's 80 (compared to the 1812-1826 period of 109 for Adams and only 49 for Jefferson.)

Adams and Jefferson could remain friends only as long as the revolutionary spirit was, in effect, the law of the land and, consequently, Adams' as well. During this period, Adams could transcend, along with so many other pillars of the community, his basic conservatism and indulge in the luxury of idealizing the 'new' beginning of America. He fantasized the extraordinary virtue of the America sprung loose from the European history of corruption and decay, and posited that virtue as the guiding rule upon which to base a political system. When that sense of the unique quality of American virtue evaporated, as it inevitably would when the rebellion was successful and people had to pick up the ordinary threads of their lives (much as in the aftermath of World War II and its victory over Hitler, or with the development of Israel after it won its fight to become an independent nation), Adams felt cheated. His consequent, abrupt movement to the 'right' was a predictable shift of a rule-skeptic who, feeling betrayed by the collapse of his guiding principle, could no longer believe in any of the going rules. Instead, Adams was to insist, one could operate politically only on disbeliefs: on the disbelief in human virtue; on the disbelief in the desire of any public official (excepting, of course, himself) to function in the public interest unless he was blocked by another public official in the pursuit of his self-interest; on the disbelief of any motivation for public service other than securing the adulation of others.

What began as a defense of the 'Constitutions of Government of the United States' became an attack upon them to the point of denying the efficacy of reason (upon which they were based): "Reason (was) insufficient to govern Nations ... Government, moreover, required new means of impressing its authority upon society." And what were these new means to be? Bestowing of titles and other trappings of aristocracy on government officials and hereditary succession to the offices of president and senators, suggestions that violated every compromise rule upon which the American constitution was based, were puffs of madness that only a rule-skeptic could have produced.

The rule-skeptic has supreme confidence in his own reason and opinions at the same time that he need constant assurance from others (whose ideas on any subject other than the rule-skeptic himself, or his production, he barely endures) that his superior talents, character, and intelligence do in fact exist. The resulting paradox arises from the abiding fear of the rule-skeptic, not that he doesn't really have such talents and intelligence (although he may pretend to such humility), but that they won't be sufficiently admired by other persons. Self-awareness of his talents, integrity, and intelligence cannot sustain a rule-skeptic who considers himself unappreciated. The consequence is depression mixed with anger, a dangerous combination. He lives by the most simple of adages: he will like those who admire him, and scorn, often even hate, those who don't.

To point up, as John R. Howe, Jr. does so graphically, the shift in John Adams's 'political thought' from a sense of American virtue to the dismal conclusion that Americans were as selfish, self-seeking, and mean-spirited as other people, leads us to the larger recognition of Adams's ultimate loss of faith in people altogether, and a consequent exclusive embrace of a concept of law and government strong enough to control human passions. Ultimately it is not, then, Adams's shift in thought but in faith that is revealed, for a rule-skeptic does have faith if only in the law as he defines it: an identity with his individual exercises of reason that permits him to question the validity of any inconsistent existing law. While the savagery and mass murders committed by mankind, in the name of liberty, equality and fraternity, and under the guise of law were shocking to the consciences of most Americans, what seemed to have disturbed Adams the most about the French Revolution was its betrayal of his sense of law.

Since the rule of law is the rule of reason, as Aristotle instructs us, I assume that by substituting 'their own reason' for the rule of reason (or law), they had glorified reason into a cause, which was perfectly willing to sacrifice reason itself (the cause) in the name of the cause. With this dismal sense of a dog biting its tail, Adams, the lawyer (the law-lover who could justify the American Revolution only by claiming it was the British who were violating the law), at the very moment Jefferson was considering it "the most sacred cause that ever man was engaged in," turned his back on the French Revolution: "The French tried making reason a natural Religion," he scoffed, "and look at the result." The idea of making reason a religion is really nothing new; the French Directory did not invent it. Aristotle, and after him the philosophers of the Enlightenment, and along with them, John Adams, were willing to genuflect before reason, and its amanuensis, law. The French version of reason was a denial of its equation with law, and that made all the difference. The ultimate horror of the French Revolution to Adams was that, in the name of reason (or equality, or liberty), the French could justify lawlessness, could, in the final analysis, justify the flaunting of reason in the name of a nameless cause.

The impact of the French Revolution was devastating to a man like John Adams already reeling from Shay's Rebellion; he had not changed that much from the man who defended the law (and Captain Preston) from the mob hysteria generated by the Boston Massacre. Although he had been caught up during the American Revolution in patriotic euphoria typical of rule-skeptics, there was really nothing to hold him back from his normal pessimism once it was back to business as usual. He waited only for justifications and they, Shays Rebellion and the French Revolution, were not long in coming.

It seems, in retrospect, almost inevitable that the relationship between the United States and France would dominate Adams' presidency and obscure any other possible consideration. For Adams, in his own mind, was at war with the French from the moment they preached their 'natural religion' of reason, and practiced sacrificial beheadings, as if at the center of reason was the invention of a cutting edge. The Alien and Sedition Laws, juxtaposed to Adams's refusal to go to war with France even at the expense of losing his own political party, can only be explained by Adams's love of liberty loved he not America more—a ready contrast with Jefferson who had expressed a preference for a free Adam and Eve as the last people left on earth to a host of men enslaved.

3

Self-Inflicted War with Mexico: James K. Polk

JAMES K. POLK had no doubt that he was a devout disciple of Jeffersonian ideology and Jacksonian action. He had no idea he was masquerading as a moralist. Ostensibly, he had no doubts about anything; at least he attempted to present to the political world, the only world in which he came alive, a 'do-gooder' mantled in an air of supreme self-confidence and firmness. But even the areas of Polk's 'firmness,' in handling the Oregon boundary dispute with England, provoking and waging the war with Mexico, exacting from Mexico the New Mexico and California territories, have been called into question. According to a congressman, Charles Jared Ingersoll, it suggests much too much the behavior of a normally cautious and reactive man determined to prove by bold and even reckless behavior his twinship with his role model, the popular idol Andrew Jackson: "And above all it is a common mistake to consider him resolute; he was not firm either personally or for measures. But having witnessed the wonders Jackson achieved by that natural endowment, President Polk affected it, inducing many to believe it his nature too."

Polk's belligerent posture with the British, of '54, 40 or fight' over the boundary to be set between Canada and the United States, terrified his admittedly timid Secretary of State Buchanan, and while it may have contributed to the settlement of the dispute at the 49` parallel (which Buchanan had advocated all along), it might equally have led to a truly unnecessary war. Again, the war with Mexico was more the act of, let us face it, a rule-skeptical bully rather than a bold, moralistic man; with almost no risk of losing, there was little to be fearless about.

There is considerable irony in Richard M. Nixon's regard of James K Polk as one "who probably ranks among our top four or five presidents in ability and accomplishments." He stoutly maintains that leaders like Polk and Eisenhower are not sufficiently appreciated because they were not heads-of-state during wartime. "It seems," says Nixon, "that waging wars, rather than ending or avoiding them, is still the measure of greatness in the minds of most historians."

Putting aside, as Nixon unaccountably seems to do, Polk's Mexican War, the irony in Nixon's admiration for Polk begins with their general distrust and proceeds through coincidental lives and careers. They were physically awkward and prone to sickliness as children— never really 'one of the boys.' They shared exceptionally devout mothers, Polk's a Presbyterian, Nixon's a Quaker, who believed religiously, for themselves and their sons, in character-building precepts of duty, discipline, hard work, and self-sacrifice intertwined with personal ambition and achievement. Neither of them could ever be called brilliant, but they were bright enough to combine their intelligence with extraordinary planning, tenacity, and concentration of purpose. Their purpose was to win out, over the athletes and super-brains of their youth, no matter what the cost in effort.

Each of them swallowed whole his mother's catechism of moral precepts and transformed them into an equation with his political progress. Morality was graded by the upward movement of his political career. People were graded good or bad in much the same way.

Both were loners. Both were terribly suspicious of the motives of others. Neither trusted anyone or really liked anyone. Both suffered devastating political defeats that would have terminated the public life of almost any other man, but they rose from their 'graves' to attain the ultimate triumph of the presidency.

They took themselves very, very seriously and, as a corollary, were impatient with anyone who derived pleasure from trivial pursuits. Pleasure in any form was a waste of time, and they were rather bitter about anyone who felt that having fun, even laughing, was a profitable activity. An immediate consequence was their inordinate necessity to 'win' in its most literal sense, since to win in any other way would involve a sense of humor they did not possess.

Above all, each devoutly believed in the strength of his own character as the gospel refined from the religious dogma they never understood or felt. Neither could, consequently, accept the immorality of any action on his part.

Each of these men was an unusual achiever and deserves so to be treated. They accomplished a great deal during their presidencies; indeed they had to or else they would have, even to themselves, betrayed that basic core of belief in the nature of success, which is to say, in their character.

Buried somewhere beneath the expressible must be intense resentment of a Nixon for an Eisenhower, or a Polk for a Jackson. (Only an Adams could voice such feelings of his Washington). Military heroes seem to reach pinnacles of success almost without effort, as if simply to breathe in and out, and wave a sword with a flourish is to reach the top of the human pyramid, at least politically, which is the only success that Polk, or Nixon, would envy. But a Polk or Nixon builds his whole career on suppressing and secreting wasteful emotions and attitudes. His genius lies in the slow, painstaking building, and then careful mending of fences until, when the heroes finally fall to the ground, the world is ready for the person who has never fought a duel, never conquered a hostile army, never chanted do's or die's. Polk was nominated as the first presidential dark horse and, for most people, remained an enigma. Yet he went about his business, the precision of which suited his nature, of fixing the Oregon boundary line and acquiring the more than a million square miles that became California and New Mexico.

M. M. Quaife, in his introduction to Polk's presidential diary, suggests with insight that the enigmatic and devious qualities attributed to Polk are unconscious emanations of his concentration upon his goals to the point of ignoring obvious complications. "Events or conditions," Quaife observes, "that would have turned aside a man less concentrated in purpose and less contracted in sympathy, were neglected or made to do service for his controlling intentions." Perhaps the clearest illustration of this, and the one which had the greatest impact upon American history, is in connection with the Mexican War from 1846 to 1848.

Americans cannot separate their wars from moral questions. They have never been able to justify wars, as other nations have, in terms of national glory, spoils, or, oddly enough, even survival. Only a moral justification can be any justification at all. This was true of even the Civil War which, at least Lincoln was well aware, was devoted to survival of the Union, with abolition of slavery a footnote that, inevitably, in the American way, gobbled up the text.

Given this premise, demanding the rhetoric of liberty or death, a world being made safe for democracy, a war to end all wars, remembering Pearl Harbor, a day that would live in infamy, the Mexican War is remarkable for its lack of moral justification, at least one that was acceptable to the general public. At the same time, there was nothing in the world that Polk wanted so much, and therefore believed in the morality of so much, as the acquisition of California and New Mexico.

Viewed from the customary American moral stance, the Mexican War was inexcusable. Its seeds were planted, beginning in 1823, with the colonization by Americans in Mexican territory that eventually became Texas. At the time the Mexican provinces, largely unsettled, consisted of the present states of California, New Mexico, Arizona, and Texas. By 1835, the Texans felt strong enough to defy Mexican rule, and decisively defeated the Mexican army on April 21, 1836. They promptly proceeded to legalize slavery (which the Mexicans had abolished in 1831) and request annexation by the United States.

Polk, whose nomination and election was premised on his unequivocal support of the annexation of Texas, was off on his transcontinental race to the Pacific. He never entertained the slightest doubt that the wrenching from Mexico, not only of Texas, but the rest of her American provinces, by hook (money) or crook (war) was as holy a crusade as he could imagine. To him, Mexico was a cruel and predatory country which provoked the United States into war, and he was puzzled and irritated by accusations of antiwar congressmen like Abraham Lincoln of being "deeply conscious of being in the wrong—that he feels the blood of this war, like the blood of Abel, is crying to Heaven against him." Polk began his presidential diary on August 26, 1845, and wasted no time building his case against Mexico: "Other matters then came up for consideration the principal of which related to our army under the command of Gen'l Taylor in Texas, and the proper means of defending that territory against the threatened invasion by Mexico." 'That territory,' however, as far as Polk and the Texans were concerned (although General Taylor had been ordered to defend the area northeast of the Nueces River, the traditional boundary of

Mexican Texas, and not to move beyond it) included the vast additional area bounded by the Rio Grande. On the previous June 6, 1845, having barely taken office, Polk had assured Samuel Houston that his extravagant territorial claim would be upheld by the United States: "We will maintain your rights of territory and will not suffer them to be sacrificed."

Several days later at his cabinet meeting, Polk again brought up the 'threatened' invasion of Texas by Mexico, and it was agreed to instruct General Taylor to consider the *crossing of the Rio Grande (not the Nueces) by a Mexican army* as an act of war. In January, 1846, Polk directed General Taylor to move south to the Rio Grande which, predictably, occasioned some four months later, a skirmish between Mexicans crossing the Rio Grande and a United States troop that suffered several casualties. This was all Polk needed. On May 11, 1846, he sent a declaration of war message to Congress: "The cup of forbearance has been exhausted. After reiterated menaces, Mexico has passed the boundary of the United States, has invaded our territory and shed American blood upon American soil."

A certain naiveté enters the picture and lies either in the concentration of Polk upon his acquisition of California and New Mexico, or in timid stabs at that larger virtue by Buchanan, which he, like Van Buren, could never quite relinquish in his long, otherwise politically dominated, career. On May 13, 1946, Polk narrated his penultimate confrontation with Buchanan, introducing a bit of drama in his otherwise pedestrian diary: "Among other things, Mr. Buchanan had stated that our object was not to dismember Mexico or to make conquests, and that ... in going to war we did not do so with a view to acquire either California or New Mexico, or any other portion of the Mexican territory ... I was much astonished at the views expressed by Mr. Buchanan on the subject."

One speculates whether Polk, mystified by Buchanan's assumption that the United States would not take advantage of Mexico's vulnerability to the land-grab, had the slightest doubt that his was the virtuous path. He was similarly baffled by the Wilmot proviso, which posited the exclusion of slavery from any land acquired from Mexico: "Slavery has no possible connection with the Mexican War, and with making peace with that country ... Its introduction in connection with the Mexican War is not only mischievous but wicked."

THE LEGAL MIND AND THE PRESIDENCY

Since ideologues tend to embrace as a faith even the careless rhetoric of such a prime mover as Jefferson, Polk is the prototypical ideologue. For, as much as any president before Nixon, he became the embodiment of what he admired in other men without ever dreaming that he might admire something originating in himself. The result is the image of a rigid, carefully controlled, contrived personality, a fabrication so patent that one is terribly suspicious of the credibility of the person it inhabits, particularly at moments of his greatest sincerity. 'Polk the Mendacious' and 'Tricky Dicky' earned their nicknames the hard way, through a total package of personality that could only pretend to define a human being. The similarities between Polk and Nixon, not only in personality, but in relation to their lives and political fortunes, are so numerous as to be startling. It is important to place Polk and Nixon where they belong, in the line of rule-skeptic presidents beginning with John Adams.

It would have genuinely disturbed Polk to be linked in any way with John Adams rather than Thomas Jefferson and yet, in significant areas, he was cast in Adams's mold rather than Jefferson's. He presented a classic rule-skeptic's posture of, having a dismal view of human character in general and an almost mystical faith in the quality of his own. The concentration upon Adams's strength of character as being his ultimate definition is familiar; his political goal was simply to acquaint the world with the purity and incorruptibility of his character, and the world to succeed need merely follow his example. To claim for 'Polk the Mendacious' a comparable vision of himself is not as obvious, but equally persuasive. Polk meant what he said when he declared, at age forty: "I resolved, from the beginning, not to separate myself from the body of (the) party, but to act with them in supporting the candidate of the … party… If, in doing this, I may have sacrificed former personal attachments for men, it is a sacrifice for principle, and on which I am ready to stand. I have changed no political opinion or principle I ever entertained; and if I shall sink, politically, I go down like an honest man, and without a regret."

Whether or not one believes, with Polk, that party loyalty to the party of the 'people' is the highest form of integrity available to a politician; it is his belief and is inextricably fused with his placing the highest priority on maintaining the purity of his character. Sellers persuasively concludes: "Somehow his religious impulses, his political principles, and his ambitions had all been fused together into a religion of democracy that he identified with the personal fortunes of James K. Polk."

Indoctrinated with the sense of the depravity and impurity of mankind by his Presbyterian mother, Polk was willing for a time to suspend this doctrine in regard to the favored American, but, like Adams, his skepticism was only waiting in the wings: "Victory had eluded him before, but never before had defeat shaken his faith that the people were essentially virtuous and wise, that they shared his nostalgic moral preference for the simpler agrarian world that was so rapidly vanishing ... the people themselves seemed to have been fatally and perhaps permanently corrupted."

The occasion of Polk's relapse into skepticism, which deeply divides him from Jefferson, arose inevitably, from the sense of not being appreciated by the very people in whose virtue he had previously had unbounded confidence. Their virtue was directly equated with their sense of his worth: "I begin, more than I have ever done before, to distrust the disinterestedness and honesty of all mankind ...There is more selfishness and less principle among members of Congress, as well as others, than I had any conception (of), before I became President of the U.S." The refrain is repeated with monotonous regularity in Polk's diary of his presidency, whenever Polk has occasion to mention his dealings with congressmen, whether they were opposition party Whigs or members of his own revered Democratic party.

If morality is based upon a preference of what human practices are to survive, what are we to make of Polk in moral terms? His notion of morality was the survival of his character, and that character reflected in his lifetime a movement from identification with the 'American people,' exemplified by the Democratic party, to a mystical fusion with 'America the beautiful,' that amorphous, incorporeal being that could never disappoint or betray him. Like a pagan offering sacrifices to his god, Polk identified expansion and aggrandizement of his immaculate America as his moral imperative, supplanting 'No American is above the law.' With his attainment of 'sea to shining sea,' he became a moral unity that could only be astonished at any other concept of morality. It would appear, ultimately, that he was not 'Polk the Mendacious,' if duplicity implies conscious intention to deceive. We are then prodded to an even more unpalatable sobriquet:

'Polk the Mean-spirited.' And if this was true of him, how can it not be true of the rest of us, we legal-minded Americans of the mid-nineteenth century, who were not about to let Mexico keep Texas, California, New Mexico, and Arizona?

4

A Great Life and Death: Abraham Lincoln

IN THE COURSE of his demonstration that the Radical Republicans were not necessarily the 'villains of the piece' starring Abraham Lincoln, David Donald observes: "All good historians are frustrated dramatists." Combine this with Clarence Darrow's conceit that in the heart of every lawyer lies a frustrated poet, and one begins to sniff out the larger than life aura of Lincoln's appeal. To modern sensibilities, his life, both privately and publicly, was intensely dramatic; it seems inevitable for this classic hero, with his tragic flaw of melancholy, to be assassinated in a theater by a typecast actor who killed to earn his exiting line, "*Sic semper tyrannis.*"

The critical impoverishment of Lincoln's childhood and adolescence, the one that made him ashamed of his parents the rest of his life, was not so much a lack of money, but their near illiteracy. Lincoln hated to talk about his childhood and, indeed, seemed to have blotted it from his memory, even thoughts other than fancies concerning his mother, who had died when he was eight. His rejection went far beyond words. When he left his father in 1831, at twenty-two, it was for keeps; he even refused to see him when he was dying or to attend his funeral. In a letter to his step-brother on January 12, 1851, he comments brusquely: "I received both your letters, and ... I have not answered them ... because it appeared to me I could writing nothing which could do any good ... I sincerely hope Father may yet recover his health ... Say to him that if we could meet now, it is doubtful whether it would not be more painful than pleasant."

It does not appear that his father, Thomas Lincoln, was a harsh or cruel father, or even that he was a silly, ineffectual man; he seemed to share, in fact, something of Lincoln's talent for anecdotes and jokes and was not dull company; yet Lincoln, as soon as he could, relegated his father to the ash-heap of his memory.

A born intellectual, burning with the ambition not to be rich, but to be educated, whose definition of success was to be respected for his mind, Lincoln was intolerant enough to turn his back on an uneducated father whose very presence reminded him of the scrubby, unschooled, supernumerary role in life he was supposed to play. His attitude was not grand or noble, particularly in his inability to come to terms with the rejection of his father even as he lay dying, but it was, as much of the rest of Lincoln, terribly human in its vulnerability.

His shame crystallized into a defensiveness that is most apparent in his wayward treatment of women he finally dared to think of marrying. It seems inconceivable that the man Lincoln was to become would be capable of such behavior until we realize that he, projecting himself as the least desirable of mates, was crying out to be found loveable anyway. The Mary episode of 1836 and the circumstances of his ultimate marriage to Mary Todd in 1842, at the age of thirty-three, reveal a man trapped between self-doubt and desire for a woman much 'above his station' in breeding and education—the only kind he could possibly fall in love with and marry.

Mary Owens first met Lincoln in 1833 when she visited her sister in Lincoln's town of New Salem, Illinois. She, a woman Lincoln, though without identifying her, was later to lampoon mercilessly, is described by contemporaries as vivacious, well-educated, and witty.

The extent of Lincoln's self-laceration can be seen in his determination to be first in a show of cruel indifference. In the guise of thoughtfulness and reason, he forced Mary Owens to reject him (unless, the hidden cry from the heart goes, she loved him beyond reason).

Lincoln had just passed the bar in the spring of 1837 and moved to Springfield, Illinois, to practice law, only a few months before his 'Dear Mary' letter. He had no idea of whether he could do well enough to support himself, much less a wife used to the 'best.' He was the same self-doubter who had written Mary Owens in May, 1837, upon his migration to Springfield, that: "There is a great deal of flourishing about in carriages here, which it would be your doom to see without sharing in it. You would have to be poor without the means of hiding your poverty. Do you believe you could bear that patiently?"

It took five more years, and his establishment as one of the foremost lawyers in Illinois, before he could mount enough of a sense of worth to brave marriage to an upper-class woman, and, even then, he had to reject Mary Todd before she could convince him that she could love and honor a man with less than a year's formal schooling, and born of illiterate parents.

As Lincoln was to prove in the later, grim years of the Civil War, his life-long refuge from pain and hurt was humor, a resource that in 1838 was triple-edged; not only did he aim a 'poison pen' at himself, but at his mother and an innocent Mary Owens as well. In a satirical, guilt-ridden letter of April 1, 1838, to a friend, Mrs. Browning, he fabricated a Western 'tall tale' full of the hyperbole and crude sweeps generic to the form; however, he sought really to exacerbate and accuse only himself, since he named no names, and even he escaped public notice; his burlesque was so broad Mrs. Browning did in fact take it for a 'tall tale.' Whatever he professes in the letter, he knew that he, not Mary Owens, had provoked the breach and that he had committed his greatest sin against himself; he had broken a promise. This was a violation not only of a personal code, but of a lawyer's greatest pride. Ethics of the legal profession were to form the core of Lincoln's sense.

Abraham Lincoln, at twenty-nine, was hardly an adolescent when he wrote his letter; yet his indulgent chroniclers, Angle and Miers, extolling his "honesty, candor, compassion, humor, humility, faith, love of family and country" are driven to fancy that he "was betrayed by his youthfulness. If he loved his family, it was reserved for wife and children—what might be termed his self-made family as opposed to the one of his birth, which he had abandoned at the earliest opportunity. If he was betrayed, it was rather by his history." His flurry of words, the flying footwork of fancy, his humorous 'tall-tales' that tend to blur and obfuscate the underlying, deadly serious thrust of Lincoln's demeaning is a mechanism compulsively employed by Lincoln throughout his life: that he was a miserable, self-hating, self-doubting man who, unless he learned (which he ultimately did) to exercise self-discipline, would inevitably betray himself and hurt others. David Donald, in his stimulating collection of essays on Lincoln and the Civil War, observes: "Lincoln's renowned sense of humor was related to his passion for secrecy. Again and again self-important delegations would descend upon the White House, deliver themselves of ponderous utterances upon pressing issues of the war, and demand point-blank what the president proposed to do about their problems ... His petitioners' request, he would say, reminded him of 'a little story,' which he would proceed to tell in great detail, accompanied by mimicry and gestures, by hearty slapping of the thing, by uproarious laughter at the end—at which time he would usher out his callers, baffled and confused by the smoke-screen of good humor, with their questions still unanswered."

The parallels evolving from Lincoln's 'scrape' with Mary Owens and his wooing of Mary Todd are striking. The two might have been sisters or even twins in appearance, education, and family backgrounds. As in the Mary Owen matter, Lincoln did his best to win and then lose Mary Todd. That he finally married her was due mainly to her refusal to let his defenses fend her off.

Mary Todd, like Mary Owens, met Lincoln while visiting a sister, Elizabeth Edwards, who considered Lincoln a totally unacceptable suitor. The Todd family strenuously and openly objected to Lincoln marrying into the family, and this was enough to destroy, at least for a time, the delicate supporting web constructed by Lincoln out of Mary's unabashed attachment, free of snobbery, and the growing success of his legal practice. He broke off the engagement and sank into a deep, prolonged, enervating depression.

It took two more years for Mary Todd and Abraham Lincoln to marry, two more years during which Mary let him know she was still available, two more years in which he was increasingly successful as a lawyer. Mary Todd now knew her man, and what she had to do: There was no public announcement, for Mary said "that the world, woman and man, were uncertain and slippery and that it was best to keep the secret courtship from all eyes and ears."

Lincoln's story, not only in his marriage probes, but in all of its phases, is, like his country's history, a study of dualism, and consequently seems to touch a vital American nerve wherever it lights. Even his body seems to be intent upon a career separated from his mind. The Paul Bunyan part of the Lincolnian legend was not too far a stretching of reality: A myth requires a rooting in fact from which to propel itself; in Lincoln's case, it involved his undeniable physical strength and athletic coordination. From there, the legends, propagated largely by people who actually knew him, but not too well, proliferated. What is evident from both fact and fancy is that part of Lincoln was a man's man, a male who enjoyed the company of men doing what men do. It began in his youth with his deep engagement in physical competition, and is exemplified by his domination of a group of rowdies in New Salem known as the Clary's Grove boys. This aspect of Lincoln's, his enjoyment at being with the 'boys,'—being one of them—was translated in later years into his compulsion, going far beyond the necessities of his profession, to travel a far-flung Illinois judicial circuit of some twelve thousand square miles. Yet, while his companions would settle for fun and games and camaraderie, Lincoln would not, because he could not. Rule-skepticism was driving him toward solitude, reflection, inwardness, and withdrawal. In the swirl and noise of his social circles, he was the calm, segregated, impenetrable eye of the tornado. According to Herndon, Judge Davis, who often rode the judicial circuit with Lincoln, told him: "I knew the man so well: he was the most reticent, secretive man I ever saw or expect to see." Herndon adds on his own: "Mr. Lincoln was a riddle and a puzzle to his friends and neighbors among whom he lived and moved … I have said and now say that Mr. Lincoln was a secretive, silent, and a very reticent-minded man, trusting no man, nor woman, nor child with the inner secrets of his ambitious soul." In his early twenties, at the same time that he was making his physical presence felt with the Clary's Grove boys, Lincoln was waging that loneliest of struggles, the fight for a life of the mind—and he had less than a year of formal, frontier education to tell him that such a life was worth the effort. Lincoln's mind, with the staying power of the long-distance runner (while his body was getting by as a clerk in a country store), storing up the tidbits of the few books available to it, impressed somewhere inside itself with its inviolateness, ("Liquor" he said, "is unpleasant to me and always makes me feel flabby and undone.") searched for and found its own sort in the New Salem Debating Society of 'intellectuals.'

A rule-skeptical dualism of mind and body takes its toll. Lincoln developed into a classic depressive, a person who not only suffers from deep and debilitating melancholy, who not only inflicts suffering upon those who love him, but literally cannot keep his mind and body functioning at the same time in the same place. Ruth Randall reports: "The disrupting effect of having one ... blind and deaf to his surroundings, was not lost on the visiting girl (Emilie Todd, Mrs. Lincoln's half-sister). Playing checkers ...one evening in the family circle, Emilie noticed how Mr. Lincoln had gone into a brown study and was not hearing a word that was being said ... Then he came out of his abstraction good-naturedly and told such a funny story that it broke up the game of checkers."

"Mr. Lincoln," Herndon noted, "continuously lived in three worlds ... First, he lived in the purely reflective and thoughtful; secondly, in the sad, thoughtless, and gloomy; and, thirdly, he lived in the happy world of his own levities. He was sometimes in the one state and then in another, and at times the transition was slow and gradual and at times, quick as a flash."

According to Stephen B. Oates: "His family was forced to endure his internal civil wars, at times poignant: 'Once a spell came over him while he pulled on of his boys in a wagon. Lost in thought, he tugged the wagon over an uneven plank sidewalk and the child fell off. But Lincoln was oblivious to the fallen boy and went on with his head bent forward, hauling the empty wagon around the neighborhood.'"

As a depressive, Lincoln's behavior, far from being mysterious, was predictable, particularly the abrupt swings between withdrawal and gregariousness. And it was not merely a question of 'whistling down sadness'; one was as inevitable as the other.

Lincoln matured at much the same time as America and in much the same way—by a surge in power of a self-confident force that, challenging a multitude of doubts, embraced the unlikely pairing of liberty and law. There had been spasms in the American past, notably Shays Rebellion that so disturbed John Adams, but nothing that had seriously eroded respect for the law of such vertically rising people as a young Lincoln who proclaimed: "Let every man remember that to violate the law is to trample on the blood of his father ... Let reverence for the laws be breathed by every American mother, to the lisping babe, that prattles on her lap... And, in short, let it become the political religion of the nation ... Passion has helped us; but can do no more. It will in the future be our enemy. Reason, cold, calculating, unimpassioned reason, must furnish all the materials for our future support and defence." Lincoln, at the age of twenty-nine, at the same time (two months later) he was drowning his memory of Mary

Owens in a vicious shower of satire, produced this paean to the Rule of Law and Reason; his emotional gear was never anything, early or late, he particularly prized, and in the middle of his journey, the life of the mind seemed to him worthy of starry-eyed worship.

His deification of law was not to last. In fact, of all of Lincoln's brilliant rhetorical salvos, this was the most short-lived. Reverence for law became a tool for him, as did reason, as did the larger morality, based upon passions instead of reason, to preserve the main chance, and that was survival of the Union, not survival of so many states, or so much land, but survival of 'the way it was' and that way was the seamless web, indissoluble and indivisible, of law wrapped securely around the 'liberty' of the colonial American 'white'. 'Liberty,' of course, to the rank and file American 'white', not only meant escape from the stifling grasp of British laws and regulations, but freedom of opportunity for the American 'white' to rise from rags to fame or fortune, or both.

By the time Lincoln was inaugurated on March 4, 1861, as President of the United States, he had been married to Mary Todd Lincoln almost twenty years. He had served as a congressman and had debated with Douglas during his unsuccessful bid for a Senate seat. He had become a distinguished trial and appellate lawyer, and, if not rich, comfortably well off. As a congressman, in January, 1848, still youngish at thirty-nine, still indeterminate in his oscillations between reason and what Justice Holmes was to call 'fighting faiths,' he cast a self-righteous first stone at Polk's deceitful but universally popular propagation of the Mexican War. His attack upon a president during a war was politically foolish, as he soon learned, much to his chagrin, from his partner, Herndon, and others back in Springfield. He had believed that he was leading a holy political crusade of words against the ungodly Democrats, but his fellow Whigs had turned mute. His only refuge at being gulled was to plead morality: "Would you have voted what you felt you knew to be a lie? I know you would not... Richardson's resolutions ... make the direct question of the justice of the war; so that no man can be silent if he would. You are compelled to speak; and your only alternative is to tell the truth or tell a lie. I cannot doubt which you would do."

But of course he had another option; he could have, like his fellow Whigs, said nothing for a time, seen how the war went, and meanwhile waved the flag with the rest of the country. After all, he was, otherwise, "an exemplary party man, serving dutifully on committees, seldom missing a roll call, never skulking a vote, and giving orthodox Whig speeches on tariffs and internal improvements." Actually, it remained only for Lincoln to take the final step of orthodox Whig speeches on tariffs and internal improvements—fusing his party loyalty to the rest of his moral side that expressed itself in his idolatry of his country as it was with the adoption of the Constitution, slavery warts and all. This step occurred when he joined and soon led the embryonic Republican Party, a party created not to abolish slavery (he would never have joined such a radical party), but to keep it substantially as the Founding Fathers might have defined it in 1787.

Thanks largely to William Herndon, Lincoln's law partner for the sixteen years preceding Lincoln's presidency, historians have noted the contradictions that mark Lincoln's personality and his presidential performance—his self-doubtings matched by his sense of superiority, his acuteness buffered by his 'spells' of depression and absent-mindedness, his 'tyrannical' acts pitted against his love of democracy and the law, his devotion to and respect for the Constitution and his flouting of it, his gregarious display of jokes and anecdotes, and his passion for secrecy. At the same time, historians, who have made their biographies of Lincoln highly engrossing dramas of conflict and ambiguities in the central figure, recognize the unprofessional carelessness of Herndon's hearsay evidence of dates, places and events, evidence collected by Herndon from quite unreliable neighbors, friends, acquaintances, and embellished both by his informants and by Herndon himself. But what emerges and what these historians cannot ignore is a persuasive portrait in its broad strokes of a double-imaged personality, sometimes coming together in a clear picture and more often, as on some television screens, offering a sharp, clear image front and center, and a blurred copy off to the side.

This is not to imply that Lincoln was schizophrenic, which he certainly was not. He was rule-skeptical. He was not two people at war with each other, but rather two eternally busy, contradictory images of self. Both images, it is clear, were united in their burning desire for center stage. As a young man still in his twenties, Lincoln warns his audience at the Young Men's Lyceum in Springfield in 1838, of the threat to democratic America of ambitious men: "Towering genius disdains a beaten path ...It denies that it is glory enough to serve under any chief. It ...thirsts and burns for distinction; and, if possible, it will have it, whether at the expense of emancipating slave, or enslaving freemen. Is it unreasonable to expect that some man possessed of the loftiest genius, coupled with ambition sufficient to push it to its utmost stretch, will at some time spring up among us?"

Edmund Wilson, acknowledging Lincoln's dreams of greatness, translates, perhaps a little too easily, this Lincolnian rhetoric into self-confession: "Now the effect of this is somewhat ambiguous: it is evident that Lincoln has projected himself into the role against which he is warning them. And a little less than two years later we find one of his political speeches winding up ... If ever I feel the soul within me elevate... it is when I contemplate the cause of my country, deserted by all the world beside, and I standing up boldly alone and hurling defiance at her victorious oppressors ... the young Lincoln, then, was extremely ambitious; he saw himself in an heroic role." Humility in Lincoln has been confused with his lack of ostentation; he continually embarrassed his wife, Mary, by his inattentiveness to dress or manners. But after adolescence he lost interest in his body; it was his mind that he prized and over which he, much like John Adams before him, might be accused of intellectual snobbery: "It is absurd to call him a modest man," said John Hay, his secretary. "No great man was ever modest. It was his intellectual arrogance and unconscious assumption of superiority that men like Chase and Sumner never could forgive." Of all the presidents, Lincoln, a great lawyer who prized being a lawyer, made the greatest use of the legal skills he had developed, not only in the exercise of logical and persuasive expression, but in maintaining his calm under stress, avoiding vindictiveness, and waiting out storms as long as he could. He would have eagerly endorsed Coolidge's maxim that: "If you see ten troubles coming down the road ... you can be sure that nine will run into the ditch before they reach you ..."

David Donald notes: "Faced with the dismal crisis at Fort Sumter, characteristically, Lincoln's final decision was neither to reinforce or withdraw; he would merely send food and supplies to the beleaguered Sumter garrison and sit back and wait. His passivity paid off. Confederate hotheads were unable to wait ... and they fired the first shot at Sumter."

At the same time, he had the rule-skeptic's boldness, even recklessness, in his scorn of existing rules once he decided to act. After the Civil War started, Lincoln, breaking every rule in the Constitutional book, made his moves and worried about Congress and the people later. With hindsight, his actions still remain hard to swallow: "To be sure," Fehrenbacher rather sorrowfully concludes, "the perilous circumstances called for extraordinary measures, and the intent of even the most repressive actions was preventive rather than punitive. Nevertheless, the secret police, paid informers, midnight arrests, crowded prisons, and suppressed newspapers were alien to the American experience ..." Samuel Eliot Morison puts it more strongly: "Lincoln wielded a greater power throughout the war that any other President of the United States prior to Franklin D. Roosevelt; a wider authority than any British ruler between Cromwell and Churchill. Contemporary accusations against him of tyranny and despotism read strangely to those who know his character, but not to students of his administration. Lincoln came near to being the ideal tyrant of whom Plato dreamed, yet nonetheless he was a dictator from the standpoint of American constitutional law."

The major complaint of Constitutionalists against Lincoln's exercises of raw presidential power is not their being unjustified, but his usurpation of congressional and judicial authority in the name of immediate necessity. This is the element, the absence of congressional sanction, that distinguishes his from Wilson's comparably autocratic reign during World War I. It points up Lincoln's indifference to the rules of the game which, rhetorically, he had extolled throughout his political career.

In the final analysis, Lincoln, as president during an awful, bloody, and morally confused Civil War, played both of his ends against the ultimate middle on which he took his inevitable stand. As a lawyer, he operated in a typically cautious, reactive, passive, calm manner, trying to abide by commitments, to honor, protect, and fight for his 'client', the pre-war United States, and constantly seeking to harmonize dissonant elements, most notably in the most irreconcilable issue of all—slavery; in short, he tried to live by the ethics of the legal profession that formed much of his life. Not that these ethics might not merge with and serve a 'higher' morality: "Negroes, like other people, act upon motives. Why should they do anything for us if we will do nothing for them? If they stake their lives for us they must be prompted by the strongest motive— even the promise of freedom. And the promise, being made, must be kept." But, as a personification of the rule-skeptical legal mind, he brusquely proceeded to disregard the cluster of legal ethics, and the majesty of the Constitution, law, and the Supreme Court as well, for the sake of the rule-skeptic's ultimate priority and faith—survival, which to him meant survival of the whole, blemishes and all (otherwise defined as patriotism), of the early white American's individualistic and opportunistic, the Horatio Alger, 'American way of life': "I happen temporarily to occupy this big White House. I am a living witness that any one of your children may look to come here as my father's child has. It is in order that each of you may have through this free governmental open field and a fair chance for your industry, enterprise and intelligence; that you may all have equal privileges in the race of life."

The middle ground on which these dual propelling forces in Lincoln met, so puzzling to many observers, was in the mediating effects, often ineffectual, of his ethical concerns upon his 'religion' of survival. Perhaps the most confusing consideration of all is the recognition that only in these terms can morality be ascribed to Lincoln; only in this framework can the exasperation he provoked in such "moralists' as Wendell Phillips and Frederick Douglass be explained. On the 'fighting faith' of the day— slavery—Lincoln made it clear to anyone who was willing to listen that he was not interested in waging a war, or even lifting a finger, to abolish slavery. Rhetorically, as early as 1837, he declared that it was founded on both "injustice and bad policy"; his arguments had already begun to form around legal and pragmatic considerations. In 1841, with the detachment and awareness of a novelist's eye, along with a disconcerting psychological obtuseness reminiscent of moviemakers in the Stepin Fetchit days, he describes twelve slaves: "strung together precisely like so many fish upon a trotline. In this condition they were being separated forever from the scenes of their childhood, their friends, their fathers and mothers, and brothers and sisters, and many of them, from their wives and children...and yet amid all these distressing circumstances … they were the most cheerful and apparently happy creatures on board. One, whose offence for which he had been sold, was an over-fondness for his wife, played the fiddle almost continually; and the others danced, sung, cracked jokes, and played various games with cards… How true it is that 'God tempers the wind to the shorn lamb', or in other words, that He renders the worst of human conditions tolerable, while He permits the best to be nothing better than tolerable."

By 1854, in the Lincoln-Douglas debates, Lincoln anticipates the European refrain running throughout the twentieth century, of the hypocrisy of the Declaration of Independence when it comes to the African-American: "I hate it because it deprives our republican example of its just influence in the world—enables the enemies of free institutions, with plausibility, to taunt us as hypocrites ..." But, in his conclusion of the same speech, Lincoln abandons rhetoric in favor of an eloquent cry from the heart for the perpetuation of his particular brand of patriotism, that longing for the whole of things as they were, even in regard to hateful slavery: "Our republican robe is soiled, and trailed in the dust. Let us repurify it. Let us turn and wash it white, in the spirit, if not the blood of the Revolution. Let us turn slavery from its claims of 'moral right,' back upon its existing legal rights, and its arguments of 'necessity.' Let us return it to the position our fathers gave it; and there let it rest in peace ..." War, as he never tired of saying, could never, for Lincoln, be a moral crusade for anything less than survival of his country. Certainly his war was not to free the world of slavery or even to make it safe for democracy, as a later lawyer moralist, Woodrow Wilson, was to proclaim on behalf of his war. The Civil War was a much greater evil to Lincoln than slavery, but he was willing to fight it through only to prevent what to him was the unimaginable—the destruction of the United States of America as he knew it—its land, its states, its history, above all, its opportunities—for white Americans. The consistent turning away by Lincoln from the moral aspect of slavery toward its impact in its various aspects upon the national interest is best illustrated by his inflexible position against the extension of slavery in the western territories, and his acquiescence of slavery where it existed in place in the South. To moralists of both the North and the South, his position was incomprehensible and contradictory, yet, despite the ugliness of its racism, Lincoln's ethical part insisted upon making his position clear: "We want them (the Territories) for the homes of free white people," he explained. "This they cannot be ... if slavery shall be planted within them... Slave states are places for poor white people to remove from... New free States are places for poor people to go to, and better their condition."

Hofstadter graphically sums up: "Lincoln took the slavery question out of the realm of moral and legal dispute and, by dramatizing it in terms of free (white) labor's self-interest, gave it a universal

45

appeal. To please the abolitionists he kept saying that slavery was an evil thing; but for the material benefit of all Northern white men he opposed its further extension." Even Lincoln's crowning achievement, the Emancipation Proclamation, was promulgated only after two years of military reverses in order to help, not the miserable pawns, the slaves, but the Queen Mother, the Union. Abraham Lincoln, his ethical gear intact, tells it the way he sees it: "If I could save the Union without freeing any slave I would do it; and if I could save it by freeing all the slaves I would do it; and if I could save it by freeing some, and leaving others alone I would also do that...What I do about slavery and the colored race, I do because I believe it helps to save the Union; and what I forbear I forbear because I do not believe it would help to save the Union... When I ... proclaimed emancipation, and employed colored soldiers ... The way these measures were to help the cause, was not to be by magic, or miracles, but by inducing the colored people to come bodily over from the rebel side to ours." It seems clear that claims of Lincoln's greatness will not be satisfied by protestations of his superior moral sense or of his remarkable power with words, or even that he happened to be the right man in the right place. The source of his greatness is at the furthest possible remove from that of his major challenger to pre-eminence in the presidency, Washington, and that is the still immediate, still overpowering sense of his dualistic humanity in all its strengths and weaknesses, its imperviousness and its vulnerabilities, its self-doubts and its assertions of superiority, its love of rules and its indifference to them, its loneliness and its gregariousness, its melancholy and its good humor. For a republic that fantasizes, so often foolishly, on the superiority of its 'common man', Lincoln lends a special dignity to the dream, and allows us to dream on.

5

An American Tragedy: Richard Milhaus Nixon

WITH ABRAHAM LINCOLN'S assassination, elements of tragic drama permeated the American consciousness and appropriated a lasting place for itself. It was not simply that Lincoln was the first president to be assassinated, or that he presided over the butchery of six hundred thousand Americans by other Americans. It was the sense generated of Lincoln, and by Lincoln through much of his life, that the American tragedy was meant to be, and that he was meant to be its leading character.

Yet the Union was preserved, the defecting states were re-absorbed, the slaves were freed, and Lincoln lived at least long enough to feel vindicated for his mauling and warping of the Constitution. He was no longer "a simple Susan, a baboon, an aimless punster, a smutty joker, someone who left the highway of principle to pursue the devious paths of expediency." Instead, he stands triumphant as the greatest presidential hero in American history. By way of contrast, Richard Milhous Nixon, at least according to many historians and political scientists in their periodical polls, is one of America's worst presidents.

If the Watergate scandal had not occurred, Nixon would undoubtedly have a significantly higher standing among historians. Even with it, I find it difficult, when considering his performance as a whole, to consign him to the lowest regions of presidential regard without giving his record and his history a decent chance to defend themselves. Going further, going past the question of judgment for sins into the larger one of a man's fate, I find myself postulating that

47

his story, more even than Abraham Lincoln's, may well be the classical tragic drama in American political history. The elements are there: his unredeemed fall from greatness visited upon him largely by that odd stroke of fate known as Watergate; his character, which, apart from the 'tragic flaw', had significant positive elements, some approaching grandeur: intelligence, courage, sympathy, sensitivity to the misfortunes of others, loyalty, love of family and country, ambition, industry. He was, after all, at least before Watergate, Garry Wills' mix labeled Nixon Agonistes: "What is best and weakest in America goes out to reciprocating strength and deficiencies in Richard Nixon."

A tragic hero, since Aristotle, has been a man whose misfortune is brought upon him by some 'error of judgment' effected not through innate depravity, but through a weakness or lack of insight within the character itself." The modern sense of the 'tragic flaw.' has been expanded, but in any case, it is not something the tragic hero, however mightily he strives, whether he is Cinyras, Oedipus, King Lear, or Nixon Agonistes, can overcome. It is part of that larger, ineluctable fate of which Lincoln and Nixon were so terribly aware: "He," Herndon comments of Lincoln, "held most firmly to the doctrine of fatalism all his life. His wife, after his death, told me what I already knew, that his only philosophy was, what is to be will be, and no prayers of ours can reverse the decree."

"Many of my friends," writes Nixon, "did not want my place in history to be determined by the defeats of 1960 and 1962... That argument never had much appeal to me, because I had a fatalistic, almost deterministic, view of history—that history makes the man more than the man makes history."

"Tragic drama," George Steiner concludes in strikingly evocative fashion, "tells us that the spheres of reason, order, and justice are terribly limited, and that no progress in our science or technical resources will enlarge their relevance. Outside and within man is … the 'otherness' of the world. Call it what you will: a hidden or malevolent God, blind fate, the solicitations of hell, or the brute fury of our animal blood. It waits for us in ambush at the crossroads. It mocks us and destroys us."

To accord to Nixon dimensions of Aristotle's pitiable, tragic figure is to invite the wrath of a significant part of a population that lived through the Nixon years, a population that, rooting Nixon's downfall in his 'vice and depravity,' denies him even a hint of virtue. This

The Legal Mind and the Presidency

includes most predominantly, of course, those adversaries that Nixon, the aggressively defensive poor boy from the West, clearly marked for his own particular villains of the piece: the Ivy Leaguers personified by Alger Hiss and Archibald Cox—his primal instances of one-on-one combat—the Eastern establishment of old wealth and old power, the intellectual community that he professed to chastise for thinking and saying too much, and doing too little, and for whose unattainable camaraderie he, a distant, loveless man, passionately yearned while settling for Charles (Bebe) Rebozo and Robert Ablanalp. They will hardly forgive him for the patronizing image he gave them of themselves—of an arrogant lack of charity for 'just plain folks', for those who had neither an Ivy league background nor 'down home' charm, for those who not only did not get jobs with Wall Street firms, but were not even invited to apply.

There is a larger constituency of outrage at the idea that Nixon should be let off the historical hook and might, in a few decades, even invite sympathy and more than a few tears. There are the hordes of moralists on both the left and right wings, those people who settle through perpetuity for their personal definitions of right and wrong. On the left, they think of Nixon as a monstrous, alien political form that, until it self-destructed, threatened to destroy the American system of checks and balances, rights and liberties. How, they marvel, did he escape the rack and the thumb-screw? How could someone so guilty not be (crucifixion would be a propriety) suitably punished? He was (the word to this group is unprintable) pardoned, as if one could possibly be pardoned for the ultimately heinous crime of being Nixon. On the right, there are those who are actually grateful to the 'radicals' for booting the apostate out; they are still purple with rage at the idea of his cavorting with Zhou-Enlai and Brezhnev, of formulating a Family Assistance Plan, when he might be out there smiting mightily the big enemies: Communists, blacks, Jews, Orientals, college students. If Nixon had listened to them, his plea of 'national security' would have meant something; 'they' got him because of his softness on Communism.

I think that there is something else in most of us that cringes from accepting at face value the idea that Nixon was the arch-villain of a twentieth century, American political comic strip. I invite from this group a willing suspension of disbelief as I posit Nixon as an American tragic hero, in suggesting that it is more fanciful to judge him a horrible unadulterated admixture of vice and depravity, than a much too vulnerable and complicated, tragically flawed human being of both large and small, narrow and generous dimensions. It might even appear, in a less skeptical age of gods of thunder, love and death, that Watergate, his Waterloo, so puzzling and inexplicable in many of its aspects, was a concoction of the 'otherness' of the world, emanating from forces over which Nixon, in the ultimate tragic sense, had no control and which, or something very much like it, was predetermined, from his earliest days in Yorba Linda, California, to destroy him; that Nixon, unhampered by the Furies, as he fancied in his purer daydreams, might even have been considered historically one of our better presidents rather than among our worst.

It is difficult to disengage Nixon from his timeworn image of unlovability and charmlessness, and even the impact of Watergate; but, in fairness, it is something we should try to do if we are to give this unforgettable, for better or worse, public figure a stab at a decent historical slot in the canon of presidents. We at least should recognize that he was in many important respects reflective of his fellow presidential rule-skeptic, Abraham Lincoln. Sometimes the analogies become frighteningly mirror-imaged; in much the same way as Lincoln revered Thomas Jefferson and was nothing like him, so Nixon, after a boyhood flirtation with Lincoln, idealized a disparate Woodrow Wilson. We should, I think, try to appreciate the diversity of the Nixonian mix—his intimate links, real or intensely imagined, with Eisenhower, Ford, Wilson, and Lincoln; they tell us a great deal about the trifurcation of the legal mind—formalists, moralists and rule-skeptics; they tell us a great deal about the American presidents.

I imagine Nixon still alive, reflecting, reading, writing, perhaps lecturing, perhaps staring out a window (to show the power of his metaphor, of the life he has lived), probably recalling, more often than not, one or other of a handful of leaders, Churchill, de Gaulle, MacArthur, Yoshida, Adenauer, Khrushchev, Zhou Enlai, Fidel Castro, the face of this or that journalist in that crowd listening to his swan song that turned into the ugly-duckling dirge of Watergate. Faced with the reincarnated image of the charmless one, I find it hard to think of him simply sitting still with his wife, Pat, or still with his daughter, Julie, or his daughter, Tricia, chatting, sipping wine, settling for the tiny, muted movements of love between people, without charging him with learning while he cavorts with his dog Checkers on the lawn, while he embraces a grandchild: *so this is how it is done.*

Yet there are the soundings of that other insular, involuted, 'self-made' man, Abraham Lincoln: "It is not merely for today, but for all time to come that we should perpetuate for our children's children this great and free government, which we have enjoyed all our lives... It is in order that each of you may have ... a fair chance for your industry, enterprise and intelligence; that you may all have equal privileges in the race of life, with all its desirable human aspirations. It is for this the struggle should be maintained, that we may not lose our birthright." This, of course, is the abiding theme of *Nixon Agonistes*: "(Woodrow Wilson's) speeches ... form a solid bridge across our recent history from Horatio Alger straight to Richard Nixon: 'What this country needs above everything else is a body of laws which will look after the men who are on the make ... I know and every man in his heart knows, that the only way to enrich Americans is to make it possible for any man who has the brains to get into the game... Business underlies every part of our lives; the foundation of our lives, of our spiritual lives included, is economic.' No wonder Nixon feels an affinity for Wilson."

But the affinity with Wilson is born of wonder; Nixon was mesmerized, much as Lincoln with Jefferson, by the dazzle of rhetoric. He could only give lip service; he, an uneasy, troubled man, was unnerved by the contemplation in twinship with an even more uneasy, even more troubled man. Lincoln's picture over his bed as a child becomes Wilson's in Nixon's presidential cabinet room.

Awe of those most confident of lawyer moralists, Lincoln's Jefferson and Nixon's Wilson, was fueled by the lifelong bouts of Lincoln and Nixon with deep, debilitating depressions. Like Lincoln, Nixon grew up in poverty and, while his parents were far from the lack of education of Lincoln's mother and father (Nixon's mother spent two years at Whittier College), he could never quite lose sight of his father's sixth-grade 'learning' The inordinate ambition of both Nixon and Lincoln stemmed, it is easily arguable, from their determination to beat fate in the American way, by a rise above one's station; at the same time the self-doubts generated by their humble origins warned them they never quite could.

Given not only their ambition to rise, but their daydreams of being great and unforgettable figures in the world, it seems inevitable

51

that each, in his own century, would mount a determined invasion of public life. They sensed from the beginning that politics was a particularly combative activity, with winning the true measure of success. Losing is devastating to a politician since he ceases, in his own mind, where it most counts, to matter. The bombardment during his campaign for office on a politician's character and intelligence attains credibility upon his defeat; he is more ready than anyone to believe he deserves it. After all, an American who spends his life running—he scorns the amateur 'joggers'—for public office is compelled to subject himself to the simple litmus test of popularity; public approval, more than money, fame, or even power, is his staff of life. Much as a movie star, he is remembered only as long as he *is* a star; those who no longer get elected are simply forgotten. For both Lincoln and Nixon, winning an election was a matter of psychic life and death.

The degree to which a politician commits himself determines the extent of his torment when he 'dies' to public office; no other president, it is easy to argue, delivered himself quite up, body and soul, as did Lincoln and Nixon to the political arena. Hofstadter assesses Lincoln in a way that makes him more Nixonian than Nixon himself: "The clue to much that is vital in Lincoln's thought and character lies in the fact that he was thoroughly and completely the politician ... It is difficult to think of any man of comparable stature whose life was so fully absorbed into his political being ... 'Politics was my life,' Nixon stated simply."

Lincoln, of course, had a limited pre-presidential public career as a state legislator and one-term congressman while Nixon spent fourteen years as a congressman, senator and vice-president. Lincoln actively practiced law for many more years than Nixon. Yet it seems clear that the apologia pro vita sua for each of them was his political existence.

Nixon, in much the same rule-skeptical way as Lincoln, puzzles analysts by the contradictions in his character and personality, by the variances between his words and his deeds, by his oblique approach to 'moral' solutions. The enigma of the 'real' Richard Nixon, rather than being solved by psychological probes, is only intensified. Mazlish ultimately settles for identifying the three personality traits he regards as dominant in the Nixonian personality, "role identification, ambivalence, and denial," and leaves it at that; he admits him to be "one of the most difficult political figures to analyze." Nixon is much less difficult to understand, and much more familiar type-casting in terms of his mental processes. There are a sufficient number of men like him engaged in the practice of law for lawyers to feel conversant with his way of thinking, and, at the same time, to feel the same uneasiness with his personality. Nixon's hard intelligence is admirable and when he is praised, it is invariably for his mind, especially his verbal facility. He is that rare example in presidential history, along with Polk, whose intellect and tenacity, blunted and frustrated by charmlessness in a career ordinarily doomed to consistent failure without it, carried him past predictable losses to the ultimate prize of the presidency.

It is unrewarding to deal with a legal mind like Nixon's in terms of an undefined morality—to accuse and keep on accusing without framing an indictment. It is essential to scrape away once again the romantic notions of a fixed 'right' and 'wrong,' and to remember that one man's 'right' is another's 'wrong'; that morality depends in any given situation upon what must, to the actors involved, at all costs, survive. For rule-skeptics like Lincoln and Nixon, or Holmes and Frankfurter, for that matter, for whom the conventional cluster of presumptions carries little weight, there is not much doubt about what fills the vacuum: it is the American flag, in all its grandeur, mystery, and lack of definition, that must, at all costs, continue to be. It is hardly surprising that Justice Frankfurter, that same Justice Frankfurter who chose in the Gobitis case the flag over the First Amendment, was for Nixon a paradigmatic justice or that the rights of the accused, as in the Manson mass murder case, meant so little to Nixon.

Nixon had no crowd to play to when, on a 1970 cruise down the Potomac, defying any possible ironic nudges from his family, he recalls: "It is the custom for all naval vessels passing Mount Vernon to honor George Washington, who is buried there. When we neared the spot, I had everyone move onto the deck and face the shore. Pat was next to me, then David, Julie, and Bebe Rebozo. As we passed by the first president's tomb, over the Sequoia's loudspeaker came *The Star Spangled Banner*. We all stood at attention until the last note died away."

The Horatio Alger story, to both Lincoln and Nixon, was part of the American Flag, but only the private part of it, the part that these secretive men squirreled away. They were triggered publicly and continuously by the public part—the national interest, the national security, the national survival—and assumed they would be prized for their patriotism. But the abolitionists and the Civil War doves did not prize Lincoln and the radical students and liberals, including many of the journalists who travelled with him, did not prize Nixon. Zhou Enlai did, and Brezhnev, and de Gaulle, and most of Europe and Asia.

Nixon despised rhetoric. There was no question in his mind, a mind that resisted a priori principles, that deeds spoke louder than words. His skill in debate rested upon his passion for logic and the clear expression of ideas, rather than upon elegance of phrasing. Unlike Jefferson or Wilson, Nixon had no faith in his rhetoric. It was as unabashedly political and partisan as his actions were patriotically motivated. Evans and Novak report his reaction to his early cabinet members: "Nothing was more irritating to the President than the style used by Romney, Hickel and Volpe: evangelistic and self-righteous, long on fury and short on facts ..."

Evans and Novak continue with a highly revelatory incident in which Volpe, nevertheless, "sold the President and did so by employing, instinctively, the one argument that would move Richard Nixon— not economic, nor ecological, nor concerned with the international balance of payments, but a plea to national pride, what Nixon himself called a 'sense of nation.'" An irony in Nixon's reputation is that it is tempting at times to applaud 'Tricky Dick,' albeit with one hand, for his 'duplicity'—at least before Watergate wrenched his behavior beyond recognition.

Unquestionably, Nixon said one thing and did another in Vietnam with the intent to deceive, and unquestionably he intended to deceive the majority of the American people who had voted him into office. If a president, to be honorable, must attempt to be the 'voice of the people,'—at whatever cost to his own sense of morality—Nixon's course was to continue to attempt to win the war, with whatever means were available to him, rather than to capitulate to the wild-eyed radical minority that demanded unilateral withdrawal of American troops, the 'peace at any price' held in such ill repute since Neville Chamberlain. He chose to lie to his American people; he told them he was holding fast when he was already committed to pulling out. The concession should be made that Nixon did a laudable job of extricating America from Vietnam; it is doubtful if he could have managed it quite so well, or even at all, if he had failed to clothe his 'radical' action with conservative rhetoric. Over and over Nixon would cry out in his silent recesses, in that tiny space reserved for non-political urges, 'Watch what we do instead of what we say.' As if it were ordained, he is brought inevitably to face what, fatalistically, after a lie to the conservatives he prized in order to quiet them down, he did what he had to do.

Nixon, as a play in three acts, delineates, in Act One, his embarrassment at his 'humble origins,' the tension generated by his educated mother's pacifism and Christian morals and his uneducated father's anger at having failed to rise in the land of opportunity, his Horatio Alger burn to rise. He is already working harder at making good than any of his friends. He is already becoming a 'loner,' going off to daydream of what might have been, what might yet be. He is already an honors student. Act One ends with a youthful Nixon, lying in bed listening to a train's whistle Pied Pipering him into imagining a success involving not only a rise to the 'top,' but embodying his mother's precept—he will be a 'lawyer who can't be bought by crooks.'

In Act Two, the scenes of Nixon's triumphs and failures pass in review: as a young congressman he exposes Alger Hiss as a communist and becomes nationally prominent; defends, with his Checkers `speech, against accusations of improprieties regarding political expenses and becomes vice-president; Kennedy and Pat Brown do him in as he loses the fight for the governorship of California; he rises from the ashes of his 1962 'farewell address' to reporters to deliver his 1969 Inaugural Address—he has risen to the top and he has brought, he fondly believes, his mother's morals with him: "When we listen to 'the better angels of our nature,' we find that they celebrate the simple things, the basic things—such as goodness, decency, love, kindness. Greatness comes in simple trappings." As Act Two ends, he is eyeing the summit of his career: he will talk to Zhou Enlai, he will talk to Brezhnev. He will extricate America from Vietnam. He will try, as much as anyone, to bring the world together in peace and goodwill.

Act Three, the final act, of course, is Watergate, and the intermingling of Watergate and Nixon's brilliant, bold moves in foreign affairs and domestic economics.

To think of Nixon as a tragic rather than simply a repellent, shabby figure who met his justly deserved shabby end, is to trace his ruination back to a larger sense of fatality, of a 'fault' within him that evoked that 'great error' of Watergate his destiny could not avoid. It involves, in other words, finding in this discredited, deposed leader of men a tragic flaw in an otherwise reasonably decent man, without being unduly distracted by his unfortunate life-long overlay of charmlessness. That tragic flaw is an unbridled rule-skepticism, with its indifference to precedent rules, its reliance on one's own superior intelligence applied to the immediate situation to see one through, its concentration on national survival, and its willingness to take large risks with treasured practices of others that get in the way. It is no accident that Lincoln, his fellow rule-skeptic, has been accused as much as Nixon of flagrant violations of the rules demanded of a president. The difference is that Lincoln's fight for the life of the nation was unambiguous while Nixon's only thought his was—a tragic difference.

To possess a rule-skeptical mind does not necessarily invite tragedy; it must, like any element of character, combine with a certain amalgam of circumstance to result in disaster. Nixon's mind—that very instrument that had carried him to the pinnacle—which had been fine-tuned to the political calling through many campaigns, betrayed him in the end by rising above itself. The more it became obsessed with love of country, the more it was indifferent to, and even scorned, the body politic it inhabited. Richard Nixon, the politician, became even more an enemy to the nation's necessities than the 'leakers' of classified information; every minute consumed by political concerns was a minute lost to the Nixon of summits and peace-making. For the first time in his life, he could not be bothered with monitoring his political troops; meanwhile, they were playing cops and robbers, and shot him down with their cap pistols. The agony of his final days, as much as anything, was being forced to think politics virtually all of the time when he no longer wanted to think of it at all. His isolation, his barbed-wire fences called Haldeman and Ehrlichman (he divined, the ex-master politician, that they would, one way or another, destroy him, but he was buying time) were designed to keep him safe from politics, and other domesticities—to divorce him from that to which he had been wedded all his life. He craved instead, with the stored up passion of a lifetime of locked-in juices, to be sequestered with his one true love, statesmanship, for which he had been conniving all his life, and which he would finally give anything up for.

THE LEGAL MIND AND THE PRESIDENCY

Conventional morality meant nothing to this rule-skeptic. Why should it? Morality meant giving up his freedom to make up his mind as he went along, as he had always done, only now he was playing hardball with the big boys, the ones who had always known that national survival, and only national survival, was the name of the game, was the only morality. He loved them, Khrushchev, Brezhnev, Mao Tse-tung, Zhou Enlai, for the best of reasons: they loved him, more than any other president they had known. He was one of them. They recognized him the moment they looked into his national-survival eyes.

Until he became president, he had lived for politics and thrived on politics; he made speeches for any Republican who asked him to, not merely because he, the grim reaper of political harvests, wanted to collect some markers, but because, then, before qualifying for the international game of national survival, this was the only survival game for him in town, the only game he knew where you could make up the rules as you went along. They were his rules and he stayed on top of them. He was a professional politician.

In the White House he surrounded himself with political amateurs, and told them to go off and handle his re-election campaign. He had no rules or use for them; all they had to do was see that he won—and stay away from him while he made the world safer for American greatness. And he did. He did make the world safer for American greatness. He did great things. But he had surrounded himself with true believers (all amateur politicians are true believers) who did not know how to make up rules as they went along and re-examine them daily—they were not people with options. True believers lived by orders, whether from God, or commanders-in-chief, and he had given them, in his scorn and indifference, only one—they were to see to it that he won the election, and this, in their narrow moralistic perspective, became their only morality. They were not told to keep him safe from tigers, only that they were to make him win. 'Knowledge is power.' 'He who hesitates is lost.' Armed with clichés, they went out to conquer the enemy Democrats and, to show their bravery, they invaded the toothless enemy's lair—the rest is Watergate.

Nixon's overriding tragic flaw was rule-skepticism; it was not pride, ego, ambition, greed, hate, vengeance, brutality, or viciousness. Nixon was a patriot. He would not hesitate to destroy himself if it meant saving the flag. And the flag meant to him that he could not save himself by menacing the system. The flag was the supremacy of the law, which meant, for Americans, the supremacy of the American judiciary. "This president does not defy the law," he sent his lawyer off to say, when he knew, and at that time only he knew, he was destroying himself to keep the system going. It seemed to be inconceivable to him to ignore any of the court orders issued against him, although he had no hesitation in refusing to honor the Senate Select Committee's subpoenas. The result was significantly to strengthen the judiciary's hand in judicial review of presidential actions.

Nixon issued no pardons; he asked for none. He trusted history to proclaim him a great president although, at the end, a terrible politician. Ah, if he had been in his political heyday what miracles could he not have wrought when first informed of the break-in. What could he not have accomplished with a real Greek chorus of say, Presidents Eisenhower, Ford, Wilson, and Lincoln, men forged on a political bellows, instead of the unanchored playboys of the western world, Haldeman, Ehrlichman, and Dean. He must have divined instantly that they were too young, pliant, and frightened to guide a rule-skeptic through the shark's jaws of moral decisions, but 'they', his furies, forbade him to listen to himself for even that one golden moment it would have taken to banish them. If he had retained the most meager of his political instincts, he would have summoned Kissinger, Laird, and Shultz, and made them make him whole: his political instinct, if it had not been dormant and tortured by Lincolnian, spaced-out vagaries of grandeur, should have told him these men could not afford to make silly mistakes, political, moral, what have you. For, although he had avoided it religiously, this, finally, was what a president's cabinet was for.

But what of our Greek chorus? "Got to be clean as a hound's tooth," Eisenhower confidently prescribes. "There is only one white when it comes to morality." The famous Eisenhower grin lights up the room. "My old 'boss,' Harry Truman, was right for once to criticize a person for not knowing the difference between telling the truth and lying. In a showdown fight I prefer one courageous, honest man at my side to a whole boxcar full of pussy-footers. Fire the whole bunch, all your campfire boys, like Haldeman and Dean, who just weren't as clean as a hound's tooth; imagine them trying to claim they were being dirty for you. Really? As if they should not be doing everything for you, anyway. Say you maybe misled them with your talk about

THE LEGAL MIND AND THE PRESIDENCY

their getting everything there was to know about the Democrats, and ranting and raving about Kennedy's 'dirty tricks' team. They should have known that tricks were out for, excuse me, you know what I mean, Tricky Dick; let's face it, you've never put your money where your mouth is, anyway. Your boys had to learn the playbook better. They should have learned, excuse me, that you're a lousy juggler, no coordination at all. They should have known that even when you're talking about juggling the truth that you're just using lawyer talk. Look here. Compared to my heart attack and my stroke, my yesterday instead of my tomorrow, you were young, you were strong, and you could have done a lot better than that. I say you should have gone on nationally, come clean to the American people, disposed of your Krauts; I mean right now, teach 'em' who's staff and who's boss. An individual who desires to remain in public life must never reject what he senses to be a sincere desire on the part of a majority of the rank and file voters, as well as the officials of his party, for him to lead them in battle. Either you run the damn show or you resign."

"I agree," says Ford. "I really do. It would tear me apart to fire a good, loyal Republican, but that's what you had to do. And if they tried to send a good, loyal Republican like Haldeman to jail for conspiracy to commit a burglary, why you just pardon them. I hate to say it, but you should have fired the whole bunch of good, loyal Republicans in that June of '72 like the General says."

"I cannot even imagine your problem, Richard," says Wilson, "even though," with a glint of his eyeglasses at Eisenhower, "you very kindly think I was the greatest President of this century, and the best-educated. I cannot believe that you might have even given, what are their names, Haldeman? Ehrlichman? anything but short shrift, much less succumbed to their connivances, propounded solutions to their personal problems. You, my dear Sir, were saving your world, remember? What is loyalty to friends, compared to that? You were covenanting with Zhou Enlai, with Leonid Brezhnev; you were making the world safe for Americans to walk the Moscow and Shanghai streets at night, teaching the backward, shameless Chinese and Russians to behave themselves, to do *right*. Your subordinates deserved only one thing: immediate dismissal."

They were all really directing their words, as board members do, to the board chairman: Abraham Lincoln. They all feel that the business of the presidency is business. Will he agree with them?

59

Will Lincoln nod through his beard in approval? They wait for the melancholy frown to thaw from its frost of inattention, from its concentration on the inner springs of man and nature. Lincoln starts, he remembers where he is, and that the Chairman has an obligation to speak the unspeakable.

"Have I ever told you about the Irishman who has forsworn liquor, but finds himself in the Watergate bar," Lincoln begins with a wink, and they smile dutifully; he must always begin with his bit of whimsy. "Since Dick is an Irishman through and through, he might especially enjoy this one." Nixon flashes his grimace that he prays, hopelessly, will yet grow into an Eisenhower grin." This Irishman," says Lincoln, slapping his knee and tugging his beard as if Nixon's world was beginning rather than ending, "after he makes sure his darlin' wife, to whom he has made his abstinence vows, is nowhere around, confides in the bartender that he is not averse to having a 'spot' added to his glass of lemonade, so long as it's unbeknownst to me."

Lincoln is doubled over with laughter. Eisenhower and Ford grin mightily. Wilson frowns. Nixon's grimace flashes on and off like a neon sign. Suddenly, as if the current has been shorted, Lincoln withdraws. He sits in front of them, but they know (how well Nixon knows) he is not there. He is in his private places and they must wait for his return. The quarter hours pass. Finally, he shakes himself and, as if he had never left, proceeds sadly: "The Irishman's whiskey tale is, after all, no joke. We must have ideas, we presidents, either for us or against us. There is no middle ground. And once we entertain an idea that we embrace as 'right' for us, however wrong it may appear to others, do we abandon the idea once it is under severe bombardment? Or do we persevere under the cloak of night, under the camouflage of quip and misdirection? Must a president mislead the American people in order to lead them to the unpromised land? I think, from time to time, he must. I have no fear of the word, 'duplicity.' All presidents have a bit of the secret agent in them: When the Pennsylvania miners broke out against the operation of the (Civil War) draft law...worried Harrisburg officials inquired whether (I) would send troops to execute the law. (What did I do? I exercised my presidential right of duplicity.) I sent a confidential message to...the...Pennsylvania governor: ... 'I am very desirous to have the laws fully executed, but it might be well ... to be content with the appearance of executing the laws...' Thus, (my) administration won the credit both for preserving the peace and for enforcing the draft.

"Now, Richard understood this when he was president. He knew that so long as it was unbeknownst to him, a 'spot' could be added to his lemonade. What a president like him or me must do is what it takes to keep our country great from sea to shining sea. His honor is defined by his devotion to his country. This is what he must make clear to his aides; and they, in turn, must understand that their reward is in his approval if they succeed in their operations; if they fail, they, as any secret agent knows, must be disavowed. All this, of course, is premised on the president's motive, however misguided. If he is genuinely and exclusively motivated by the national interest in the issuance of his guidelines, he is an honorable man—and only then. It is a long way from the splendor of emancipation to the shame of Watergate, and yet a line of historical influence runs between them ... It is accordingly possible to conclude that my use of executive power was wise and appropriate in its context, but not an unmixed blessing as a presidential tradition.

"I like to believe, for instance, that my suspension of habeas corpus, my suppression of newspapers, my secret police and their midnight arrests, my paid informers, were purely and unequivocally triggered by my deep and abiding commitment to the national interest in a time of extreme peril. I can no more be persuaded that the government can constitutionally take no strong measure in time of rebellion, because it can be shown that the same could not be lawfully taken in time of peace, than I can be persuaded that a particular drug is not good medicine for a sick man, because it can be shown not to be good food for a well one.

"I believe—all my life I have believed, and in very little else, I'm afraid—that we have the greatest country on earth because I, the son of illiterate parents, with one year of formal schooling to my name, could become the chief magistrate of one of the most literate populations in the world. A country in which a person with but willing hands and an agile brain can, without even being named Jackson, 'kill' the bank; this is a country which merits one's last full measure of devotion. I believe we can accept a genuinely felt patriotism in Richard equal to my own.

"It is easy for most Americans to say that a patriot is one who is willing to die for his country and let it go at that. It is not so easy for a president from whom patriotism requires that he *live* for his country as well. Richard is, and I understand his doing so, equating his situation with mine, but mine was war, literally, and his was metaphorical: 'war' in the streets, 'war' on the campuses, 'war' against law and order.

"Richard's behavior in the cover-up was, however, impeachable and criminal. He was advised of a crime committed by his subordinates and, regardless of whether or not it was occasioned by his own neglect, he knew, was required to know, as a patriot who loved his country and its system of government under law, that justice must be served over politics. He knew, was required to know, that we are a nation founded more on rights than on democracy and its political processes.

"My concern here is not with Richard's guilt, but whether we might not, with malice toward none, charity toward all, unearth an extenuating circumstance. I find it readily, since it is so reminiscent of my own, in his cast of thought. He simply did not think in terms of a political 'right' or 'wrong,' but rather an 'effective' or 'ineffective' one. While he would not dream, himself, of physically performing 'dirty tricks, imbibing a 'spot' unbeknownst to him, well, that always had to at least be considered—so long as it worked, and it remained unbeknownst to him. Is it immoral not to think in terms of conventional morality when it leads loyal supporters to commit very, very dirty tricks? I shouldn't think so if it helps to win a war; I should think so if it helps merely to win an election.

"It's this, finally—a matter of perspective. My prime virtue was his tragic flaw. I am filled with both pity and terror at his misfortunes (there but for the sake of God go I), I offer him my best cotton kerchief to bind up his wounds. I know that if our roles were reversed he would do the same for me."

Mr. Lincoln falls silent and stares into space for several minutes while the others fidget. Finally he lets out a hoot of laughter and slaps his knee: "Have I ever told you of that friendly Kentuckian I once rode with in a carriage? The man offered me a chew of tobacco, then a cigar, and finally a sip of brandy from a flask. Each offer I politely declined. As we were parting, the Kentuckian said good-humoredly, 'See here, stranger, you're a clever but strange companion. I may never see you again, and I don't want to offend you, but I want to say this:

my experience has taught me that a man who has no vices has damned few virtues. Good day.'"

Nixon's tragedy has ended. Since his death, he lives on only in memory, past Washington, D. C, past California and beyond, but his political curtain has come down. He has written about leaders, other leaders, and even there, in the text, there are no new revelations, no new clues, about what the real Nixon was really like. A sad truth is that we know all we need to know and that we knew all along. An even sadder truth is that to know Nixon was to know a more decent and honorable man than he seemed, until as if to play out his pre-destined string, he reconstructed himself into the indecent and dishonorable man that he never had been before. Only then, only when he had finally become the Nixon that reporters could no longer kick around (not even reporters kick a dead horse) did he pay his dues to the fatality that shaped his ends. An essential condition of a tragic hero's death is that it pulls his convulsed nation back together again. Nixon's political death may go that way into history—a new generation of Americans perhaps will insist on it.

PART TWO

LAWYER MORALISM IN THE PRESIDENCY

6

A Bird's Eye View of Lawyer Moralist Presidents

APART FROM WHAT intellectuals have made of fellow traveler Thomas Jefferson on the one hand, and Andrew Jackson as a diamond in the rough on the other, embedded in each of their guiding stars is a morality that forms a simple equation, simple for democratic rhetoric at least, between democracy and virtue. At the same time, the seeds of de Tocqueville's repeatedly quoted observation, conceived in the age of Jackson, that the American lawyer was the American aristocrat bloomed in this moral climate.

Jefferson, Jackson, Wilson, and Franklin Roosevelt, presidential lawyer moralists, particularly used the idea of speaking for and only for 'the people', to embrace, in its fullest sense, an 'aristocratical' life for themselves as presidents.

A signal characteristic of the presidential lawyer moralist is his patrician scorn of the judiciary when it interferes with his individual sense of the 'rights of the people'. This is indeed paradoxical, because Americans are generally considered to have no rights that the courts won't enforce for them; at least they have no constitutional rights enforceable in any other way than revolution or the difficult process of amendment. This is not to say that the lawyer moralists consciously exhibit contempt for the law itself, that centerfold of the Constitution; at least their rhetoric usually is respectful, while never even remotely approximating the respect of the non-lawyers for both the law and the judiciary, or the lawyer formalist for the Constitution.

Rights, oddly enough, are marked by what Keats labeled as the 'negative capability' of a man of achievement, especially in literature, of "being in uncertainties, mysteries, doubts, without any irritable reaching after fact and reason." In a very direct way, rights protect the doubters both from the rule of reason and the inexorable will of the 'people.' A cluster of vagaries protects the individual's search for self-expression from a government bent upon preservation—of itself, its society and, however reluctantly, its citizens. By injecting a streak of romanticism into the heart of a legal system bedded in reason, rights have glamorized the otherwise pedestrian sense one has of being not under man, but law.

Jefferson, Jackson, Wilson, and Franklin Roosevelt were true believers in the 'rights' of the 'people.' The problems that evolved from this faith lay not primarily in flaws in their presidential characters, which quite often manifested highly personal, capricious, and high-handed tendencies, but in the uncertain nature of rights themselves. The consequence of an attitude that resisted reason was for each of these lawyer moralists to rely confidently upon his own visionary scheme of rights and wrongs. This more often than not led to a lawyer moralist presidential rule of a highly personal, capricious, and high-handed nature. In Jackson's case, whether it involved the Bank of the United States, the Cherokee Indians in Georgia, or South Carolina and nullification, what seemed right to Jackson became a right of the American 'people', and those who opposed the 'right' became, not merely hated by Jackson, but divested of any share in communal rights.

Since the Constitution is a codification of the rule of reason, the pervasive politician's reference to 'the people' qualifies as a convenient cover for negative capability. It is important, I think, to point out that the element of negative capability in literature is not derogatory. Its negation is a capability; it is the commendable quality of being able to transcend the rigid, inflexible mandates of reason and making of the human experience something richer, by way of instinct and imagination. In literature it may result, as John Keats tells us, in Shakespeare. In politics, however, it may lead us, by an unprecedented sacrifice of reason to instinctual pressures, into peril, since the body politic is involved. It leads us to those tense, self-righteous moments in American history provided us by a Jefferson with his embargoes, a Jackson with his destruction of the monetary system, Wilson with his Veracruz and League of Nations, and a Roosevelt with court-packing and internment of Japanese Americans.

7

Words Speak Louder Than Actions: Thomas Jefferson

ADRIENNE KOCH, A writer deeply involved with Jeffersonian thought, characterizes Thomas Jefferson as "the child of the European Enlightenment and in himself the superb fulfillment of the American Enlightenment." Even in this brief statement, Koch indicates the depth of her understandable reverence for Jefferson, a devotion, however, that blurs with his behavior during such equivocal incidents as his tainted governorship of Virginia, his defense of the bloodiest of the French revolutionaries, his secret 'nullification' acts while vice-president, his unbending hostility toward the English, his relentless prosecution of Aaron Burr, and his frenzied enforcement of the Embargo Acts.

To defend Jefferson's virtue is to defend the praiseworthy deepest, and at the same time most vulnerable, part of him. Garry Wills is persuasive when he views Jefferson as a 'child' of the Scottish Enlightenment, with its fundamental emphasis on an innate "moral sense," independent of reason, rather than the English Lockean version of morality discoverable only through reason. As Jefferson writes in an August 10, 1787 letter: "He who made us would have been a pitiful bungler if he had made the rules of our moral conduct a matter of science. For one man of science, there are thousands who are not. What would have become of them? Man was destined for society. His morality therefore was to be formed to this object. He was endowed with a sense of right and wrong merely relative to this. This sense is as much a part of his nature as the sense of hearing, seeing, and feeling; it is the true foundation of morality... The moral sense, or conscience, is as much a part of

THE LEGAL MIND AND THE PRESIDENCY

man as his leg or arm. It is given to all human beings in a stronger or weaker degree...State a moral case to a ploughman and a professor. The former will decide it as well, and often better than the latter, because he has not been led astray by artificial rules."

This often-quoted letter displays much of the rhetoric that forms a significant part of our vision of Jefferson. There is the trust in the 'common' man, and springing from that 'the people.' There is the suspicion of 'artificial rules,' which is to say, suspicion of the application of reason or precedent laws to moral behavior. We might safely enough predict that judicial decrees, being, after all, rules governing human behavior, would come under Jefferson's fire when they opposed his moral vision.

It seems odd, then, to recall that Thomas Jefferson was formally educated to be a lawyer, more exhaustively so than virtually all his contemporaries, and that he practiced law full time for seven years, An intellectual complicity with an 'innate' moral sense would seem to impel one more toward the pulpit than the courtroom, and indeed, Hutcheson and Reid, leaders of the Scottish Enlightenment, were trained in the ministry. The commingling in Jefferson of legal training, with its concentration upon reason and analysis of precedent rules, and faith in a moral sense that preceded and operated outside of, and often in resistance to, reason and rules, gave rise to remarkable contradictions and paradoxes in his character.

A thoughtful and prominent, but far from objective, critic wrote in 1836, some ten years after Jefferson's death: "I read over the portion of Jefferson's correspondence during that period (of the Alien and Sedition Acts), published by his grandson. It shows his craft and duplicity in very glaring colors. I incline to the opinion that he was not altogether conscious of his own insincerity, and deceived himself as well as others. His success through a long life, and especially from his entrance upon the office of Secretary of State under Washington until he reached the presidential chair, seems, to my imperfect vision, a slur upon the moral government of the world. His rivalry with Hamilton was unprincipled on both sides ... continued reading the letters of Jefferson from 1793 till August, 1803... His duplicity sinks deeper and deeper into my mind. His hatred of Hamilton was unbounded; of John Marshall, most intense; of my father, tempered with compunctious visitings, always controlled by his ambition..." This writer, of course, is John Quincy Adams.

Transcending the dark side of Jefferson's moon are the loyalty and high regard, even affection, for him, displayed by such profound and not easily captured social scientists as John Adams and James Madison. While John Adams and Jefferson were estranged and hostile toward each other for eleven years, they were friends and intellectual communers for thirty. He possesses as well the intense admiration of such respected biographers as Dumas Malone and Adrienne Koch, and ranks fifth best president in both the 1948 and 1962 Schlesinger presidential polls. Of special interest is the 1982 Murray-Blessing poll of historians specifically classified as liberals or conservatives, both of which rated him as fourth best.

Biographers of Jefferson are extraordinarily stubborn in dealing with the contradictory aspects of his character; they prefer to land on one side and either explain the other side away or ignore its existence. Certainly Jefferson offers enough material to convince a liberal historian that he is the archetypal liberal; nevertheless, a conservative historian would have little trouble identifying with him. His radical rhetoric is more than met by the conservatism and caution of his so-called revolution of 1800.

He was not flamboyant. Even as a lawyer he stuck primarily to the solicitor side of law business-such matters as land title determinations, collections, and the drafting of wills and deeds. He had little or no sense of humor, a fairly common trait of moralists. The Swiftian rapier did not suit Jefferson. He disapproved of satire and hid what little humor he had under 'the pale cast of thought.' What was ludicrous in life was cause for regret rather than amusement. Expecting so much of men, and nations too, he could not laugh at their follies, least of all his own. His inability to laugh at himself triggered a distaste for opposition that moved from irritation to hatred in short order, a hatred far from rhetorical in nature that translated itself, wherever Jefferson had, or thought he had, the power, into efforts to destroy utterly the object of his hostility. Jefferson was a remarkably talented human being but could be a perverse and vindictive one as well.

There is a ring of psychological truth about John Quincy Adams' surmise that Jefferson "was not altogether conscious of his own insincerity, and deceived himself as well as others." His moral override tended to blur for him the shabby consequences of much of his behavior; otherwise how, for example, could he have equated his

70

vendetta against one man, Burr, with his strenuous efforts to protect the rights of all the American people: "Should we," he asked, "have ever gained our Revolution, if we had bound our hands by manacles of the Law?"

Adrienne Koch's glossing over, in the name of an abstract idealism, Jeffersonian attacks upon Burr, upon the judicial system in general and Justices Chase and Marshall in particular, is an act of critical charity, particularly when measured against Jefferson's early extravagant praise for the judiciary, as in 1789 when he wrote to James Madison, "In the arguments in favor of a declaration of rights, you omit one which has great weight with me; the legal check which it puts into the hands of the judiciary. This is a body, which, if rendered independent & kept strictly to their own department, merits great confidence for their learning and integrity. In fact, what degree of confidence would be too much for a body composed of such men as Wythe, Blair & Pendleton?"

His later judiciary utterances sprang out of his activities as president in bitter, unsuccessful disputes with Marshal, such as *Marbury v. Madison* and the Burr treason trials.

The intensity of Jefferson's verbalized contempt for the judiciary and juridical law has no parallel among the other presidents, although comparisons can be made with Jackson, Wilson, and Franklin Roosevelt, fellow travelers in the lawyer moralist group. Jefferson's rhetoric was entirely intractable in this area. The mere thought of Marshall at any given moment could enflame him: "...what I dare say our cunning Chief Justice (Marshall) would swear to, and find as many sophisms to twist it on out of the general terms of our Declarations of rights ...as he did to twist Burr's neck out of the halter of treason. May we not say then with him who was all candor and benevolence 'Woe unto you, ye lawyers, for ye lade men with burdens grievous to bear.'"

Even old age failed to soften him: "Experience has already shown that the impeachment (of judges) ... is not even a scarecrow ... The Constitution, on this hypothesis (that 'the judiciary is the last resort in relation to the other departments of the government') is a mere thing of wax in the hand of the judiciary, which they may twist, and shape in any form they please... The judiciary of the United States is the subtle corps of sappers and miners constantly working under ground to undermine the foundations of our confederated fabric... The great object of my fear is the federal judiciary. That body, like gravity, ever acting, with noiseless foot, and unalarming advance, gaining ground step by step, and holding what it gains, is ingulphing insidiously the special governments into the jaws of that which feeds them."

As a constant, there is the divorce of Jeffersonian rhetoric from action. Earlier, his immediate reaction to the Constitution was, "I should have liked it better had the Judiciary been associated for that purpose (presidential veto), or invested with a similar and separate power."

A revelatory instance of Jefferson's tendency to turn a deaf ear to his own warning voices involves his participation in the Kentucky and Virginia resolutions of 1798, passed in reaction to the Alien and Sedition Laws The determined secrecy regarding his draftsmanship of the initial resolution, the Kentucky proposal, gives pause to his most sympathetic apologists.

Jefferson was Vice-President of the United States, serving under John Adams, with the minimal duty to be loyal to the government of which he was a part. Yet, in his original draft submitted to the Kentucky legislature, he conceived and pushed for the nullification doctrine, a concept that was later to torment Jackson and Lincoln. The Kentucky legislature removed Jefferson's language inviting all the states to 'concur in declaring these acts void and of no force.' This was a pure example of Jefferson's willingness to employ a radical rhetoric that he was not personally compelled to enforce, and whose consequences he was not obligated to face.

Jefferson was not an either-or man like Patrick Henry; he didn't take a bold overt position when he could avoid it, as in his secret preparation of the Kentucky Resolutions. He merely proposed radicalism and readily accepted the refusal of others, such as the Kentucky legislature, literally to act out his rhetoric.

To cast Jefferson in the role of civil libertarian is inevitably to entangle his apologists in contradictions. It would seem to be impossible to call him, during the Burr trial, a protector of the rights of man. Marshall's formulation of treason that resulted in Burr's acquittal was actually occasioned, and properly so, by the failure of the government to provide the constitutionally required proof of overt acts by Burr, to support its charge of his raising troops against the government. To recognize Jefferson's flaws, then, to realize that there is something menacing about the split between his acts and rhetoric, the kind of self-deception that sends others out to die for revolutionary freedom while he pursues intellectual curiosities, is still to admit that Jefferson is, nevertheless, a legendary American, one of those vital people out of whose mix contemporary America is composed. This is 'self-evident' even to those who might respond, impulsively and cynically, that what America now is should not happen to anyone, that it is defined by murder, rape, drugs, pollution, suicide bombers, wars, nuclear leaks and, worst of all, by political betrayals of that governmental responsibility which Locke, at least, considered a sacred trust. A political leader, Locke stoutly maintains, holds his power in trust for the people; he is responsible, by law, to the people for their lives, liberties, and property, a commitment that transcends rhetorical professions.

It is difficult to rail against Jefferson, an undeniable genius. His Declaration of Independence was a gem. His political theories were indispensable in the formulation of American democracy at its best. But who is to say that a genius must have a good heart? It is here, divorced from protestations of good will to the common man, that Jefferson comes off so poorly. Such hearts, in the early days of the American Republic, belonged to James Madison and John Adams, and each of them, in his own way, was a victim of Jefferson's failure of character.

Jefferson's famous, self-composed epitaph moves us from his nasty side to his ineradicable claim upon our respect, if not our love: "Here was buried Thomas Jefferson, author of the Declaration of American Independence, of the Statute of Virginia for Religious Freedom, and father of the University of Virginia."

After all, in authoring ideas that stimulated one of mankind's grand historical processes, Jefferson was performing in the same epochal arena as Jesus Christ, Karl Marx, and John Locke. His rhetoric made a scavenger hunt of the search for America's future that seemed so direct and straightforward under Constitutional directives. Jefferson's contribution in the age of Lockeian reason, and in the teeth of a deistic embrace of 'freedom' from religion, was a mystical wash of faith, in 'the people', in a moral sense as real as a leg, in revolutionary change, in transcendental mind over mundane matter, in Jeffersonianism, a political form of Swedenborgianism, with its own set of true believers. We have no Madisonian, Adamsonian, Washingtonian or even Lincolnian, but we do have Jeffersonian democracy (along with that other American form of Swedenborgianism that is known as

Emersonian democracy). And Swedenborg, after all, did have his own meticulous devotion to detail (reports on smelting and assaying), and invention of various machines and contraptions (ear trumpets for the deaf, flying machines), even as Jefferson did.

8

The Bank is Trying to Kill Me, But I Will Kill It: Andrew Jackson

ONE OF THE most intriguing linkages between presidents is that which joins Thomas Jefferson and Andrew Jackson, the early patron saints of the modern Democratic party, particularly at fund-raising dinners. Yet each knew enough to scorn the other. Jefferson, according to Daniel Webster, commented: "I feel much alarmed at the prospect of seeing General (Andrew) Jackson, President. He is one of the most unfit men I know of for such a place. He (taking one to know one?) has had very little respect for Laws or Constitutions ... His passions are terrible. When I was President of the Senate, he was a Senator; & he could never speak from the rashness of his feelings. I have seen him attempt it repeatedly, & as often choak with rage... he is a dangerous man."

Jackson was equally vitriolic: "Mr. Jefferson has plenty of courage to seize peaceable Americans (Burr) ... and persecute them for political purposes. But he is too cowardly to resent foreign outrage on the Republic ... The Federalists will jump Burr, tooth and toenail, and when they do Jefferson will run like a cottontail rabbit. He's the best Republican in theory and the worst in practice I've ever seen."

Jackson's assessment of the Jeffersonian 'fault' manages an uncanny psychological accuracy that lends credence to Jacksonian devotees who label him an intuitive, untutored genius of sorts. Amos Kendall, his Postmaster General, stated: "His reasoning was like lightning and his action like the thunderbolt... though he acted rapidly, he never acted rashly. The difference between him and other men was more in the rapidity of reasoning than in the prudence of action. Louis McClane (Jackson's Secretary of the Treasury, then State) said of him: 'General Jackson was the most rapid reasoner I have ever met with. He jumps to a conclusion before I can start on my premises.'"

James K. Paulding, a writer and Martin Van Buren's Secretary of State, goes even further: "To him (Jackson) knowledge seemed entirely unnecessary. He saw intuitively into everything, and reached a conclusion by a short cut while others were beating the bush for the game."

Jackson had no trouble disdaining Jefferson the man (to him, the coward) at the same time that he was a 'Jeffersonian' democrat. He felt that he practiced what Jefferson could only preach. He was outraged at Jefferson's equation of government with self in the Burr case, and yet he promptly mirrored such personification in his own dealings with Biddle and the Bank of the United States.

The truth is that Jackson was more like Jefferson than either of them could admit, once one puts aside the fearlessness of one and the physical timidity of the other. As presidents, the 'untutored' mind of Jackson and the 'academic' mind of Jefferson met and were twins in that hidden staging area where thoughts prepare for action, and are all too often translated into their opposites. Significantly enough, affected by their tenure as practicing lawyers at the height of their evangelical imperatives, their abandoned lawyerdom colored their moral decisions. Jackson was a lawyer and a judge for some sixteen years, from 1788 to 1804; he was active as a military commander for only six or seven, from 1812 to about 1819. It is understandable that the dramatics of Jackson's brilliant victory at New Orleans, at or after the end of the War of 1812, and his highhanded invasion of Spanish Florida while chasing hostile Seminole and Creek Indians, climaxed by his execution of two British subjects as Indian collaborators, should overshadow Jackson's legal career, but that his lawyerdom should be summarily dismissed, or even excused away, by historians is astonishing. Other military heroes, after all, such as Washington, Grant, and Eisenhower were trained for the military; their training initiated and prescribed their adult careers. They were professional soldiers, in other words, while Jackson, as his supporters delighted in saying, was a 'citizen soldier': "Supporters toasted Jackson as the 'Farmer of Tennessee.'" When he died, a eulogist summed it up: "He wielded the axe, guided the plough, and made, with his own hands,

THE LEGAL MIND AND THE PRESIDENCY

the most of his farming utensils-as nature had made him a farmer and a mechanic, besides making him a statesman and soldier."

Undeniably, Jackson was not a John Adams, John Quincy Adams, Daniel Webster, William Wirt, or John Marshall in his relationship to the law. Relatively few lawyers were then, or are now. On the other hand, there were many lawyers, and not all of them were practicing on the frontier, whose legal careers were equivalent to that of Jackson. Stripped of a military coating, no one, in summing up, would fail to concentrate on the corpus juris of such a life.

To say that Jackson was not a scholar of the law is not to say that Jefferson, or Woodrow Wilson, or Franklin Roosevelt was. Yet they were all lawyers and two of them were 'bookish' though not precisely in the law. Jefferson and Wilson were not legal scholars because, to put it mildly, the study of law was distasteful to them. Jackson and Franklin Roosevelt were not scholars of anything, which, at least, is to give them the nod for the purity of their resistance to 'book learning.'

Unlike Jefferson, Jackson liked being a lawyer and spent a large amount of his life struggling to become, and becoming, a judge. Yet as late as 1977, Burke Davis, a noteworthy biographer, nevertheless is so impelled to depreciate Jackson's legal career that he transvaluates a striking example of Jackson's legal mindedness: "Judge Jackson occasionally revealed a disregard for precedent that perplexed lawyers who practiced in his court. In 1803, he heard a complex land case in Nashville involving titles that had been clouded years earlier in a decision by Judge McNairy—with the assistance of District Attorney Jackson. Jackson reversed McNairy's decision. An appeal was filed that cited one of Jackson's own arguments, but he denied the plea on the grounds that the federal court had no appellate jurisdiction, and because McNairy's decision had been contrary to the law and the facts. When a complaining attorney pointed out that the decision was based on the arguments of District Attorney Jackson, Judge Jackson replied that his oath as district attorney had bound him to protect the interest of the government, but that his oath as judge bound him to rule impartially between private citizens... The decision stood."

No Holmes or Marshall could have behaved in a more judicial fashion. To bind a judge to his prior arguments made while a state prosecutor is unthinkable to a responsible lawyer. To hold to what he obviously considered a bad prior decision under the law was equally unthinkable.

The principal grounds for general ignorance of Jackson as a lawyer are the assumptions, not only that he was 'untechnical, unlearned,' but that this resulted in a superior, native wisdom. The contrast between Jackson and John Quincy Adams, the New England lawyer intellectual, often proved irresistible. Accordingly, Henry A. Wise observes: "Jackson was the very man to d—n Grotius, Puffendorf and Vattel; and Adams was the very man to condemn him for that above all other things as a great malefactor. Jackson cared only for his justification; but Adams was horrified at its mode. Jackson made law, Adams quoted it.

"That Mr. Adams is possessed of learning (wrote the Republican General Committee of New York City) we are willing to admit... That he is learned we are willing to admit; but his wisdom we take leave to question...to know that which before us lies in daily life, is the prime wisdom. That wisdom we believe Gen. Jackson possesses in an eminent degree."

Jackson was the first Gary Cooper 'High Noon' hero, the first Clint Eastwood 'High Plains Drifter', the first Natty Bummpo (who, after all, surfaced at much the same time as Jackson). 'High Noons' and 'High Plains Drifters' are fashioned from the betrayal of law and order by the prevailing legal system; the man on the white horse, even more violent than the criminals, must then gallop to the rescue of us all. The idea that such a hero might temper his individual sense of justice with a resort to protracted litigation is repugnant to most moviegoers.

The practice of the average lawyer in the smaller firms and the rural areas minimizes the intellectual stress of appellate work, and such specialties as corporation, tax, and equity law. Jackson's cases, 'disputed land titles, assault cases, and bad debts,' were and remain typical. Jefferson was practicing a similar law in Virginia a decade or so earlier; his cases dealt with 'land ownership, debts, the recovery of slaves, slander, assault, and battery.' He never liked being a lawyer, and it was during his seven years of practice that he was the best sport he was to be; yet his lawyerdom, unlike Jackson's, has been faithfully extenuated and accommodated. Being a lawyer is not especially antagonistic to intellectuality (it is, to Jacksonian instinctualism), and in its higher planes of performance is considered apposite.

In a way that has been defined as peculiarly American, Jackson manifested a great respect for the law at the same time that he did not hesitate to take it into his own hands for the sake of the 'right'. He was capable of saying, and meaning, when judges were being arbitrarily removed in Kentucky in 1821: "Let me tell you, that all the rights secured to the citizens under the constitution is worth nothing, and a mere bubble, except guaranteed to them by an independent and virtuous Judiciary ... I hope the enlightened freemen of Kentucky will assert their rights, and preserve the independence of the Judiciary unimpaired by faction, or the designing demagogues of the day."

However, after imposing martial law on New Orleans following his victory in 1814 over the British, he was equally ready to arrest both a Louisiana state legislator as a spy for censuring his acts, and a Judge Dominick Hall for issuing a writ of habeas corpus to release the legislator. This high-handed disregard of the judiciary illustrates the curious mix of rhetoric balanced against action in Jackson, a mix that invites the same accusations of duplicity leveled against Jefferson before, and Wilson and Franklin Roosevelt after him.

Robert V. Remini, an intense admirer, is impelled, nevertheless, to acknowledge the self-deceiving split in Jackson: "A slave owner all his adult life, he regarded liberty as the priceless heritage of all men. A staunch advocate of equality, he thought only in terms of white adult males. Women, blacks, and Indians did not enter his thinking about liberty or equality, and his public statements to Congress invariably included the most racist ideas prevalent at the time."

An interesting reading of Jackson's flirtations with raw morality on the one hand and seasoned law on the other emerges from a running commentary by Justice Story. The tension between Jackson and the Supreme Court arose over the challenges of the States of Georgia and South Carolina to the supremacy of the United States Supreme Court in determining constitutional questions. The particular controversies arose through Georgia's claim of sovereignty over Indian lands within its borders, and South Carolina's resurrection of Jefferson's nullification doctrine in resistance to the Federal tariff of 1828.

It was predictable that Jackson, with his background as an Indian fighter, should favor Georgia as the Supreme Court became locked in a terrifying, literally life-and-death struggle with the State of Georgia. This situation initiated one of Justice Story's pessimistic views of Jackson's anti-court bias: "I have for a long time known that the present rulers and their friends were hostile to the judiciary ... The recent attacks in Georgia, and the recent Nullification doctrine in

South Carolina are but parts of the same general scheme, the object of which is to elevate an exclusive State sovereignty upon the ruins of the General government.".

After the Supreme Court voided the Georgia statute, Justice Story expected the worst from Jackson: "We have just decided the Cherokee case, and reversed the decisions of the State Court of Georgia, and declared her laws unconstitutional ... Georgia is full of anger and violence. What she will do, it is difficult to say. Probably she will resist the execution of our judgment, and if she does, I do not believe the President will interfere ... The rumor is, that he has told the Georgians he will do nothing."

The reluctance of Jackson to apply pressure upon Georgia to honor Supreme Court mandates in favor of the Cherokees is clear; his unwillingness, if it came to that, to jeopardize the Constitutional system under which he operated is equally clear. His unyielding stand against South Carolina's Nullification Ordinance, another frontal assault on the Supreme Court's jurisdiction, in a situation where his head and heart were not at odds, illustrates this and resulted in Justice Story's marveling accolade: "But what is more remarkable, since his last Proclamation and Message, the Chief Justice and myself have become his warmest supporters, and shall continue so just as long as he maintains the principles contained in them. Who would have dreamed of such an occurrence?"

Even in Jackson's vaunted personal crusade against Nicholas Biddle and the Bank of the United States, even with such melodramatic battle cries as: "The bank, Mr. Van Buren, is trying to kill me, but I will kill it," Jackson's victorious annihilation of the bank was accomplished in decorous legal fashion. He neither arrested Biddle nor took over his bank with troops; he simply exercised a presidential veto over the Congressional bill rechartering the bank. When Congress failed to override the veto, that, and not the veto in itself, signaled the death of the bank.

What ultimately surprises us about Jackson's presidency is how uncharacteristic it was of our military presidents in general, marked as it was by questions of constitutionality rather than by scandals and ineptitude, and a parade of homilies. The crises of Jackson's terms involved complex explorations into the nature of our political and economic system, into the allocations of power between the branches of the federal government and the national and state governments. In

THE LEGAL MIND AND THE PRESIDENCY

his presidential battles, his veto of the bank charter bill, his stand against South Carolina's nullification, his posture during the Cherokee cases, he did not avoid, but invited and precipitated, constitutional debate. There was obviously more of the lawyer buried in President Jackson than he dreamed of in his moral philosophy. There was even obviously more of the lawyer moralist in him, and the threat which that implied, to judicial law and individual rights. There is more menace than heroism, after all, in his martial law arrest of a New Orleans judge for issuing a writ of habeas corpus, or for standing idly by while the Cherokee Indians were picked clean by Georgia.

9

The Man Who Would Save the World: Woodrow Wilson

FORREST MCDONALD, A bold historian, finds it necessary, from time to time, to cut a decent path in the thickets created by other historians. Disposing tidily in 1958 of Charles Beard's unpalatable definition of the Constitution as a primer of Marxian economics, he turned his machete upon the Jeffersonian apologists in 1976. McDonald, while giving Jefferson his due, refuses to sentimentalize him, and along the way forges an interesting link that was over a century in the making: "The name of the scheme was embargo. In its name, Thomas Jefferson conducted a fifteenth-month reign of oppression and repression that was unprecedented in American history, and would not be matched for another hundred and ten years, when Jefferson's ideological heir Woodrow Wilson occupied the presidency." The ideology to which McDonald refers, operating in multiple disguises—freedom here, rights there, majority pulsations everywhere, forms swirling around the grandstand, bedecked with pastoral myths, of simplicity, goodness and truth—may be summed up as lawyer-moralism.

There is a beguiling innocence about the morality of the non-lawyer presidents, at the same time that it invites patronization. When thinking about the quintessential moral nature of a Washington, Grant, Taylor, Eisenhower, or of an Andrew Johnson, Harding, Truman, or Reagan, I am pressed not to admire unreservedly their lack of guile. At the same time they seem painfully vulnerable to unprincipled, devious admirers and to dangerously simple solutions to complicated problems. A very different reaction to a Jefferson, Jackson, Wilson, or Franklin Roosevelt occurs. Innocence is the last attribute that suggests itself. Instead we long to preserve inviolate our admiration for their energy, will, intelligence and imagination from a repulsion at their easy divorcement of rhetoric from action—of, to put it ungraciously, their duplicity. Their dissimulation is made all the more perilous in being both conscious and unconscious.

Talleyrand, the artful French politician who orchestrated the XYZ affair during the Adams administration, and compromised Jefferson's Francophilia, once observed (along with others such as Voltaire) that man was given speech not in order to reveal his thoughts, but to conceal them. This is, of course, as any practicing lawyer knows, only a half or quarter-truth. Man speaks (his purpose, not someone else's, divine or satanic) in order to not only both reveal and conceal his thoughts, but, perhaps more importantly, his emotions. Morality, a term commonly associated with the way men behave more than how they talk, suffers a small death each time preachment contradicts conduct. Talleyrand and most European politicians would argue that at least they are honest about their Machiavellian practices whereas the Americans are preposterous with their claims of candour. Europeans have derided the intensity of the American Dream, which originally and stubbornly persisting, has claimed from 1776 that saying 'from rags to riches' or Horatio Algerism will make it so, and a later more humble, more attainable, Clintonian perspective of 'from 'rags to the middle class.'

The Horatio Alger ('from rags to riches') arm of the American Dream posits 'riches' as enormous liquid assets, or the triumph of individualism via Ayn Rand and the Republican Tea Party, or God as the American commander-in-chief, or a preeminent show of intellectuality—in short, any category considered to be the ultimate in wish fulfillment.

The keen observation made of Wilson by Linley M. Garrison, Wilson's Secretary of War, is equally applicable to other lawyer moralists, "He was a man of high ideals but no principles," which translates itself readily into the recognition that ideals are the preached morality of the lawyer moralist.

These willful, lawyer-trained men infected their rhetoric with a moral passion that, disconnected from action, was nevertheless expected to overcome any deterrent in the physical world. When it did not, the moral passion became diseased, and as life-threatening in its way to the American body politic as the simpler equation of morality with action (the doing of good) of the non-lawyer moralists, the generals, the movie stars, the heroes on horseback: "A man does what he must," proclaimed John F. Kennedy, "in spite of personal consequences, in spite of obstacles and dangers and pressures, and that is the basis of all human morality." "I have a perfect horror of words that are not backed up by deeds," was Theodore Roosevelt's reaction to Wilson.

Once again, as in the case of Jefferson, biographers are struck by what they feel to be inexplicable contradictions in Wilson's character. Once again, they are so pulled in the direction of his rhetoric that they cannot easily stop to accommodate the contrariness of his actions. Paradoxes so common to lawyer moralists abound: "Wilson's political philosophy was rooted in the enlightenment and drew sustenance from the great liberals of the nineteenth century, who saw their fellow human beings as rational creatures, capable of settling almost any difficulty if only they would use their reason ... Yet, combined with this sincere and heartfelt confidence in man's reasonability, was Wilson's almost perverse conviction that he, himself, was perpetually right."

It becomes extraordinarily difficult for Wilson's most thoughtful and conscientious biographer, Arthur S. Link, to present a balanced view of him: "Wilson's exaltation of intuition, his egotism, and his indulgence in personal prejudice were at the same time sources of strength and of weakness. Perhaps they help to explain why the American people admired his boldness, and thrilled to his noble visions and the cadence of his oratory, and yet did not love him as an individual ... How can we reconcile the curious contradictions in Woodrow Wilson—his craving for affection and his refusal to give on equal terms, his love of the people en masse and his ordinary disdain for individuals, the warm idealism of his speeches and the coolness of many of his official relationships, the bigness of the political visions and the pettiness of his hatred? Being neither mind reader nor psychiatrist, the biographer can only agree with Colonel House that Wilson was 'one of the most contradictory characters in history.'

Hanging heavily behind the image of Wilson as intuitive and moralistic is the fact of personal history, parallel to Jefferson's, that the most respected teacher (surrogate father?) in his life was a law teacher: "the head of the Virginia law school, Hohn B. Minor ... widely known as a scholar and professor; to the end of his life Wilson thought of him as one of the greatest men he had known, and next to his father, his greatest teacher."

Yet Wilson's special cross, perhaps triggered by his dismal experience as a practicing lawyer in his early career is his exaggerated contempt for lawyers in general. Upon quitting the law at the age of twenty-six, he confided uncharitably to his friend, Robert Bridges: "I cannot breathe freely nor smile readily in an atmosphere of broken promises, of wrecked estates, of neglected trusts, of unperformed duties, of crimes and of quarrels. I find myself hardened and made narrow and cynical by seeing only the worst side of human nature... it was never my wish to be a mere lawyer and I have found this out, that ... a man must become a mere lawyer to succeed at the bar; and must, moreover, acquire a most ignoble shrewdness at overcoming the unprofessional tricks and underhand competition of sneaking pettifoggers... The practice of the law, when conducted for purposes of gain (he made very little or nothing after a year of practice), is entirely antagonistic to the best interests of the intellectual life... The philosophical study of the law ... is a very different matter from its scheming and haggling practices."

Later in 1902, as a Princeton professor, in a speech on patriotism, he went out of his way to contrast "good men" with lawyers: "The only way to get good government is to elect good men to conduct it, and then good men to interpret it. We have bred in this country a race of subtle lawyers, and they read the statutes very subtly, and you cannot frame a law in American grammar and punctuation, but he can get out of it, and drive a coach and six horses through it, and then he will make you believe that was the law that was meant."

Wilson was duplicitous in much the same way as Jefferson; he was not the deceiver— his rhetoric was. The fact that he might believe in his rhetoric as gospel did not save him from deceit but, rather, created a form that is baffling; the deceiver is at the same time the most deceived. Wilson never imagined he could be speaking falsely because his words for him were the truth and nothing but the truth. They were truth because no deed and no history could violate them. When he went into the Caribbean, Central America, and Mexico from 1913 to 1917, an officious intermeddling revived by later presidents in Nicaragua, Vietnam, and Iraq, and when he practiced both dollar and bayonet diplomacy, his motive power was an oratorical morality, utterance become belief. What was good in his gospel had to be good for Santo Domingo, for Haiti, for Mexico. Wilson's is more modern United States Iraq War policy proclaimed in an age when the United States could moralize for others and make it stick—except in Mexico where the ultimate decision to withdraw parallels the Vietnamese 'solution'.

His record south of the border is so shabby that it deserves J. M. Blum's extended recitation: "(His) complex of attitudes not only beclouded the national interest but also conflicted with Woodrow Wilson's sincere abomination of imperialism and war ... so it happened that in the name of friendship Woodrow Wilson ultimately took up a white man's burden scarcely distinguishable in form or reward from that of less altruistic statesmen ... (He) perpetuated a kind of dollar diplomacy he would not allow in China ... let Bryan (William Jennings Bryan, Wilson's Secretary of State) sustain unpopular, reactionary administrations in Nicaragua and Santo Domingo ... used American marines to establish protectorates in Santo Domingo and, against fierce resistance, in Haiti ... there was no virtue in confusing administrations Bryan sponsored or that the marines created with just governments based on laws... the President made of a minor episode an excuse to intervene with force (he ordered the U.S. Navy to seize Vera Cruz) in a Mexican revolution ... his armed reprisals, and violations of Mexican sovereignty, brought the two countries perilously close to unnecessary war ... The United States ... could ill afford ... by intrigue or force to try to teach its neighbors to elect good men. That tendentious effort generated the smug bombast that can breed ... war."

At the same time, Wilson could say, and, incredibly enough, believe it: "We must respect the sovereignty of Mexico. I am one of those—I have sometimes suspected that there were not many of them—who believe, absolutely believe, in the Virginia Bill of Rights, which was the model of the old bill of rights, which says that a people have the right to do anything they please with their own country and their own government. I am old-fashioned enough to believe that, and I am going to stand by that belief."

Prior to America's entry into World War I, Theodore Roosevelt, in a typical two-fisted outburst, expresses exasperated frustration at the president he scornfully labels the 'pacifist hero', (to him an obviously self-contradictory label): "Nothing is more sickening than the continual praise of Wilson's English, of Wilson's style. He is a true logothete, a real sophist; and he firmly believes, and has had no inconsiderable effect in making our people believe, that elocution is an admirable substitute for and improvement on action... our people are now all confused and weakened and incapable of giving any coherent support to our own rights or the rights of others in the teeth of Germany's ruthless and cruel efficiency. This is directly due to the action of Wilson—the worst President since Buchanan, an even worse President than Taft, a considerably worse President than Andrew Johnson... I have a perfect horror of words that are not backed up by deeds. I have a perfect horror of denunciation that ends in froth... I do not believe in neutrality between right and wrong. I believe in justice."

Wilson's leap into national prominence itself involved a difficult moral question. His 'morality' demanded that immediately upon being elected Governor of New Jersey he break with James Smith, Jr., the party boss who had done much to get him nominated and elected. In the same pattern, later he broke with Colonel George Harvey, heavily responsible for his political career, as part of his switch to progressive from conservative during the presidential campaign of 1912. These easy betrayals of loyalty and commitment to persons in the name of a 'higher' ethic did not go unnoticed: "He who abandons a friend will abandon a principle ... and what a man does to an individual he will do to a people," declared the New York American. A friend of William Howard Taft, then president, wrote to him: "If the people of this country were what they used to be, this exposure of the school teacher's treachery to his friends would be sufficient to make him impossible as a presidential candidate." The defense by Wilson's supporters is predictable: "'Ingratitude' is one of the rarest virtues of public life. 'Gratitude' is responsible for many of our worst political abuses. Upon 'gratitude' is built every corrupt political machine."

Unquestionably, the choice between the betrayal of a friend and of principles is difficult. In Wilson's case the problem is compounded by his renunciation of principles formerly dear to him. At the same time his defenders argue for the virtue of his pursuit of the 'right' at all costs, his detractors complain bitterly of his lack of character. Taft was to say of him: "My contempt is based on the fact that I regard him as a ruthless hypocrite, and as an opportunist, who has no convictions that he would not barter at once for votes. His is a man who has a certain kind of tenacity that can not be characterized as firmness, because that is to be regarded as a virtue when it is exhibited in the maintenance of a cause, not in support of pride or opinion or because of personal spite, or for some personal advancement. On the other hand, he surrenders a conviction, previously expressed, without the slightest hesitation, and never even vouchsafes to the public the arguments upon which he was induced to change his mind."

While Taft was a Republican and Wilson a Democrat, I feel that much more than a political attack is involved. Taft, whatever he was not, is conceded to have been, much like Grover Cleveland, preeminently a man of character, a common characteristic of most formalist lawyer presidents. That such a man should prize character above anything else is no accident. Indeed, a principle that transcends familiar virtues would have little attraction for Taft. The linkages between characters, morality, principle, loyalty, steadfastness, integrity, and forthrightness make it difficult to match questions of character and morality in a one-on-one confrontation. A betrayal of a commitment would seem to lack moral sanction; lawyers are particularly horrified by breaches of faith or understanding between themselves. They are much less likely to condemn a fellow lawyer on questions of moral niceties, since the guidelines are usually so much more ambiguous. While the extent of the responsibility of a lawyer to defend a morally reprehensible client, or to be publicly concerned with the general welfare of his society, are continuing sources of concern to the ethical lawyer, the simple breach of his word by one lawyer to another is regarded as the gravest of professional sins.

From this perspective, the excessiveness of lawyer Taft's contempt for lawyer Wilson's breaches of promise and character becomes understandable, and even appropriate, however extenuating the 'higher principle' involved may be to others. The same level of rage is reached by John Quincy Adams in his venomous portrait of Jefferson, and for much the same reason.

It is very easy, and predictable, for an intense concentration upon a 'higher principle' in a person of power to lead to a philosophy of ends justifying means. A seduction, not only of the leader, but of his followers occurs. An ideologue will always find the words, much the same words, revolving around means and ends, and so Jefferson's line of rhetorical defense is a familiar paradox— the ultimate resource for a democracy when its survival is at stake is a 'temporary' dictatorship. "Congress must legalize all means (to effect the Embargo) which may be necessary to obtain its (read, my) end," he notified his tough, brilliant, skeptical Secretary of the Treasury, Albert Gallatin. To justify the unconstitutional purchase of the Louisiana Territory, he argued, "To lose our country by a scrupulous adherence to written law, would be to lose the law itself, with life, liberty, property and all those who are enjoying them with us; thus absurdly sacrificing the end to the means." It never seems to have occurred to him to apply such reasoning to John Adams and the Federalists in the enactment of the Alien and Sedition Laws, laws on much more solid Constitutional grounds than his Louisiana purchase, his enforcement of the Embargo Acts, or his Kentucky nullification resolutions.

Andrew Jackson, no happier with Jefferson than Jefferson with him, nevertheless is in total accord with the sentiment that 'good' ends (with the good defined exclusively by him), justify dubious means. Martial law, however willful and unnecessary after the Battle of New Orleans, was one of these means: "Whenever the invaluable rights which we enjoy under our happy Constitution are threatened by invasion, privileges the most dear ... may be required to be infringed for their security...Is it wise, in such a moment, to sacrifice the spirit of the laws to the letter, and by adhering too strictly to the letter, lose the substance forever, in order that we may, for an instant, preserve the shadow? It is not to be imagined that the express provisions of any written law can fully embrace emergencies which suppose and occasion the suspension of all law, but the highest and the last, that of self-preservation."

On the way to President Monroe's careful comment that Jackson, in his invasion of Spanish Florida, had "transcended the limits of (his) orders," and had "acted on (his) own responsibility," Jackson responds: "Allow me fairly to state that the assumption of responsibility will never be shrunk from when the public interest can be thereby promoted. I have passed through difficulties and exposures for the honor and benefit of my country, and whenever still, for this purpose, it shall become necessary to assume a further liability, no scruple will be urged or felt." Woodrow Wilson marches to much the same tune: "The very necessity of bending to war's unwelcome insistencies made him believe with frenetic intensity that its end would justify its means. He came gradually to employ concentrations of authority and to indulge debaucheries of spirit tolerable to him only because of his now urgent, now wistful faith that out of war would emerge a Utopia of remembered yesterdays that never were. In an ironic, dovetailing of historic events, Wilson, Jefferson's 'ideological heir,' upon America's entry into World War I, fashioned an updated version of the Federalist sedition laws, and added some refinements of his own, beginning with the Espionage, and Trading With the Enemy, Acts of 1917, and culminating with the Sedition Act of May 16, 1918.

The question at this point, raised in exasperation, is why, then, is Woodrow Wilson considered to be one of our greater presidents? The answer certainly does not lie in those critical areas of liberal concern such as civil rights or liberties, or even with social welfare. While giving Wilson credit for his 'New Freedom' program designed to restore individual competition, which resulted in establishment of such noteworthy progressive objectives as the Federal Reserve System, tariff reduction, and the Federal Trade Commission, Blum indicates that he 'buried (as) unwise and unjustifiable' a bill establishing government banks to extend inexpensive, long-range credit to farmers, shelved a measure prohibiting child labor, and permitted several of his cabinet members to segregate, for the first time since the Civil War, whites and blacks within the executive departments. His reaction to a bill of the California legislature offensive to the Japanese was to suggest toning down the language, and he side-stepped the woman suffrage movement by regarding it as a state issue. Earl Latham is no less critical of Wilson's civil liberties record, but shelves his displeasure in a larger attempt to account for his greatness, and in the accounting I am reminded once again how much most assessments of presidential quality depend on the quality of presidential rhetoric and how little on their actions: "Woodrow Wilson ... is not only an exemplar of the intellectual in political life, but he stands... for the best in the American liberal tradition. This tradition rates high the integrity of common men, the improvability of social life, the value of the human personality, and the use of social techniques to promote these ideals ... It appeals to the intelligence, to the adjudicative and rational faculties ... It is humble about the truth and hostile to arrogance ... It is more a temper and an attitude than a dogma and a creed. But it does not lack the supreme morality, which is charity through understanding,

THE LEGAL MIND AND THE PRESIDENCY

without patronage or bigotry, with deliberate and condign force to keep open the system through which each finds his own salvation."

Americans are probably more easily captivated and seduced by idealism than any other national group. It is a quality that both redeems and betrays one's sense of life. To others, trying to accommodate beautifully expressed dreams with ugly manifestations of reality, it is scorned as the ultimate hypocrisy. The ultimate opinion of Americans entertained by the French is summed up by Georges Clemenceau's cynical evaluation of Wilson: "If the Creator needs seven days to organize a couple of creatures of which the first born instinctively tore each other apart, Mr. Wilson, in one sovereign word, is going to create men such as have never been seen, whose first need will be love and universal harmony."

Few Americans, even in hindsight, would substitute Clemenceau for Wilson in the American presidency. The harsh, razor-sharp, unmitigated Gallic skepticism is alien to the American grain. Yet, the exaggerated concentration and embodiment in Wilson (which may help to explain our sense of his greatness) of our national obsession upon the word as fulfillment and the action as some extenuating circumstance, is demonstrably frightening.

10

The Fox and the Lion: Franklin Delano Roosevelt

WHILE HISTORIANS HAVE frequently referred to the puzzling or inexplicable nature of presidents like Lincoln and Nixon, a special emphasis on contradiction and paradox has been reserved for the lawyer moralists This feature of the personalities of Jefferson, Jackson, Wilson, and Franklin Roosevelt has inevitably led to expressions of bafflement, but the essential ingredient seems to be the recognition of a type of personality that 'gives' with one hand and 'takes' with the other. Of Jefferson, Dumas Malone comments: "A more extended quotation would show that he (Charles Francis Adams) admired many things in Jefferson and saw a contradiction, not merely in this particular statement and episode, but in his career and character as a whole." Henry May, in his delightful exploration of *The Enlightenment in America* concludes that "Jefferson at first seems clear and consistent, but those who have really tried to get beneath the calm and ordered surface have found understanding ever more elusive."

Colonel House observed of Wilson, "It is not the President's face alone that changes. He is one of the most difficult and complex characters I have ever known. He is so contradictory that it is hard to pass judgment on him." Burke Davis felt that, "The contradictions of his (Jackson's) fierce, unyielding spirit were inexplicable. His 'exasperating tendency' to regard issues as opportunities for personal combat conflicted with his habitual inclination to study problems in exhaustive detail..."

It should, however, hardly be surprising that a mind which judges primarily in a mix of moral and legal terms will tend to dispute with itself. I suggest that a good part of the frustration of historians is due to their reluctance to leave a historical narration poised in the tension that characterizes each of us as a living person rather than a literary (historical) figure.

The linkages between Franklin Roosevelt and morality are especially important because, even more than the Civil War, the Great Depression of the 1930s remains the most significant 'moral' test America has faced in regard to its survival as a practice, in the form in which it was conceived and developed by Jeffersonian democratic rhetoric and Madisonian constitutionalism. The Civil War was, as Lincoln understood and expressed it, a matter of preservation (physical survival) of the Union; the Great Depression posed our most serious challenge to the perpetuation of that unique and difficult matrix we like to call the American way of life. It is hard to imagine a political leader who more symbolized that way of life than Franklin Roosevelt in its paradoxes and contradictions swirling around American law and American morality.

While Burns adopts, for FDR, Walt Whitman's penetrating view of the American as a creature of contradictions, he goes much further when he titles his biography, *"The Lion and the Fox,"* and uses as his epigraph Machiavelli's cold-blooded description of an ideal ruler: "A prince must imitate the fox and the lion, for the lion cannot protect himself from traps, and the fox cannot defend himself from wolves. One must therefore be a fox to recognize traps, and a lion to frighten wolves. Those that wish to be only lions do not understand this. Therefore, a prudent ruler ought not to keep faith when by so doing it would be against his interest, and when the reasons which made him find himself no longer exist. If men were all good, this precept would not be a good one; but as they are bad, and would not observe their faith with you, so you are not bound to keep faith with them."

Burns, who has written an impressive and generally laudatory biography of FDR, seems to mean what he says about Roosevelt's Machiavellian methods, however he may extenuate them, or at least attempt to, with the argument that 'moral' ends may justify 'amoral' means.

To posit Franklin Roosevelt as Machiavellian, with its nuances of self-interest, cunning and cruelty, above all, with its basic idealization of amorality as a basic instrument of a prince's survival in power, is to cut harshly across the American rhetorical grain. The coin of the rhetorical realm is composed of an alloy of simplicity, candor, truthfulness, and humility. The American president is fabled as the man rendered uncommon, not by charm or intellect, but by the very extent of his community with us, and his genius as a president is measured largely by that extent. The ultimate American conceit is that our greatest presidents speak for all of us, as all of us. In MacIntyre's sense of a shared community, the great president creates a nation-wide community for us to share.

Alluring though it may be, the encapsulation of a personality in a metaphor invites massive distortion. To Machiavelli's prince, perpetuation of power is the overriding concern, the obsessive practice, in the pursuit of which he is obliged to disregard any other end, and use whatever means he possesses to survive as Prince, including cruelty, deceit, and force. The prince does not arbitrarily discard mercy, truthfulness, peaceableness or generosity; they, too, may prove to be useful tools in the perpetuation of his power. So also he may attempt to satisfy the needs of his people, but only if this seems valuable in maintaining his power.

It appears to be, finally, arguably inappropriate, by Mr. Burns' own criteria, to attribute dominant characteristics of a Machiavellian prince to Franklin Roosevelt. Adolph Hitler, or Richard Nixon, perhaps (although, as we shall see with Nixon, not really so) might be more apposite. It is not the amoral lengths to which the prince will go to accomplish his objective that distinguishes him; it is rather his objective of perpetuation of power, a reason for being that is unclouded or unqualified by any mediating element such as the good of, or the voice of, or the will of, the people being governed. The presidency, to Franklin Roosevelt, however, as a lawyer moralist, involved a fusion with 'the people.' He embraced Grover Cleveland's maxim that "public office is public trust." He was never more sincere than when he marveled: "This country is fortunate, not alone because of the devotion of the many people who are running 'your Government,' but chiefly because these persons... are using their minds to achieve visions and ideals for the permanent benefit of the average citizen."

The image of Roosevelt as Machiavellian is something of an American "tall tale" constructed out of his shiftiness," exemplified usually by historians, without much precision, by the contrasting tones of the so-called First and Second New Deals. A renewed sense emerges of the inevitability in a lawyer moralist president of contradictory elements of personality, character and modes of thought. What is often most frustrating to historiographers is the sense that their final diagnoses of a public personality as complex and baffling is somehow off; they suspect that like the discovery of a scientific 'ultimate cause', their man, if run to earth, will turn out to be fairly simple and straightforward. No president lends himself more to this suspicion than FDR.

Roosevelt is historically entrenched as an artist of politics. He was, after all, the only (and last, saving a Constitutional amendment) American president to be elected for more than two terms. This in itself makes him suspect; longevity in an American public office is loaded with sinister, anti-democratic implications. At the same time, he was idolized. The impact of this admirable, memorable man upon the American people was enormous. The American Heritage's History of the Presidents paints an admirable picture of him: "In the twelve years and forty days of his Presidency, Franklin Delano Roosevelt aroused a loyalty and an opposition unequaled in American history. To his enemies, Roosevelt was a dictator, a charlatan, a grinning poseur—'that Red in the White House.' Crowning his domestic treason, they cried later, Roosevelt had personally plunged America into war with Germany and Japan only to sell out to Stalin. To those who admired F.D.R.—a decisive majority of Americans in four presidential elections—he was the friend of the poor, the champion of minorities, the defender of labor, the patrician savior of capitalism from a menacing American communism in the nation's worst economic depression, the inspiring architect of the Allied victory over the Axis powers, and the prophet of a new world order under the United Nations."

One is easily shocked by a review of a great man's life before the demonstrated fact of his greatness. How, one wonders, does a Napoleon or a Shakespeare get from here to there? In Roosevelt's case, there was literally no hint that he would become FDR. Born on January 30, 1882, into wealth and social prominence, a pampered only child, he joined the American 'elite', during which journey he was an unflappably mediocre student. Combined with his 'C' average was the snobbish intensity of his disappointment at not, like his fifth cousin, Theodore, in an earlier era, making Harvard's top social club, Porcellian.

Searching for clues to the flavor of Roosevelt's presidency, Burns makes much of the Groton education: "The more that mask and costume are stripped away from Roosevelt, the more the turn-of-century man of Hyde Park, Groton, and Harvard stands out. Roosevelt, for all his deviousness, was basically a moral man in the sense that he felt so intensely the need to do right that he had to *think* he did right. He believed in doing good, in showing other people how to do good, and he assumed that ultimately people would do good. By 'good' he meant the Ten Commandments and the Golden Rule, as interpreted by Endicott Peabody. He meant the 'simple rules of human conduct to which we always go back,' as he said in 1932."

Having acquiesced in the general affirmation of FDR's contradictory nature, Burns cannot, nevertheless, resist an attempt to reduce FDR's personality to a simple common denominator of the Golden Rule as divinely told to Reverend Peabody and divinely absorbed by Roosevelt. But he was not simple because, a divided and self-deceiving man, he was another instance in which the lawyer moralist's rhetoric deceives not only himself, but others. Self-deception practiced by an expert in rhetoric, as Jefferson taught us, is highly seductive; it excites reverence and faith. It also invites contempt from those who are not deceived.

If we define morality simply as goodness, we still must explore standards of goodness (the virtues), and are back to difficult and demanding exercises in moral philosophy. To determine whether FDR was 'moral,' we must go beyond the euphemism that he felt the need to do right and thought he was doing right. We need to know whether, at least in his role as president, his sense of right and his practice, based upon that sense, can be termed moral. I believe that they can.

When Franklin Roosevelt was inaugurated for his first term as president on March 4, 1933, the United States was facing its greatest crisis of faith. The Civil War had brought into question the survival of the country as a single union, and whether blacks could be defined as human in order to have rights, but neither side disputed the essential nature of the existing institutions. The Great Depression, having thrown some twelve million people, about one-fourth of the labor force, out of work, having created as a national phenomenon soup kitchens, breadlines, and 'Hooverville' communities of paper shacks, chopped at one of the deepest roots of the American 'way of life,' variously referred to as economic individualism, the free enterprise system or laissez-faire. Whatever it was called, lodged in the Fifth and Fourteenth Amendments to the Constitution as an American commonwealth's (common wealth) sine qua non, was the premise that equally precious and private to the individual, as his life and liberty was his property.

In 1905, Holmes commented in one of his celebrated dissenting opinions: "The liberty of the citizen to do as he likes so long as he does not interfere with the liberty of others to do the same, which has been a shibboleth for some well-known writers, is interfered with by school laws, by the post office, by every state or municipal institution...for purposes thought desirable, whether he likes it or not. The Fourteenth Amendment does not enact Mr. Herbert Spencer's Social Statics." He was arguing against the majority opinion that a New York statute limiting the work hours of a bakery employee was unconstitutional. With his usual verbal facility, Holmes raises interesting questions about 'liberty' in a 'libertarian' society. He, in effect, points out that government for "purposes thought desirable" may put its thumb on the scales weighing individual performances, and thereby affect division of the spoils.

His examples, such as school laws and post office, however, beg the question since these are prime examples of constraints universally conceded to be beneficial to each of us as an individual, and to which most of us fully subscribe. Other examples would be fire and police protection. It is easily arguable that liberty is not impaired by restraints to which one voluntarily agrees. (This, in effect, is argued by classical theorists, such as Rousseau and Machiavelli, against contractarians—Hobbes, Locke and company—who maintain that only in public service can the individual truly attain liberty.)

In the area of personal liberties, where he was not particularly strong, Holmes might find stiff modern opposition to his notion as to what constitutes a shibboleth. It is only in connection with economic liberty that Holmes' application of laissez-faire to judicial non-interference with Congress marches to the same tune as twenty-first century liberals, a tune that first became a national hit with the New Deal.

If, as Holmes suggests, it is unworkable to conceive of liberty as a total absence of governmental constraint, we must then think of liberty in relative terms. That is, we might view liberty with Holmes as a *reasonable* absence of governmental constraint. We would then, like him, have only to ask whether it is arguably reasonable for the State of New York to limit the number of hours a bakery employee may work. Holmes did indeed think it was arguably reasonable and, consequently, that New York had not, under the Fourteenth Amendment, deprived anyone of his liberty, in that case, to contract for hire. All Fifth and Fourteenth Amendment questions become computerized with the simplified proposition: liberty exists if the potential victim is not unreasonably constrained.

The problem with this definition of liberty is that it depends upon the exercise of reasonableness, the most slippery and subjective of words of legal convenience. It is for this reason that I prefer to regard liberty as the degree of tolerance a rational society has for its non-rational elements. A totalitarian society, it seems to me, has as little tolerance for its non-rational elements (Utopian or unorthodox philosophy, art or schemes) as its citizens have liberty; it operates at the same time on its initial (to an American liberal, insanely unreasonable) premises in a completely rational manner. This is the primary characteristic of a 'planned' society.

We may now take the leap into the New Deal and its onslaught on the laissez faire rules of the American game that existed virtually intact until the Great Depression of the Thirties. We may also begin to understand the extent of the fury of Roosevelt's social class against him when we realize its irrational base. Economics, dressed out though it is in the accoutrements of reason, claiming to be the most hard-headed of the social sciences, as any sensitive Wall Street analyst will finally admit, bobs in a sea of unpredictable emotions.

One of the intriguing results of the New Deal, at least what is called the First New Deal, is that it unsettled the common premise upon which both American liberalism and conservatism had theretofore been based, and that was the priority of individualism, couched in the rhetoric of 'rights'. This, of course, has occasioned a great deal of confusion as to what a modern American liberal or conservative really is, and can allow Garry Wills in his fine book on Nixon to endow him with "an older sense of what can only be called liberalism," and for James McGregor Burns to label FDR "in the broader sense a conservative, at least in his first two years in office." However, the view of Nixon as a liberal, or Roosevelt as a conservative, in both instances twenty-first-century reflectors of individualism, loses its initial shock effect when one realizes that every American, Republican or Democrat, from the Civil War to the New Deal, was something of a 'classical liberal'—i.e. someone hypnotized by Horatio Algerism. In

The Liberal Imagination, Lionel Trilling had already gone beyond Wills and, discounting the political thrust of the New Deal, claimed in 1949 that, "In the United States at this time liberalism is not only the dominant but even the sole intellectual tradition. For it is the plain fact that nowadays there are no conservative or reactionary ideas in general circulation."

It is unrewarding, then, at least in political terms or parties, to speak of a 'liberalism' that by definition includes 'conservatism,' and I am drawn to Trilling's estimation of liberalism as a "large tendency rather than a concise body of doctrine." Trilling's elaboration focuses upon his concern that liberalism, impelled initially by an emotional, imaginative vision of "a general enlargement and freedom and rational direction of human life (that paradoxically) ... drifts toward a denial of the emotions and the imagination." He seems to feel that liberalism, having lost its energy through the bankruptcy of conservative ideas and the consequent loss of a dialectic, must somehow reinvigorate itself, must be recalled "to its first essential imagination of variousness and possibility." Trilling's ultimate whipping boy emerges as our old double agent, reason, stripped this time of emotion and imagination, much as MacIntyre condemns reason in an Enlightenment divorced from a shared sense of community. (Although Trilling cannot resist a glancing pat on the back for liberalism's 'rational direction of human life.') But Trilling does manage as well to convey the importance of variousness as an essential ingredient of liberalism, and this, the insatiable itch for variety of human experience, is likely to be that "large tendency," highly emotional, characterizing liberalism rather than, say, belief in a package of rights, or tolerances that embodies individualism. This is hardly a startling proposition, since conservatism would, unless encrusted with complicating notions, seem simply to involve that opposite 'large tendency' equally emotional, to hang on to, to conserve what one has and considers valuable, especially in the terribly difficult world of ideas, rather than risk its loss for something new.

From this vantage point, Franklin Roosevelt assumes a more comfortable stance as a prototypical liberal, while Nixon drifts with the mainstream of the Republican tradition, exemplified by Coolidge and Hoover, of conservatism. If this perspective tarnishes the glamour of paradoxes in presidential personalities, it heightens the deeper contradiction that drives presidents to personify their country's endless debate between reason and feeling, between law and democracy, between law and morality.

It is as difficult for people to remember that Franklin Roosevelt was a lawyer as with Jackson and Wilson. From 1904 to 1907 he attended Columbia Law School and, although he failed to complete his courses and never received a law degree, passed the New York Bar in 1907. For three years, until 1910, he practiced law with a Wall Street firm, but was clearly not a 'Wall Street' lawyer. Through his connections he got a clerkship at the old Wall Street law firm of Carter, Ledyard, and Milburn. It was an unpaid job the first year, and his work was rather routine. But cases came his way—many of them from his rather litigious family—and he enjoyed the practical higgle and haggle of legal negotiation. He was surprised and depressed at the gap between legal education and legal practice. He saw little connection between legal 'grand principles' and the problems of a relative's trunk destroyed on a Le Havre dock, the interpretation of a will, or a deed of transfer of land. Roosevelt was not excited by the broader points of law. If he had been, his future at Carter, Ledyard, and Milburn—and his whole career—might have been much different. The firm defended such clients as Standard Oil of New Jersey and the American Tobacco Company against the government's attacks on the trusts; it was saturated with the spirit of sober, responsible defense of corporate interests in the face of progressivism. As it turned out, Roosevelt was influenced far more by his everyday contacts with clients, lawyers, claimants, and the politicians, and the would-be politicians around the courts than he was by office ideology.

I believe that, instead of speculating on what kind of lawyer FDR might have been, it is more important to emphasize what kind he actually was. If he had not been born into the American 'upper class,' with his gentleman 'C's,' he would never has been offered a job at Carter, Ledyard, and Milburn. This is not to say that given the same mind, unearned income, and personality, his career would have been much different. For he was, after all, a lawyer, a more typical one, in fact, than the Wall Street brand concentrating exclusively on legal formalisms, such as those involved in taxation, corporate organization, planning, administration, acquisitions, mergers, reorganizations, public issues of securities, liquidations, corporate responses to the activities of the various governmental agencies, and the personal business emanating from corporate executives, such as wills, trusts, estate

THE LEGAL MIND AND THE PRESIDENCY

planning, personal taxes and investments, possibly even pre-nuptial or divorce settlement agreements; i.e. the matrix of a Wall Street firm's business.

Roosevelt did not, like Wilson, turn his back on lawyerdom with utter distaste and a sense of personal failure; on the contrary, after his ten years as New York State Senator and Assistant Secretary of the Navy, and his nomination as vice-president in the losing 1920 Democratic campaign against Harding, FDR returned for eight years to a combination of law practice, the vice-presidency of Fidelity and Deposit Company of Maryland, and a sprinkling of other business investment activities.

We may say that three years at Columbia Law School, followed by an admittedly undiscriminating law practice for three, then eight years, led to the sense in FDR that the legal mind had value, if only as a *sine qua non*. Frances Perkins, that keen analyst of Roosevelt's mental processes, posits him accurately, if inadvertently, as the senior member of the law firm who must argue a case in court after its preparation by an assistant: "He was a man of high intelligence, but he used all his faculties when he was thinking about a subject... He had to have feeling as well as thought. His emotions, his intuitive understanding, his imagination, his more and traditional bias, his sense of right and wrong—all entered into his thinking... The popular literary picture of a statesman is a man who reads volumes of information, studies profound reports, compares the views of experts, analyzes the details of their agreement and disagreement, and then by a process of pure logic arrives at a conclusion. I have never seen a man of action proceed in this way, which is the technique of the legal analyst who must prepare a case for the senior member of the law firm who must argue it in court... Of course, he followed a pattern of logic in his thinking, arraying the facts, comparing them, and drawing conclusions, but he did not rely solely upon logic as a guide to action... I remarked that man acting on pure logic is often untrue to his nature. The president said, "This is exactly right; that is the way I feel."

More often than not, particularly if we are headed for Wall Street, when we are talking of law and of the legal mind, we are referring to an exaggerated bias toward the art and the practice of reasoning, the mind measured, as it were, by Law Scholastic Aptitude Test scores. And a person who scores the best on a preliminary test may be expected to prefer future professional solutions in terms of test scores.

Yet, on the whole, unless all else is stymied, the rule of reason merely receives lip-service from the evolutionary legal mind. Lawyer formalism wrestles with its counterpart, rule-skepticism, or with the lawyer moralist, that hybrid who insists that the heart has its own reasons.

We are involved, if we admire FDR, and he is admirable, with the fact that he was a 'C' student at Groton, Harvard, and Columbia Law School, that he flunked two courses in law school, and that he failed to get his law degree. We are involved because somewhere in all this mediocrity and failure of intellectual performance is a sense of betrayal of at least a part of the 'riches' American dream, perhaps the key part: success at any stage, and in any aspect, of the 'riches' dream. Not ultimate triumph through failure and suffering and transvaluation (Horatio Alger wins not because of hard knocks, but despite them), but the naked success of a fair start and a sequence of proximate ribbon-breaking finishes.

Discomfort at FDR's lapses from intellectual grace is reflected in much of the treatment he has received from historians, and much of their insistence at his complexity might be explained by their compulsion to 'save' him from 'C-dom.' They are generally academicians, after all, who initially signaled their superiority through SAT scores.

It is readily apparent that no one functions as the pure embodiment of reason. Men, all men, have feelings, and are persuaded from time to time to act upon those feelings although they may refuse to admit it. American law allows space for irrationality and its clutch of moralities in order to isolate and quarantine them; legal fictions serve as its health wardens. As I have suggested, most of the battles in moral philosophy over the source of morality have pitted reason (Aristotle, Cicero, Kant) against irrationalism (Hobbes, Hume, Nietzsche, Kierkegaard), which is to say that the instincts and will are respectable forces in any moral consideration.

The divergence between law and morality is not based upon an inherent immorality or amorality in law, but rather in law's 'last resort' reliance, in stressful, unorthodox situations, upon reason as man's mechanism of survival to the sweeping exclusion of other possible modes. When reason threatens rather than protects survival, it tends to separate from morality. American constitutional law, a freeze of Enlightenment deification of reason, is extraordinary in the degree of its dependence upon reason. In this light, the liberal 'moral'" frenzy against the Supreme Court during New Deal days becomes understandable, as do the gaps, ambiguities, and inconsistencies in Rooseveltian thought. Analysis of Roosevelt's personality rather than his way of thinking does much to muddy the waters.

James McGregor Burns translates his sense of FDR's complexity into "a lingering between two worlds." By this he means that Roosevelt operated, on one level, on the nineteenth century gentleman's ethical code of *noblesse oblige*, characterized by an optimistic and progressive view of man's nature, and on another level, adapted his methods to the impact of twenty-first-century cynicism and despair over the most devastating economic depression in American history. "The result," Burns concludes, "was a man of no fixed convictions about methods and policies, flexible as a broker because he had to mediate among conflicting worlds and experiences... Indeed, even to some of his friends he seemed almost in a state of anomie, lacking any guideposts at all, because he rejected so many doctrines and dogmas. Quite naturally, because the mask often was almost impenetrable, they could not see the inner compass of certainty and rightness."

Having gone this far, Burns is unfortunately led to picture Roosevelt once again as that rather menacing type of leader whose devious and unscrupulous means (Machiavellian) are justified by his high-principled ends. Burns has brought us full circle, back not to Machiavelli, but to Jeffersonianism: "Was there then no hard center, no core personality, no final commitment in this man? ... The more that mask and costume are stripped away from Roosevelt, the more the turn-of-the-century man ... stands out... Roosevelt, for all his deviousness, was basically a moral man in the sense that he felt so intensely the need to do right that he had to think he did right. He believed in doing good, in showing other people how to do good, and he assumed that ultimately people would do good. By 'good' he meant the Ten Commandments and the Golden Rule, as interpreted by Endicott Peabody. He meant "the simple rules of human conduct to which we always go back... How explain, then, the 'other side' of Roosevelt, his shiftiness, his compromises, his manipulations, his foxiness? ... So sure was he of the rightness of his aims that he was willing to use Machiavellian means..."

Isaiah Berlin, an admirer in common with Roosevelt's enemies, goes so far as to compare Roosevelt to Hitler and Mussolini, but makes of the comparison a virtue: "He was accused of many weaknesses. He had betrayed his class; he was ignorant, unscrupulous, irresponsible.

He was ruthless in playing with lives and careers of individuals... He made conflicting promises, cynically and brazenly, to individuals and groups, and representatives of foreign nations... What attracted his followers were countervailing qualities of a rare and inspiring order: he was large-hearted and possessed wide political horizons, imaginative sweep ... he was in favor of life and movement, the promotion of the most generous possible fulfillment of the largest possible number of human wishes... He had all the character and energy and skill of the dictators, and he was on our side."

G.W. Johnson also is impelled to distinguish FDR from Hitler: "Both had risen to power on the crest of a wave of protest set in motion by the same sort of grievances. Both took over countries economically in a state of collapse and virtually disintegrating socially. Both faced the problem of putting millions of idle men back to work immediately, and the even more urgent problem of putting some spirit into an apathetic and despairing people ... If we came out with the New Deal and the Germans came out with Nazism, the main reason is because we had chosen the author of the Commonwealth Club speech and the Germans had chosen the author of *Mein Kampf*. There is at least this much in the 'leadership principle.'"

These defenses share the common assumption that Roosevelt is to be excused because, resembling one, he was not a dictator 'at heart'; that is, his heart was in the 'right place.' But, as we have noted, 'goodness' as a priority practice exists in the eye of the beholder, and to many Nazi true believers, Hitlerian goals were the essences of Germany's survival as a great nation. To them he was not only great, but a terribly good leader. The distinction between a beneficent FDR and the horror that was Hitler rather lies in the degree of coherence of their respective visions. Frances Perkins records: "He used to laugh ... at the dire predictions that he would make himself a dictator. He was totally incapable of comprehending what a dictator is, how he operates, how he thinks, how he gets anything done. A man like Mussolini was a puzzle to him; Hitler worse than a puzzle. He didn't like concentrated responsibility." In this area I find it difficult to think of Roosevelt (and easy regarding Hitler) in Machiavellian terms, even metaphorically, because they imply a carefully considered master plan, an ordered philosophy of the uses of power, and the means of maintaining it, particularly against juridical law, concepts alien to any of the Americans who have become president, and particularly to

Roosevelt. If there is general agreement on the Rooseveltian mind, it is that he had no integrated, synthesized intellectual system. What he did have, and to a remarkable degree, was a mind at war with itself. That war was not primarily between Groton ends and Machiavellian means; it was rather characterized by the familiar Jeffersonian split between rhetoric and action, and once again was vitally engaged in the American wrestle between those ultimate choices of survival tools, law, and morality.

In the ideological debate carried on between FDR and Herbert Hoover during the critical 1932 presidential campaign, the issue was joined over the question of survival. For Hoover, it was survival of individualism, which to him was a euphemism for the American way of life. Without it, life for him, however otherwise bountiful, would become meaningless.

Hoover deserves more sympathy than he has received. He was a good man. His heart was in the right place. He was not led by political forces, but by a philosophy which defined the country he loved, a philosophy that, for him, triggered America's rise into greatness from its humble beginning is 1787.

He, ordinarily prosaic, was passionate in his defense of this philosophy: "This campaign is more than a contest between two men...between two parties. It is a contest between two philosophies of government ... We are told...that we must...have a new deal. It is not the change that comes from the normal development of national life to which I object, but the proposal to alter the whole foundation of our national life, which has been built through generations of testing and struggle, and the principles upon which we have built the nation...

"Our system is the product of our race and of our experience in building a nation to heights unparalleled in the whole history of the world. It is a system peculiar to the American people. It differs essentially from all the others in the world. It is an American system. It is founded on the conception that only through ordered liberty, through freedom to the individual and equal opportunity to the individual will, his initiative and enterprise be summoned to spur the march of progress.

"It is by a society absolutely fluid in the movement of its human articles that our individualism departs from the individualism of Europe... there can be no rise for the individual through the frozen strata of classes...I deny that the promise of American life has been fulfilled, for that means we have begun the decline and fall. No nation can cease to move forward without degeneration of spirit... We have heard a great deal...about reactionaries, conservatives progressives, liberals, and radicals. There is one thing I can say without any question of doubt—that is, that the spirit of liberalism is to create free men; it is not the regimentation of men."

Hoover, the man of science, the mathematical mining engineer, not the lawyer, FDR, as a political being was guided more by faith than reason. (This is typical of the scientist who turns to politics, such as Oppenheimer or Pauling). Liberalism, Hoover's umbrella word for Horatio Algerism and individualism in general, is "a force truly of the spirit." Even though reason points to a severe threat to the economic survival of a people, a Hoover, to be faithful, must be blind to reason's solution, such as governmental invasion of private enterprise. One must pray with Hoover: "that some extraordinary force (of the Devil?) has been thrown into the mechanism, temporarily deranging its operation ... One must believe that the difficulty is not with the principles upon which our American system is founded and designed through all these generations of inheritance..."

Hoover pointed his finger in singularly eloquent language at the American dilemma that has not gone away since Roosevelt: on the deaths of what American practices are the American people prepared physically to survive? Machiavelli's Prince would answer that for himself all custom, habit, and usage serve only as long as they permit his 'Third Reich' to persevere. Translated into American terms, if freedom of speech, press, religion, due process of law, individual privacy and property, all must go to preserve the Prince, so be it. Hoover believed that "expansion of government in business" would poison "equality, free speech, free press, and equality of opportunity," and that "without such freedom the pursuit of other blessings is in vain." For Hoover, life without "freedom to the individual and equal opportunity to the individual" would reflect a simple physical survival not worth having. But was FDR so Machiavellian that he was prepared to sacrifice the Constitution, its Bill of Rights, and its Fourteenth Amendment to secure the economic survival of America? His enemies, then and now, say so with great vehemence and conviction. Burns' lion and fox metaphor evokes this implication. Or did, as I think he did, Roosevelt sincerely believe (the detachment of rhetoric from action) that while his government might batter property's due process protections to promote the general welfare (i.e. allow Americans physically to survive), he trusted that the personal freedoms and liberties would not only be left intact, but that he was treating them with traditional reverence.

As early as his first presidential campaign, he conceived of a new 'economic declaration of rights,' consisting of the right to job and savings security, to justify the deprivation of classical due process property rights. The right of protection from government was being translated into the right of protection by government, since God evidently was not helping too many of those who tried to help themselves. The characteristic that most confounds Rooseveltian observers is his lack, not of intellectuality, but of a coherent philosophical base. It was this exasperating 'hole' at his center, the sense of internal emptiness that swallowed up even his overwhelming external charm and energy, and left him ultimately friendless among many friends, that shapes FDR in Keats' "vast idea" of him that goes far beyond "minist'ring reason."

It is misleading, in several ways, to regard Roosevelt as "a man of no fixed convictions about methods and policies" who, at the same time had "absorbed a core of beliefs ...he would never lose." Apart from the distracting emphasis on means divorced from ends, it implies that because one believes there might be more than one way 'to skin a cat', one way is just as good as another, even though it might violate a "core of beliefs." In Roosevelt's case, since his "core of beliefs" consisted, in large part, of a code of conduct (the 'turn-of-the-century man of Hyde Park, Groton, and Harvard') rather than a philosophical system, there was a fusion in him of means and ends that rendered qualifications between them meaningless, and the choice of method much more significant.

The tension generated within Roosevelt, as he faced one of the most serious threats in American history to national survival, evolved from his devotion to the often contradictory mechanisms of reason and faith, a faith not only in the Grotonian code of conduct, but in the same tenets of classical liberalism so passionately embraced by Hoover. It is intriguing to speculate upon the outcome of Roosevelt's presidency and its impact upon the American future if FDR had had a unified philosophy of life concentrated upon, say, the creation of a welfare state. In the pursuit of such a philosophy, he might well have viewed the liberal anchors of individualism and laissez-faire as mortal enemies, to be uprooted and destroyed forever. His program of the first hundred days, instead of the blurred and tentative N.R.A., could have been a socialization of the utilities and railroads, for starters.

The necessity of historians to distinguish between a 'first' and a 'second' New Deal emphasizes more than the lack of a unified vision in FDR; it suggests a startling substitution of one mode of thought for another which, in turn, implies that, rather than his having one stable definition of 'good', such as "the Ten Commandments and the Golden Rule, as interpreted by Endicott Peabody," he had at least two.

The "basic change in 1935," according to Arthur M. Schlesinger, Jr., "was in atmosphere ... The First New Dealers had a utopian and optimistic, and moral cast of mind; the Second New Dealers prided themselves on their realism. The First New Dealers thought well of human rationality and responsibility... The Second New Dealers accepted Brandeis's maxim, 'Man is weak and his judgment is fallible'; they said with Frankfurter, 'We know how slender a reed is reason ... how deep the countervailing instincts and passions' ..." Schlesinger has here combined the vital concepts of morality and reason in an interesting way. Admittedly, the First New Dealers were dominated by a "moral cast of mind: In their belief, radical in America, that economic governmental planning and supervision were essential for survival, they were knights of faith. Just as obviously, the Second New Dealers, exemplified by Brandeis and Frankfurter, were distillations of reason. Yet, as Schlesinger observes, it was the First New Dealers who "thought well of human rationality," and the Second New Dealers who noted "how slender a reed is reason."

What is unsaid, pretending to paradox, is that moralists tend to idealize reason in others while not, themselves, acting upon it, while rationalists, at least the rule-skeptics among them, like Brandeis and Frankfurter, have serious doubts about the capability of others than themselves to reason. In the middle of all this was FDR. Roosevelt entered the White House with what is probably a president's greatest asset, a self-confidence built upon a distaste for introspection. To such a personality it is obscene to finger the "phenomenal coruscations of the souls" and much more rewarding to collect stamps. Yet, to many intellectuals, his quality of mind, cloaked by his prodigious personality and energy, in itself constituted a betrayal—of exactly what they were not quite sure. Scorn triggered the conclusion that "Roosevelt was a nonintellectual—a man who lived and thought on the skin of things."

The First New Deal was inevitably moralistic, because it was a time clearly to try anything that might overcome the nightmare of the Great Depression; even reason dictated that any means of survival that had a chance to work should get its chance. FDR's "radical" First New Deal lieutenants, such as Tugwell and Moley, were ultimately disenchanted with Roosevelt's drift away from a planned economy, but his 'morality', unlike theirs, allowed for the exercise of whatever survival options appeared reasonable; his 'shiftiness' was the result of rational moves evolving in reactions to current events. His refusal to continue programs whose early promise faded, to Moley a betrayal of the 'faith', was rather, in terms of concentrating on the continuing existence of the nation, a significantly high moral stance.

It is important to remember that the great 'philosophical' transformation of America which began with the New Deal, in this sense, an indivisible New Deal, was not collectivism or planned economy programs, but the rise of a 'welfare state.' It was not so much planning as massive relief that distinguished FDR's administrations from Hoover's. The Second New Deal did not evolve out of a drastic shift in FDR's thinking, occasioned by prodding from new counselors such as Brandeis and Frankfurter, or from his reaction to the Supreme Court's invalidation of First New Deal programs, but very simply from his realization that the threat to the country's physical survival was no longer critical: "Some of the things they have done in NRA are pretty wrong, though I think it is going better now. We have got the best out of it anyhow. Industry got a shot in the arm. Everything has started up ... I think perhaps NRA has done all it can do. I don't want to impose a system on this country that will set aside the antitrust laws on any permanent basis."

The Second New Deal, involving a less ominous period in terms of national physical survival, allowed FDR the breathing room to seek the preservation of the practices he preferred. Frances Perkins seems to have swallowed wholesale FDR's conception of his basic ground-rules: "Roosevelt took the status quo in our economic system as much for granted as his family. They were part of his life, and so was our system; he was content with it. He felt that it ought to be humane, fair, and honest, and that adjustments ought to be made so that the people would not suffer from poverty and neglect, and so that all would share. He thought business could be a fine art and could be conducted on moral principles. He thought the test ought to be whether or not business is conducted partly for the welfare of the community ... He was willing to do experimentally whatever was necessary to promote the Golden Rule and other ideals he considered to be Christian, and whatever could be done under the Constitution ."

It is likely that Roosevelt wholly believed that whatever he did "was necessary to promote the Golden Rule and other (Christian) ideals ..." It was also possible for him to act out the role of a proper Christian gentleman in securing the passage of the Social Security Act and National Labor Relations Act: "adjustments ... made so that the people would not suffer from poverty and neglect, and so that all would share." But, of course, it is absurd for a political leader to sincerely imagine that he can actually lead a nation under the precept of the Golden Rule, and it is this self-deceit that gives rise to so much suspicion of FDR's motives.

It becomes especially pointed by the time of World War II when we realize how indifferent FDR was toward civil liberty questions. Civil liberties, one of the major concerns of twenty-first century politics, was largely invisible during the New Deal with its concentration on economic survival. The extent to which Roosevelt's rhetoric and actions diverge is illustrated graphically by James McGregor Burns' account of the shocking World War II internment of many thousands of Japanese-Americans: "the President ratified an action that ... came to be viewed in later years as one of the sorriest episodes in American history. This was the ... incarceration in concentration camps (of tens of thousands of Japanese-Americans)... Few Americans have paid more glowing homage than had Roosevelt to the democratic idea of individual liberty. A week after Pearl Harbor he had proclaimed Bill of Rights Day ... After flaying Hitler for crushing individual liberty, he said, "We Americans know that the determination of this generation of our people to preserve liberty is as fixed and certain as the determination of those early ... Americans to win it ... We will not, under any threat, or in the face of any danger, surrender the guarantees of liberty our forefathers framed for us in the Bill of Rights ... The American Civil Liberties Union would call it "the worst single wholesale violation of civil rights of American citizens in our history ... Only a strong civil-libertarian President could have faced down all these forces, and Roosevelt was not a strong civil libertarian. Like Jefferson in earlier days, he was all for civil liberties in general but easily found exceptions in particular. He related to friends that at a Cabinet meeting (in March 1942) he had told Biddle that civil liberties were okay for ninety-nine percent but he ought to bear down on the rest ... The supreme irony of the evacuation was that while Germans and Italians offered the same alleged threats to military security as the Nisei and Issei, their guilt was established on an individual basis, not a racial basis. Roosevelt was quite aware of the distinction."

Roosevelt also follows the familiar, treacherous path of lawyer moralists in his condescension toward the Constitution, lawyers, and the Supreme Court. Of the Constitution he remarked, on the occasion of his second inauguration, "When the Chief Justice read me the oath and came to the words 'support the Constitution of the United States,' I felt like saying, 'Yes, but it's the Constitution as I understand it, flexible enough to meet any new problem of democracy." He went so far as to write out the lawyers from any part in creating the Constitution: "The Constitution of the United States was a layman's document, not a lawyer's contract. That cannot be stressed too often ... This great layman's document was a charter of general principles, completely different from the 'whereases' and 'the parties of the first part' and the fine print which lawyers put into leases and insurance policies and installment agreements... for one hundred and fifty years we have had an unending struggle between those who would preserve this original broad concept of the Constitution as a layman's instrument of government and those would shrivel the Constitution into a lawyer's contract."

His animus against lawyers, like Jefferson's before him, reached a predictable boil when, as judges, they presumed to judge *him*. His 'court-packing' scheme involved very little ideology and a great deal of personal vendetta in very much the same way that Jefferson went after the Supreme Court to get Marshall. The plan failed, like Jefferson's, because neither Jefferson nor Roosevelt respected the Constitution or Supreme Court in general enough to appreciate the reverence in which they were generally held.

Hoover is an eloquent spokesman for the pervasive view, particularly of non-lawyers, that "the citadel of the rights of the poor against the oppression of rulers and against the extortions of the rapacious is the judicial system of the country, that the impregnable apex of that system is the Supreme Court..."

Franklin Roosevelt was, to put it simply, a marvelous 'crisis' president. He came in during the nation's most severe economic crisis and went out during World War II. He was a president who not only expressed, but had, confidence in the future and faith in the 'old-fashioned' virtues, who (ah, there's the rub) even at the expense of such virtues (unwittingly for the most part), probed for survival mechanisms, whether for the nation, for democratic principles, or vulgarly, for FDR's perpetuation in the White House. His major flaw, self-deception, became an asset during crisis: genuine confidence and fearlessness in a charismatic leader are contagious. Yet he left behind ineradicable doubts about the future of those very American virtues clustered around self-reliance that he, in concert with Hoover, most prized. The ultimate test of the value of a president, after all, is how successfully he has preserved in each American an historical sense of himself. Franklin Roosevelt, in spite of his greatness, because of it, seriously eroded that sense.

PART THREE

LAWYER FORMALISM IN THE PRESIDENCY

11

A Birdseye View of Lawyer Formalism Presidents

THE DESIGN OF a lawyer formalist is to establish the relevancy of an existing rule in order to guide his resulting behavior. When his mosaic of guiding principles is settled in place, he tends to be brisk and efficient; before then, he seems timid and tentative. His decisions are slanted toward stable, uncomplicated procedures. In contrast, a rule-skeptic, having discarded the notion of necessary relevant rules, tends to avoid the necessity for action at all, or, if an action is unavoidable, to delay it as long as possible, and then, almost at random to select any premise available, possibly even a radical one, on which to proceed. A formalist, rule-ridden, tends toward conservatism of action, while a rule-skeptic is susceptible to rashness since his behavior must ultimately depend upon a premise in which he has no faith. Going beyond these distinctions to recognize the ultimate respect for law, if not its institutions, tenaciously retained by both the formalists and rule-skeptics, we collide with the lawyer-moralist who more often than not finds the law itself an exasperating irrelevancy. Albert Gallatin, who had served both Jefferson and Madison as Secretary of the Treasury, outlines the menace of such a view: "In avowing that he would have punished, through the medium of a court-martial, men presumed to be guilty of political offences in their civil character and who did not belong to the army, General Jackson has expressed a greater and bolder disregard of the first principles of liberty than I have ever known to be entertained by any American, or, indeed, by any person professing himself to be...a friend to a government of laws ... He entertains, I believe, very sincere but very erroneous and most dangerous opinions on the subject of military and Executive power. Whenever he has been entrusted with the first, he has usurped more than belonged to him; and when he thought it useful to the public, he has not hesitated to transcend the law and the legal authority vested in him."

The formalists comprise the largest section—seventeen of the twenty-seven legal-minded presidents—and, fairly predictably, the least flamboyant. On the average, they were the most successful lawyers in practice, and their presidencies, by and large, were decently handled. Their memory does not make our pulses pound. There is no Washington, Lincoln or Roosevelt among them. On the other hand, there is no Harding, Grant, or Nixon either. They are distinguished by an earnest desire to abide by the rules. None of them evinced much desire to gain power at the expense of the Supreme Court or Congress; rather, their major concern was whether they, as president, might ever stray, or even threaten to stray, beyond Constitutional bounds.

They are not, to historians at least, generally a distinguished list. Of the group, apart from founding fathers, Madison and Monroe, with their special references, and Clinton and Obama with their Ivy League law school degrees, Cleveland emerges with a considerable reputation for integrity and incorruptibility, traits which come naturally to the formalists, and Coolidge is remembered for possessing the driest wit in the White House. The most that the rest can hope for is not to be chastised too severely, as Buchanan has been for not doing something about preventing the impending Civil War (although what he could have done is never made clear), or Fillmore and Pierce for not being more than Fillmore and Pierce, or Van Buren for having been too sly and too political (neither of which he was during his presidency). And yet ... and yet ... there are questions of balance and restraint, there are matters of special respect for, and sensitivity, toward the rights of individuals. Let us, then, give the formalists some breathing space, at least until we compare their overall quality and impact with that of the more celebrated lawyer-moralists and rule-skeptics. I believe that they deserve more respect and admiration than they have received. I believe more. I believe the lawyer formalists have been, and remain, the best chance a democracy has to check the

American people when they are, as de Tocqueville put it: "...intoxicated by passion or carried away by the impetuosity of their ideas." De Tocqueville questioned whether "without this admixture of lawyer-like sobriety with the democratic principle, democratic institutions could long be maintained."

12

Founding Fathers: James Madison and James Monroe

SUCCEEDING THOMAS JEFFERSON, their mentor and patron, James Madison and James Monroe stand historically, as presidents, in his shadow. The originality or independence of their presidential vision or imagination seems blurred around the edges in most historical accounts.

Madison and Monroe were, in a political sense, slavish imitators of Jefferson and, at the same time, nothing like him. Jefferson was a lawyer turned moralist, a man with a flair for the language, if not the firing line, of revolution, a radical political thinker who chafed under presidential checks—Constitutional, Supreme Court decisions, or otherwise. Technically not a lawyer (he did get law books together and prepared for the bar), Madison was the apotheosis of legal-mindedness and well earned the right to be included among the lawyer formalists. He was a first-rate legal thinker and doer, a man who, brilliant in spearheading that remarkable set of rules, the United States Constitution, suffers a curious fading as president. This is not surprising, but largely unfair. A formalist has a talent for both organizing rules and living by them, but his adherence to rules is hardly as spectacular as his composing a legal system.

Although he studied law under Thomas Jefferson and was admitted to the Virginia bar in 1786, Monroe practiced law only briefly after being elected to the Virginia assembly the same year. He was a U.S. Senator by 1790, Minister to France in 1794, governor of Virginia in 1799, minister to England in 1803, again governor of Virginia in 1811,

Secretary of State the same year, Secretary of War in 1814, and finally president from 1816 to 1824.

The quality of formalism that may demonstrate itself, as in Hugo Black on the Supreme Court, to be fiercely active, has a reverse spin in the presidency and emerges frequently to critical eyes as passiveness and timidity. This results primarily from a formalist's subservience and devotion to that dominant collection of rules known as the United States Constitution. In its name, Justice Black can resist any congressional or presidential action that threatens individual rights under the First Amendment. The First Amendment (not a drive for personal aggrandizement, but the reverse) thrusts him into the active role of expanding Supreme Court power. Under the umbrella of that same Constitution, formalistic presidents find themselves blocked from pushing programs they find desirable and would otherwise attempt to bulldoze through Congress. They go further. When they act, they do so in much the same reactive way as the Supreme Court; they veto or otherwise frustrate the will of Congress without having previously manifested a will of their own.

Madison, the legal minded 'non-lawyer,' seems paradoxical in his major roles in American history. As the seminal architect of the Constitution, he looms as a mythical hero of the intellect, a genius at structure. As a president, this same man, with his same brain, initially startles us with the recollection that he served two full terms, so unheralded is his performance and so blatant are the charges of his presidential weightlessness. He emerges in most historical treatments as one of the larger proofs, if the American public required it, that intellectuals do not belong in the presidential list, that 'eggheads' lack the pragmatic, common-sense touch, required of the top man in an egalitarian society. It is generally conceded that, after John Adams, Jefferson and Madison, what one might call the 'hard intelligence' took over —men more concerned with pragmatic political results than with generalized intellectual concerns and speculations. This so-called hard intelligence is applicable to the whole series of formalists succeeding Madison: Monroe, Van Buren, Tyler, Fillmore, Pierce, Buchanan, Hayes, Arthur, Cleveland, Benjamin Harrison, McKinley, Taft, Coolidge, Ford, Clinton, and Obama. Recalling the vulgar jokes about Gerald Ford's mental gear (such as Lyndon Johnson's gibe that he could not chew gum and fart at the same time), we should consider Ford's competency as Minority

THE LEGAL MIND AND THE PRESIDENCY

House Leader and his background as a lawyer to realize how relative and self-serving definitions of intelligence can be.

Historians have gone out of their way to lean on Madison as president. Their gravamen is not even that he was such a poor president as that he was such a great constitutionalist. They are annoyed at having to admire a person's intellect extravagantly one moment and to patronize it the next for the very same qualities. Samuel Eliot Morison, Henry Steele Commager, and William E. Leuchtenburg corral the general irritation: "James Madison must be accounted a great statesman, owing to his labors on the Federal Constitution, but he was a very poor politician ... He had a talent for writing logical diplomatic notes; but logic was of little use in dealing with Europeans locked in a deadly struggle. Negative in his dealings with Congress, he allowed Jefferson's personal 'strings' for influencing House and Senate to rot from disuse. And he was stubborn to the point of stupidity."

Morison's most intriguing indictment is Madison's stubbornness. Stubbornness about what? Certainly, moral 'stubbornness,' such as Truman's, is not stupid. But Madison was not inflexible in the moral mode; his was too much of a legal mind for that, as his major shifts, on the Bank of the United States and on states' nullification rights, suggest. If any characteristic defines the formalistic cast of the legal mind, it is stubborn adherence to the precedent rules by which such a mind is governed trigger Madison's inflexibility, his general deference to Congress, his rules of reason applied to international affairs—all of the ways of thinking that illumined his remarkable career as a constitutional architect did not make him a mediocre president—only one so rated by most historians. An argument, and a persuasive one, can be made that Madison's presidential talents have been seriously underestimated. Henry Clay, no mean contemporary observer, thought so, according to Mrs. Samuel Harrison Smith: "Last Sunday Mr. and Mrs. Clay passed with us, in a social, domestic manner ... The characters and administrations of Jefferson and Madison were analyzed... Mr. Clay preferred Madison and pronounced him after Washington our greatest statesman... He thought Jefferson had most genius—Madison most judgment and common sense—Jefferson a visionary and theorist, often betrayed by his enthusiasm into rash and imprudent and impracticable measures. Madison, cool, dispassionate, practical, safe. (Samuel Harrison Smith) would not yield

Jefferson's superiority and said he possessed a power and energy, which carried our country through difficulties and dangers...(Clay insisted that) the power of Madison's less energetic character and caution would have produced the same results."

A presidential maxim might be that small wars make small reputations and big wars, big ones. The War of 1812, the Spanish American War, and the Mexican War did little to enhance the names, respectively, of Madison, McKinley and Polk. Unlike the 'big war' presidents, there is no automatic linkage. The names of Lincoln, Wilson, and Franklin Roosevelt are indelibly impressed with their wars. Still, an argument can be made that Madison was the greatest wartime president in American history, if one judges performance not in terms of *Sturm und Drang*, but of the formalistic triumph of republican principles and human rights over wartime pressures.

Any attempt to restore a historical period to immediacy points up the difficulty of highlighting the areas of concern, the lives or events, or marketplaces or current commentaries, that generate a decent feel of the time. Yet it is not that difficult to imagine the general anxiety still fluttering over the ground rules governing the infant republic when Madison took office. The government of the United States had been running for a meager nineteen years, by a series of chief executives, none of whom had a part in constructing the Constitution. Only one, in fact, Washington, had even been present at the convention. And, rather obviously, neither Adams nor Jefferson had much affection for a document that had, unthinkably, been composed very well without them; each, in his own way, was disposed to disparage it when it contradicted their separate and opposing notions of the way to run a country. It is interesting that while neither Adams nor Jefferson, regarded, in contrast to Madison, as individualistic and independent thinkers, vetoed a single Congressional act, Madison vetoed seven bills, including (his last act as president) a bill for internal improvements (which he very much favored), on Constitutional grounds.

The collision between Hamilton and Jefferson, which resulted in the creation of the opposing Federalist and Democratic-Republican parties, arose from an irreconcilable difference of opinion as to the ultimate rule by which the new game, called the United States of America, was to be played. Hamilton's strategy was to use any means available to concentrate power in the national government; Jefferson's notion, at least before he assumed the presidency, was to, at all costs, minimize that power. Only in contrast to Madison can Hamilton and Jefferson become fellow travelers; they are linked in their treatment of the Constitution as a convenient instrument by which they might justify their divergent political visions or which, when convenient, they might ignore. Neither of them, Hamilton as a rule-skeptic or Jefferson as a lawyer-moralist, were especially fond of, or committed to, the idea that a collection of commandments could command them, might have the arrogance to codify their philosophies. To humble themselves before Constitutional premises was to violate their sense of self.

These were very real distinctions when played out in the political arena. It is no accident that one of the crucial Constitutional issues during the Madison and Monroe terms was not even a problem during Jefferson's presidency. Madison and Monroe, each in his turn, agonized over whether the Constitution allowed Congress to authorize the building of roads and canals. But Madison, writing to Monroe in 1817, observes: "The Cumberland Road having been a measure taken during the administration of Mr. Jefferson, and, as far as I recollect, not then brought to my particular attention, I cannot assign the grounds assumed for it by Congress, or which produced his sanction. I suspect that the question of Constitutionality was but slightly if at all examined by the former. And that the Executive consent was doubtingly or hastily given." It was no small matter to Madison and Monroe that they were forced to veto bills for urgently needed internal improvements. It was even more important to them, however, to live by the Constitutional frame of reference.

Irving Brant, incensed, and justifiably so, at the disparagement by historians of Madison as president, insists that, "If James Madison was not a great President, greatness has no meaning." He emphasizes Madison's unusual concentration on civil liberties during war-time: "Both during Madison's life and thereafter, the deepest underrating of his work has been as President and wartime Commander-in-Chief. His talents were not military, but he kept a firm hand on the helm during a contest that rent the American people asunder. Most of all, the underrating resulted from the quiet methods of President Madison and from historians' disregard of the titanic difficulties heaped on him by the refusal of New England to take part in the war. By his unflinching stand for freedom of speech and press, he prevented sedition from flaring into civil war."

American history is filled with examples of how easy it is for a president, in the name of national security, particularly in wartime, to invade civil rights. Lincoln, Wilson, and Franklin Roosevelt are prime examples. Even abuses committed by Nixon might have been condoned during a major war period. Madison's restraint in dealing with New England's insurgency during the War of 1812 is unique in American presidential history. Further, it serves to illuminate a commendable characteristic of the formalistic presidents. They generally tend to soft-pedal the demands of national security in favor of a steady insistence upon the survival of the Constitution and the individual rights secured by it. Yet, ironically, civil libertarian presidents get a bad press compared to the excitement and drama generated by the presidents who gallop on white horses on high roads.

Another dominant characteristic of Madison as president exemplifies the formalistic trait of initial indecisiveness (while fumbling for the proper premise) followed by firmness amounting to intractability once his mind has zeroed in on the applicable rule of conduct. "Mr. Madison," observed Albert Gallatin, who had worked with him during Jefferson's presidency and much of his own, "is, as I always knew him, slow in taking his ground but firm when the storm arises."

While Madison was intellectually much superior to Monroe, the similarities in their mental processes, the way they arrived at decisions, may be divined from John C. Calhoun's assessment of Monroe: "Tho' not brilliant, few men were his equals in wisdom, firmness & devotion to the country... I have known many much more rapid in reaching a conclusion, but very few with a certainty so unerring." Of neither man, Madison or Monroe, can one say comfortably that he was brilliant, in the way that Hamilton, say, was brilliant, but it is with confidence that one judges them, along with the lightly regarded Van Buren and Tyler, as among our wiser, safer presidents.

13

The Little Magician: Martin Van Buren

WHATEVER MARTIN VAN Buren said or did before the presidency, as president he felt compelled to play by the rules. The way he formalized his presidency and thereby dignified his political sleaziness was remarkable. Formalism is, finally, a way of 'wising up.'

Van Buren is the originator of a presidential line regarded, and justly so, as mediocrities who transcend themselves by falling back upon the originality and moral fervor implicit at the core of long-standing premises. Van Buren's confounding of the critics who had labeled him the American Talleyrand, the Fox, and the Little Magician would hardly have been possible if he had not possessed a formalistic mind honed upon a successful career in the practice of law. His presidency, successful when viewed historically, was founded upon a sturdy reliance upon the United States Constitution and its restraints upon governmental power: "The principle that will govern me in the high duty to which my country calls me is a strict adherence to the letter and spirit of the Constitution as it was designed by those who framed it. Looking back to it as a sacred instrument carefully and not easily framed; remembering that it was throughout a work of concession and compromise; viewing it as limited to national objects; regarding it as leaving to the people and the States all power not explicitly parted with, I shall endeavor to preserve, protect, and defend it by anxiously referring to its provision for direction in every action."

There was nothing evasive or equivocal, in the face of tremendous pressure to alleviate the Panic of 1837 with Federal funds, about the insistence of 'the Fox' on constitutional guidelines: All communities are apt to look to Government for too much ... especially at periods of sudden embarrassment or distress. But this ought not to be. The framers of our excellent Constitution ... acted at the time on a sounder principle. They wisely judged that the less Government interferes with private pursuits the better for general prosperity."

Nor does Van Buren, intent on preserving the Union, back away from an anguished but determined stand of later 'Northern' formalists on slavery. "Have not recent events made it obvious ... that the least deviation from this spirit of forbearance is injurious to every interest, that of humanity included? Amidst the violence of excited passions this generous and fraternal feeling has been sometimes disregarded; and ... I cannot refrain from anxiously invoking my fellow-citizens never to be deaf to its dictates ... now, when every motive for misrepresentation has passed away, I trust that they (my sentiments) will be candidly weighed and understood ... I must go into the Presidential chair the inflexible and uncompromising opponent of every attempt on the part of Congress to abolish slavery in the District of Columbia against the wishes of the slaveholding States, and also with a determination equally decided to resist the slightest interference with it in the States where it exists." Van Buren's devotion to constitutional principles is equally firm in regard to the question, hotly debated during the early presidencies, of internal improvements: "Convinced ... of the inexpediency as well as unconstitutionality of the construction of works of internal improvement under the direct or indirect authority of the Federal Government, so long as the Constitution remained as it was, I became earnestly solicitous not only to arrest the course of legislation on the subject ... but to devise some ... better and a safer footing ... I proposed an amendment of the Constitution, the object of which was to make that lawful which was then illicit and to protect the public interest against abuses by wholesome constitutional restraints ..."

Much is made by historians of Van Buren's aversion to the 'people' as opposed to affection for, and ability with, smaller groups. For example, Holmes Alexander feels that "if a single positive belief can be ascribed to the man who made his name synonymous with evasiveness, it is that he dreaded and distrusted, above all, the will of the People." This suggests, as in the later case of Lyndon Johnson, that it was not so much that he dreaded the people as that he was reacting to their distrust of him. Van Buren's envy of a people's champion is evident in his summation of Andrew Jackson: "... the conciliation of individuals formed the smallest, perhaps too small a part of his policy. His strength lay with the masses and he knew it. He first, and, at least in all public questions, always tried to be right and when he felt that he was so he apprehended little—sometimes perhaps too little—from the opposition of prominent and powerful men; and it must be admitted that he seldom over-estimated the strength he derived from the confidence and favor of the people and his consequent ability to cope with his political opponents. Seldom if ever had he to contend, as is so often the case with public men, with that lurking suspicion, common and perhaps natural to the public mind, that the most zealous and seemingly the most earnest efforts for the public good have their origin in motives of personal ambition or self interest."

Holmes Alexander, measuring the transformation of Van Buren from a political manipulator to a president with a sense of integrity and national purpose, has perceptive words to say about the capability of a formalist like Van Buren to rise above himself: "though no one ... seemed to have guessed it, Martin Van Buren ... was no longer the Little Magician nor even the Red Fox. He was not the first ... man whom a sacred trust, no matter how undeservedly achieved, has suddenly sobered and ennobled, but the courage, wisdom and unselfishness he would show as Chief Magistrate was far and away the most astonishing miracle he ever performed... Those talents, so long directed toward personal ends, were actually to be applied ... for the good of his country. This is not to say that Martin Van Buren became overnight a seer and a statesman. His was never the profundity of mind to permit that. What he did was what any man with ordinary intelligence, a sense of balance and a practical education in government could have done—were he willing to take the consequences."

It is much too easy to condemn formalists for their lack of flair or their refusal to exploit the dramatic potential of situations, if only in words. Their trademark, and this holds true of such maligned presidents as Tyler, Fillmore, Pierce, and Buchanan as well as those, better regarded, like Cleveland, is a "sense of balance" that often, in retrospect, is regarded as excessive caution. This quality, even though usually accompanied as well by character and integrity, has led many historians, often quite unfairly, to disparage their presidential performances.

Although, for example, John Tyler, much like Van Buren, is considered to have scored significant successes in foreign policy, such as avoiding flare-ups with England over the Maine and Oregon boundaries, and paving the way for annexation of Texas, he is denigrated both for his refusal to propose legislation to Congress and his alacrity in vetoing bills (mainly related to internal improvements). His stance was due, of course, in both instances, to his adherence to Constitutional directives as he saw them. And historians have laid a large part of the blame for the Civil War upon the inaction of the "dough-face" triumvirate of formalists preceding Lincoln—a dubious charge.

14

The Dough-Faces: Fillmore, Pierce, Buchanan

MILLARD FILLMORE FROM New York, Franklin Pierce from New Hampshire, and James Buchanan from Pennsylvania are among the most unfortunate of American presidents; it is dismal to be vilified for being what you most prize in yourself. Their sin was that they were unmitigated examples of formalism in a radical period. By this I mean a period that used the law, where possible, as a support for moral positions that otherwise treated it as the enemy, to be destroyed in the name of a higher ethic. Radicalism in America can only mean resistance to, and overthrow, not of a ruling class, but of the dominant rule of law—a radicalism not duplicated even during the bloody rise of unionism or the Franklin Roosevelt years of depression and experimentation.

Defining American radicalism simply as opposition to the rule of law evidently is not nearly romantic enough for most radicals, who are usually very romantic indeed. Furthermore, radicals like to think of themselves as affirmers rather than destroyers, even though their affirmation involves an inevitable prior destruction of existing human beings and structures. Staughton Lynd, for example, conceives of the radical tradition in America as affirming "that the proper foundation for government is a universal law of right and wrong self-evident to the intuitive common sense of every man; that freedom is a power of personal self-direction which no man can delegate to another; that the purpose of society is not the protection of property but fulfillment of the needs of living human beings; that good citizens have the right and duty, not only to overthrow incurably oppressive governments, but before that point is reached to break particular oppressive laws; and that we owe our ultimate allegiance, not to this or that nation, but to the whole family of man." Much of Lynd's book predictably deals with emanations of the Jeffersonian rhetoric in the Declaration of Independence while the rest concerns itself mainly with the abolitionist movement. These, the Jeffersonian rhetoric combined with the abolitionist movement, form the most unequivocal expression of opposition to the rule of law in American history.

An interesting question is, why, in this instance, did radicalism triumph? It is not enough to refer the problem to slavery. The impetus for the progression from 'disruption' to an extravagantly bloody war, cannot be claimed, however dearly desired, by the radical abolitionists. They were joined by too many people who had little interest in the movement. The terribly complex answer lies more in a primal American hostility to the law itself, that was able, in this one case, with the immensity of the moral force behind it, to overwhelm the Constitutional legal system.

The formalistic cries in the wilderness of the pre-war presidents were clear and unequivocal, and were endowed, consequently, with considerable dignity. That position was simply that there was no higher law than the Constitution, at least not for Americans, and that any other position betrayed the rule of law to which the United States was irrevocably committed. It recognized that even more than slavery, the law was under attack. Repetition of this theme among Fillmore, Pierce, and Buchanan is remarkably common:

"In our domestic policy the Constitution will be my guide, and in questions of doubt I shall look for its interpretation to the (Supreme Court) ... and to the usage of the Government, sanctioned by the acquiescence of the country. I regard all its provisions as equally binding. In all its parts it is the will of the people expressed in the most solemn form, and the constituted authorities are but agents to carry that will into effect. Every power which it has granted is to be exercised for the public good; but no pretense of utility, no honest conviction, even, of what might be expedient, can justify the assumption of any power not granted. The powers conferred upon the Government... are as clearly expressed in that sacred instrument as the imperfection of human language will allow, and I deem it my first duty not to question its wisdom, add to its provisions, evade its requirements, or nullify its commands." (Millard Fillmore)

"The dangers of a concentration of all power in the general government of a confederacy so vast as ours are too obvious to be disregarded. You have a right, therefore, to expect your agents in every department to regard strictly the limits imposed upon them by the Constitution of the United States ... Our Government exists under a written compact between sovereign States, uniting for specific objects and with specific grants to their general agent. If, then, in the progress of its administration there have been departures from the terms and intent of the compact, it is and will ever be proper to refer back to the fixed standard which our fathers left us and to make a stern effort to conform our action to it." (Franklin Pierce)

"Our only safety consists in obedience and conformity to law. Should a general spirit against its enforcement prevail, this will prove fatal to us as a nation. We acknowledge no master but the law, and should we cut loose from its restraints and everyone do what seemeth good in his own eyes our case will indeed be hopeless." (James Buchanan)

J. Buchanan Henry, Buchanan's nephew, offers this insightful view of his uncle's formalism: "If there was any more marked political bias of Mr. Buchanan's mind than any other it was that of an almost idolatrous respect and reverence for the Constitution. He had been educated and lived in the old constitutional school of statesmanship, and wholly believed in the wisdom and perfection of that great organic law ... He fully and ardently believed in its sufficiency for all purposes, whether of peace or war ... I cannot close without a few words upon my uncle's views upon slavery. He simply tolerated it as a legal fact under our Constitution. He had no admiration for it whatever ... He was only desirous to see the Constitution and laws obeyed, and did emphatically, not believe in the so-called Higher Law."

This particular concept of the 'higher law' of conscience surfaces again, it will be recalled, during the Nuremberg Trials of the Nazis after World War II. From this perspective, the impact of abolitionist accusations of immorality upon Southerners can be imagined.

Fehrenbacher persuasively suggests that: "In the end, it may have been the assault on their self-respect—the very language of the antislavery crusade—that drove many southerners over the edge." The real bite of that language, more than its accusations of Southern immorality, was its scorn for the law, its shredding of the Constitutional parchment, which Fillmore, along with the other 'doughfaces', clearly recognized: "Some objections have been urged against the details of the act for the return of fugitives from labor, but it is worthy of remark that the main opposition is aimed against the Constitution itself, and proceeds from persons and classes of persons, many of whom declare their wish to see that Constitution overturned. They avow their hostility to any law which shall give full and practical effect to this requirement of the Constitution."

To Southerners, if Northerners were insisting that in the name of conscience men were above the law, the United States of America had already ceased to exist. The language of the abolitionists was unabashedly a direct attack upon the Constitution. The fear of a lawless civil war, of perhaps even contributing to it by not more vigorously fulfilling their Constitutional vows, haunted the dreams of Fillmore, Pierce, and Buchanan. They have been, perhaps irretrievably, tarred with the abolitionist's rhetorical brush. They have been condemned by historians for having, in effect, fulfilled their oath "to the best of (their) ability, preserve, protect and defend the Constitution of the United States,"—an obligation, ironically, the South deeply felt it had the right to demand. They are, as I have said, unfortunate men; they dreaded to provoke a war over what they considered irrational demands that violated the basic premises upon which the Constitutional document was based. The Constitution, after all, was, no less than that of 1850, or the Missouri-Kansas Act, itself a compromise. It was unthinkable to these formalists, not only that a sacred compact should be broken, but that the violators should then rub salt in the wound by accusing the other party, the South, of causing the breach. The result was the tragedy of the Civil War, as well as the miseries of the Reconstruction Period, involving the crucifixion of Andrew Johnson by the Radical Republicans, and the mercilessly prolonged debasement of the South.

It is virtually impossible to defend a rational position from a moral one when they are diametrically opposed. The idea of slavery, so repugnant to modern sensibilities, will hardly entertain the possibility of mitigating circumstances. Where, for example, does a rationalist begin to counter Van Wyck Brooks in The Flowering of New England: "They (the abolitionists) were members of a family of minds that had appeared in all the Western countries, in Italy, in Germany, in France, to defend the religion of liberty, poets militant, intellectual men who were glad to fight and die for their beliefs, figures that were

THE LEGAL MIND AND THE PRESIDENCY

appearing in flesh and blood on battlefields and barricades in Europe. Brothers of Mazzini, heirs of William Tell, men of the world themselves and men of culture, they roused the indifferent minds of the thinking masses and made the American anti-slavery movement a part of the great world-struggle of darkness and light."

But, oh, how few of the poets militant died—how many of the masses. Where is the unqualified wisdom in mass death?

15

The Golden Age: Hayes, Arthur, Cleveland, B. Harrison, McKinley

IF A FORMALIST could pick a time when he would be president, he might well choose the period after the Civil War until the turn of the nineteenth century. History has, on the whole, treated Hayes, Arthur, Cleveland, Benjamin Harrison, and McKinley relatively kindly, especially when compared to Fillmore, Pierce, and Buchanan. These five formalist-lawyer presidents, serving from 1877 to the fall of 1901 (divided only by Garfield's nine months in 1881), managed to attain a commendable composite rating of fifteenth compared to the pre-Civil War trio's twenty-sixth in the 1948 and 1962 Schlesinger polls.

Yet only the dates have changed; the basic qualities of the nineteenth century formalists are so similar they might have been cloned. It is as if they were a relay team passing the baton from one to the other without a break. If the criticism of Fillmore, Pierce, and Buchanan is based upon their addiction for the letter of the Constitution, their exasperating exercises in legalism, their caution and delay in making decisions, then what are we to make of biographical summations of these others: "… calm and deliberate. He could never be stampeded into hasty or ill-advised action." (Hayes) "Deliberate, often procrastinating, in coming to a final decision." (Arthur) "…vigorous, deliberate and logical … He would display the utmost caution in making up his mind. But once he reached a conclusion, no force could compel him to quit it." (Cleveland) … his temperament became more and more judicial. When he reached a conclusion after thoroughly examining a question, it was generally irrevocable of a deliberate habit of mind and not only took his own time but kept his own counsel... one of those lawyers who often take weeks to make up their minds." (B. Harrison) "His reticence and caution were ingrained into habit by the time of his presidency ... Once decisions were made, he seldom reflected on them; he did not rehash what might have been. His basic problem was making up his mind, and he often moved with maddening slowness, his ingrained caution impeding his way. Once his course was clear, however, he was inflexible." (McKinley)

Harry Barnard, biographer of Rutherford B. Hayes, the first, and prototypal, post-Civil War formalist, observes that "... his pronounced instinct for reconciliation caused him to view settlement of the race issue in the South as a matter for the slower, though more permanent (he felt) process of education ..." Fillmore, Pierce, or Buchanan could not have agreed more, but reconciliation of a moral issue after it is tested in blood is one thing, and before is another. (The quarrel over whether the United States should have dropped its atomic bombs on Hiroshima and Nagasaki will rage eternally, but the tremendous deterrent effect of having dropped them, and having proved how horrible the consequences were, is undeniable). The price of the victory over slavery, some 600,000 American lives, was not considered too high by the abolitionists, but while Pierce was scorned and derided for his alliterative reference to the Civil War as a "fearful, fruitless, fatal civil war," Hayes, by 1877, would be lauded as the 'healer of strife.' His 'calm and deliberate' temper, his caution and common-sense, trademarks of the 'doughfaces', could once again be regarded as virtues rather than demonstrations of unconscionable behavior. Once again, a display of character and integrity became commendable. Hayes was permitted to concentrate upon the civil-service reform dictated by the scandals of the preceding Grant regime.

Hayes's administration is credited with effectively concluding the Reconstruction period, but actually the South had not been occupied to any extent by Federal troops since 1871, during Grant's first term. In South Carolina and Louisiana, small contingents of Federal troops were still monitoring the political processes; in removing these troops, Hayes received an exaggerated amount of credit for affirmative action.

His efforts toward improving the civil service and eliminating the residuum of graft, nepotism, and cronyism left over from Grant's tenure foreshadow the praise accorded Arthur and Cleveland in succeeding periods. Of Arthur, presumed to be a political hack, after he assumed the presidency, George Frederick Howe could maintain, "The last thing the public expected from President Arthur was leadership or sincere support of the civil service reform cause. His record as a machine politician seemed to augur ill for any kind of reform. Yet it was Arthur who helped lead the fight for civil service reform as President." Hayes, like Cleveland, was forced to react to a national strike during his presidency and, like Cleveland, broke the strike with Federal troops. While he waited until requested to do so by state officials, he first, like Cleveland, had to satisfy himself that his action was constitutional—a *sine qua non*, of course, of formalistic behavior. Interestingly enough, both at the time were praised for their firmness in meeting the threat (of strikers) to property, and the suggestion by liberals that the president was unfairly putting his thumb on the scales in favor of the capitalist over the laborer went unheeded. That a moral imperative could be imposed in favor of the worker no less than a black slave awaited a later period, and, bloody though the history of unionism is, it still was no Civil War. It was basically a class struggle which never became a revolutionary movement; it, consequently, gained its ultimate successes within the law.

16

The Golden Age's MVP: Grover Cleveland

EXCEPT PERHAPS FOR the presidencies of William Clinton and Barak Obama at the turn of the twenty-first century, Grover Cleveland, all two hundred and fifty pounds of him, makes a good case for being the quintessential lawyer-formalist president. To begin with, he is the only formalist who was considered a 'near-great' in the highly regarded Schlesinger polls of 1948 and 1962, and while this would seem to make him an aberrant form, it becomes evident that it is in the intensity and extent of his formalism that he invites admiration. Cleveland is not explained simply by maintaining, as so often is done, that he was perfect for his time, although, admittedly, the latter half of the nineteenth century, succeeding the Civil War, the formalist's 'Golden Age,' was tailor-made for an exhibition of formalistic virtues of caution and conservatism, for a concentration upon individual rights and the tradition of American character instead of upon the 'riches' American dream, equally traditional, of perfecting the society.

On his way to writing a memorable biography, Allen Nevins says of Cleveland: "It is as a strong man, a man of character, that Cleveland will live in history. For all his shrewdness of judgment, he was never in any sense a great intellectual force. It was his personality, not his mind, that made so deep an impress upon his time … His character is one upon which it will always be refreshing and inspiring to look back … It was guided by a sense of rectitude that in the end became second nature to him, and which led him sometimes to remark deprecatingly to his intimates: 'It is no credit to me to do right. I am never under any temptation to do wrong.'"

The terms 'right' and 'wrong' have very special connotations when applied by, or in respect to, legal formalists. We are really dealing with ethical rather than moral questions; Cleveland's 'right' was playing by the rules. To a social reformer, almost nothing that Cleveland thought or did was remotely connected with 'right.' He had, for instance, no feel for blacks or industrial workers, or any minority struggling to get a decent slice of the American pie. Cleveland, Nevins admits, viewed social legislation as heretically bad. To do 'wrong,' for Cleveland, carried with it no philosophical density, for his was the most prosaic of minds. It meant, simply, never to break the rules governing a decent (as opposed to a predatory) nineteenth-century businessman's code of behavior. This stance, in itself, compared to Gould's or Rockefeller's, was refreshing to most of his fellow Americans. Where moralists (such as abolitionists, Al-Qaeda terrorists, Nazis, French resistance fighters in World War II, Communists, Christian Crusaders, and the United States Central Intelligence Agency) can justify cheating, lying, stealing, and even killing in the name of a 'higher' law, to Cleveland it was unthinkable that anything could justify a lie, a breach of contract, or other failures to abide by the rules. Contracts are sacred because they establish the given conditions without which formalists tend to disintegrate. This, as Nichols said of Franklin Pierce, is equally applicable to Cleveland: "He was always confident when he did not have to use discretion. If he had a rule or a statute to follow, he would stick to it through thick or thin. It was only in connection with matters that were without rules ... that he floundered."

The latter half of the nineteenth century deserves serious consideration as the strangest period in American history. The Civil War, involving an unprecedented focus upon moral principles countermanding the traditional reasoned approaches, had been fought and won. The slaves were declared free and equal but not, until 1896, separate. The radical Republicans, abolitionists elected to power, were powerful enough to impeach and come within one vote of convicting a president for the 'crime' of being 'soft on the South'; nevertheless, by 1877, only twelve years after the war, Rutherford B. Hayes is elected president, and the rest of the century is devoted to questions of civil service reform, gold standard versus bimetallism, and tariff fluctuations, with Grover Cleveland's terms (1885-1889 and 1893-1897) the apogee of the curve. It was as if the governing of the American society consisted of board meetings of a giant corporation, and as if the only real goal was to satisfy the shareholders.

Yet, during Cleveland's first administration the Haymarket Square riot occurred. This event, which arose out of a workers' strike for an eight-hour day and resulted, on the flimsiest of evidence, in the hanging of four 'anarchists,' if nothing else, concentrated attention on the fact that America was not one big, happy corporation. By the time of Cleveland's second administration, it was clear that the struggle between business and labor had reached a boil, and Cleveland's role as strike-breaker invited tremendous criticism, not only from the liberals of his age, but the historians of ours. That criticism, however, as portrayed by Nevins, has remained peculiarly apologetic: "Undoubtedly, Cleveland did his duty as he saw it, or rather as Olney unhappily showed it to him. He acted with all his usual conscientiousness and his course really required courage: Governor Altgeld and Mayor Hopkins both opposed his use of troops; they were the Democratic leaders in Illinois, and they had done more than anyone else to help Cleveland carry the State in 1892 ... But any observer who possesses a due sympathy for the rights of labor must feel that Cleveland was led sadly astray ... by his impetuous and bellicose Attorney-General."

The classification of Cleveland as 'near-great' obviously has its ironies when considering the extent to which he personifies the weaknesses ascribed to the other formalists. His high ranking is largely explained by the instinctual admiration of the American people, shared by historians, for the apolitical, amateur politician, for that person divorced from guile and deception, whose tongue is never forked. Regardless of the quality of their performances, Van Buren and McKinley are denigrated because of their projection as, simply, professional politicians. The consequence is that only Cleveland is excused for exaggerated and exasperating formalistic traits. His cautiousness is extenuated by Morison et al's observation that: "...once he reached a conclusion no force could compel him to quit it... Both by initial caution and subsequent firmness he was thus admirably equipped for the work of an executive who acts under constant fire." His lack of imagination is transformed by Merrill into a virtue: "The very narrowness of Cleveland's interests contributed not a little to his success. By concentrating on a few things, he was able to do those well on the strength of his industry, common sense and integrity." His conviction that what was good for business was good for the country was sympathetically received by a nation which later excoriated an Eisenhower cabinet member's statement that what was good for the country was good for General Motors and vice versa.

17

Twentieth Century Formalists: Taft, Coolidge, and Ford

THE 'REAR-DOOR' ADMIRATION for formalism persisted in varying degrees during the twentieth century, tentatively beginning with William Howard Taft, and continuing with Calvin Coolidge and Gerald R. Ford. Its form is an indulgence, laced with both affection and contempt, which relies heavily for its sympathetic component upon nostalgia. The American society, having come of age, no longer laying claim to being the 'new world' of hope for the poor, the ignorant, the homeless, but comprising an inextricable part of the old, having engaged in two World Wars and two hopeless, ideological land wars in Asia and the Middle East, armed with an irrelevant idiom, having suffered an economic collapse of cosmic proportions, no longer fantasizing about being number one, but suffering the torments of actually being pre-eminent among nations—this twentieth-century America dreamt of the good old days when character in a president was enough, and evident in all too few.

In Taft's case, indulgence is complicated by a symbiosis with Theodore Roosevelt. The relationship between Roosevelt and Taft, interesting enough in its love-hate aspects, becomes even more intriguing when considered as morality pitted against legal formalism, for it is upon these abstractions that their deep friendship and mutual respect foundered and ultimately turned sour. The story of Roosevelt and Taft is no less powerful a metaphor for American history than that projected by James Fenimore Cooper in *The Pioneer*, and it takes little imagination to equate Roosevelt with Natty Bumppo and Taft with Judge Temple. It also tells us a great deal about the American psyche; in the play of the 'heart' against the 'head,' to recall Perry Miller's division. Even when the 'head' registers one of its occasional wins, it loses out to the 'heart' in its public relations.

American memories of Theodore Roosevelt are infused with great affection and admiration. He is associated with an amalgam of trust-busting, creation of the Panama Canal, a charge up San Juan (actually Kettle) Hill, and, generally, an abundance of courage and conviction. Taft, on the other hand, when he is remembered at all, is regarded as a rather inept, ultra-conservative legalist. For Roosevelt's daring, Taft substituted caution; for his dislike of the judiciary, reverence; for impatience with the Constitution, abiding respect.

An objective analysis of their respective mental attitudes, stripped of a confusing overlay of personalities, suggests that historical reputations, nurtured by even the most thoughtful of analysts, depend largely upon emotional rather than reasoned reactions. A man like either of the Roosevelts or John F. Kennedy evokes strong feelings that linger long after logical probes digress. In the same way, the lack of a strong initial emotional tug identifies the ultimate sense of mediocrity of a Taft or Hoover.

Yet it is clear, or should be clear, that there are frightening aspects to a Theodore Roosevelt in the presidency. He not only lived dangerously, but thought that way. His view of war could not be more alarming: "The amiable peace-at-any-price people, who in our country have been prancing about as anti-imperialists are, not invariably, but generally, weak in body or mind, men who could not be soldiers because they lack physical hardihood or courage ... there are undoubtedly large sections of the population ... (who) would become utterly appalled by slaughter in the field. In the Spanish war ... our generals ... had to grapple with a public sentiment which screamed with anguish over the loss of a couple of thousand men ... a sentiment of preposterous and unreasoning mawkishness."

His complicity in the revolt of Panama from Colombia, after Colombia refused to ratify the treaty that would have given the United States the necessary strip of land for a canal, is ominously similar to Wilson's high-handedness in Mexico and to modern presidential adventures in Vietnam and Cambodia, and for much more venal purposes; yet he carves out a virtuous path: "I feel we are certainly justified in morals, and therefore justified in law, in interfering summarily and saying the canal is to be built and that they must not stop it." His attitude toward the law was uncomfortably and threateningly patronizing. When discussing his actions in pensioning Civil War veterans whether or not disabled, even though the Congressional Act was limited to the disabled, he observed: "There were two sides to the matter … The first was the situation I had to face as regards the party in Congress. The second was the moral justification of what was actually done." Viewed against the backdrop of Roosevelt's abuses of the Constitutional system of government rather than the way his enthusiasm and energy captivated people's imagination, it is not difficult to relax with some contentment into Taft's so-called deficiencies.

Understandably, Roosevelt would be captivated by Taft while Taft was his obedient servant and become violently angry with him when, hand-picked by Roosevelt for the presidency, Taft nevertheless became his own master. Roosevelt felt betrayed. Here were hundreds of pounds of efficient and responsive deference as civil governor of the Philippines and Secretary of War in a man who, upon being elected president, instead of impulsiveness, reverted to his own judicious temperament: conciliatory instead of belligerent, law-loving instead of law-hating. While Taft, as president, sought to maintain his image as a loyal Rooseveltian lieutenant, it still could not have suited a 'bully' without his pulpit to settle for nothing less from Taft than the playing out of Roosevelt's moralized fantasies, whatever those fantasies might be. It could not have been simply principle and conviction that drove Roosevelt to attack Taft in his Achilles heel, the judicial system. The effect of Roosevelt's demand for recall of judicial decisions, to Taft a mortal invasion of judicial independence, was to make Taft, probably for the only time in his life, 'fighting mad.' It led to the irreconcilable rift in the Republican Party, to the formation of Roosevelt's Bull Moose third party, and to the election in 1912 of the Democrat, Woodrow Wilson.

Political contests in the twentieth century were still to be fought on the Constitutional terrain. That is how Taft saw it, and expressed it, in his acceptance of the Republican nomination in 1912, when he defined the issue as "whether we shall retain, on a sound and permanent basis, our popular constitutional representative form of government, with the independence of the judiciary as necessary to the preservation of those liberties that are the inheritance of centuries."

Donald F. Anderson concludes, "It is difficult to conceive of a president who was more concerned with defending the judiciary than himself, but this was clearly true of Taft." The quarrel, then, between Taft and Roosevelt was not, at least for Taft, ultimately personal, even though he was reduced to calling Roosevelt a 'dangerous egotist' and a 'demagogue' while Taft, to Roosevelt, was a 'puzzle-wit' and 'fat-head.' It finally resolved itself into the familiar American clash between law and morality. Only a lawyer formalist like Taft could, in all sincerity, reduce a political attack to an attack upon the law: "One who so little regards Constitutional principles, especially the independence of the judiciary; and one who is so naturally impatient of legal restraints and of due legal procedure, and who has so misunderstood what liberty regulated by law is, could not be safely trusted with successive Presidential terms."

In a penetrating summation, Paolo E. Coletta concludes that: "Taft was not a bad president but rather a good one. We should therefore seek reasons for his inability to achieve more than he did." Some of the "reasons" developed by Coletta point to the political pitfalls built into the very virtues of the formalistic spirit: "Of absolute integrity, high-minded, just-minded, and clean-minded, he was in no way devious. He never posed, had small capacity for self-delusion, and was completely free of the arts and practices of the demagogue... Trained in the law, Taft took a conservative and legalistic approach to government. He must find authority in the Constitution or in law prior to acting ..." Donald R. McCoy observes: "In the face of the increasing complexities of the twentieth century, the luxury of having a passive president would seem to be less and less affordable. Yet Americans ushered in the century with a "Taft (who) was torn by indecision at critical times. When subject to opposing pressures he took the path of least resistance and did nothing." And in 1924 they elected Calvin Coolidge, the apotheosis of inaction (followed by Gerald Ford in 1974).

"If you see ten troubles coming down the road," Coolidge is reported as saying, "you can be sure that nine will run into the ditch before they reach you and you have to battle with only one of them." His taciturnity is legendary; his comparable reluctance to act is in the formalistic tradition and flavored his presidency. In a curious fashion, while Taft is censured for being the calm between the dramatic and volatile administrations of Theodore Roosevelt and Wilson, Coolidge invites an amused affection that relieves him of any connection with the scandals of Harding or the stock market crash and depression attributed to Hoover. Yet the Teapot Dome scandals actually broke while Coolidge was president, and the crash came only seven months after he left office.

Coolidge's major contribution to the stability of the presidential office, like Gerald Ford's to follow, and Taft's before him, was in those very formalistic character traits that led so largely to his denigration: "Our country has prospered, our Government is secure. But that prosperity and that security flow from the school and the church. They are the product of the mind and the soul. They are the result of the character of the American people." Coolidge's code of ethics, that "the development of character was the highest ideal," was required to restore dignity to a presidency tarnished by the Harding scandals just as "openness and candor," divorced from questions of ability or intelligence, were the necessary traits required of Ford after Nixon's Watergate. It is inevitable that once the crisis of faith is over, these men are derided as old-fashioned and obsolete. Americans are invariably ashamed at being caught out adopting the "country-boy" air of admiring, simply, and good character.

Coolidge, like Taft and Ford (as if to say that the twentieth century will settle from time to time for nothing less) is the embodiment, for better or worse, of the formalistic mentality. Claude M. Fuess comments: "He sometimes took more time than even his friends could have wished, but it was not laziness or procrastination which caused the delay. He wanted to be sure of his ground ... By nature he was prudent and logical, and his acts were the consequence of long meditation ..." Donald R. McCoy adds: "(Coolidge) was like the naval officer who runs his ship according to the letter of the book, on the premise that nothing can go wrong that way. Coolidge's book was the Constitution and he interpreted it almost literally as far as the Chief Executive's powers were concerned. He addressed himself only to those problems clearly provided for in the Constitution and by judicial interpretation of it."

One cannot leave Coolidge without expressing admiration for his rhetorical power, atypical of formalists, often surrounded though it is by platitudes. His laconic wit is proverbial; not so readily recognized is the power frequently generated by his language: "We do not need more material development, we need more spiritual development. We do not need more intellectual power, we need more moral power. We do not need more knowledge, we need more character. We do not need more government, we need more culture. We do not need more laws, we need more religion. We do not need more of the things that are seen, we need more of the things that are unseen ... Civilization is always on trial, testing out, not the power of material resources, but whether there be, in the heart of the people, that virtue and character which come from charity sufficient to maintain progress."

It is remarkable, when assessing strength of character in the White House, as opposed to charisma or greatness, or brilliance or power, how often we turn to formalists like Cleveland, Benjamin Harrison, Taft, Coolidge, or, finally, Gerald Rudolph Ford, Jr. Upon reflection, however, it seems inevitable. Good character is defined by an aggregate of virtuous qualities which, particularly in the case of lawyers pursuing a code of ethical professional behavior, consist of such things as integrity, promise-keeping, caution (avoidance of trouble for oneself or others), reasonableness, common sense, steadiness, dignity, respect for the rights and opinions of others. On the contrary, the moralist is all too often characterized, as in the case of a Theodore Roosevelt, by impetuosity, carelessness, deviousness, and indifference both to the rights of others and to principles other than one's own. While these moralistic traits, accompanied as they so often are, by charm, courage, flair, and a commitment to the 'right' (especially when it turns out right), can be catapulted into greatness, they are rarely summed up by the word 'character.'

Ford can be said to have been made a president purely and simply because of his character, which can be argued to be, in his case, primarily a desire to abide by ethical rules. It has been cynically suggested more than once that Nixon picked him as his vice-president, following Agnew's resignation under fire, with the expectation that even the Watergate fiasco could be tolerated more than the prospect of Ford becoming president; that Nixon would thereby survive even Watergate. Whatever may have been Nixon's motives, it is clear that to obtain Congressional approval he had to select a man with the most unimpeachable character imaginable. Nothing else, just character. The man selected and universally approved was Gerald Ford and, ironically, with his pardon of Nixon on September 9, 1974 (a day that for many will live in infamy), exactly one month after Nixon resigned, imputations of the dubious quality of that character became the most lively criticism leveled at him during his entire term. John J. Casserly, one of his speech-writers, noted in his journal: "The only conclusion I have been able to ascertain over the past year is that as a congressman, Mr. Ford became accustomed to cloak-room compromises. He had been conditioned to feel comfortable with accommodation. The difficult decisions reaching the White House involve deep personal and professional principles. Apparently, Mr. Ford doesn't want to face—I do not believe he cannot see—the difference between compromising moral principles and compromising legislative positions. Men and women sometimes cannot and will not compromise their principles— and they should not be expected to do so."

Richard Reeves, evaluating Ford's first hundred days, continues the guarded, qualified estimations: "Gerald Ford ... built his career and life on avoiding offending anyone. Ford's discovery, shared by many in modern America, was no small thing. It was that the highest national honors and rewards could be won by limiting oneself to commonplace virtues—ambition, perseverance and caution ... The worst Ford has ever been accused of on Watergate and the ensuing cover-up is devoted, perhaps calculated, blindness," It remained for Clark R. Mollenhoff, a member of Nixon's house staff in 1969 and 1970, to pull off the velvet gloves in early 1976: "Ford's first nineteen months as President have given us little to praise and much that is highly vulnerable to criticism. This should have been expected because, in all of Gerald Ford's political life, he has demonstrated no commitment except to the Republican Party and within that party only to the extent that it did not entail any risk for his only longtime political goal—to be Speaker of the House of Representatives. He was less irritating than other ambitious politicians because he was a professional 'nice guy' ... Ford's record for duplicity has matched and, for the time period involved, surpassed Nixon's ... Ford spoke of openness and vetoed a Freedom of and Information law. He spoke of candor and weaseled away from his seeming promise not to pardon Nixon. He spoke of cooperation with Congress and the need to be accountable, but used 'executive privilege' to cover up for Secretary of State Henry A. Kissinger's evasions and falsehoods."

In a summation of the nature of Ford and his presidency, he, perhaps, has been harder upon himself than even his critics, for he idealized as his model the president most difficult for him to emulate: Harry S. Truman. It is understandable that Truman might invite

The Legal Mind and the Presidency

Ford's admiration. Here was, after all, another professional politician, a man linked to sordid machine politics as well, a person who had been scorned and derided for his mediocrity of mind and personality. All of this endeared Truman to a man of whom Nixon would say, "Can you imagine Jerry Ford sitting in this presidential chair?" Richard Reeves concludes: "The vital difference between Truman and Ford, a distinction which crystallizes the pathos in a career like Ford's, is that Truman was guided by a rigid and uncompromising moral base that never let him forget that politics was only the servant of his morality, while Ford equated decency of character with loyalty to party and accommodation of political friends, an equation that was not disputed until he was dipped into the White House fishbowl."

Unfortunately for Ford, his presidential actions were intertwined with politics to such an unprecedented degree, due to Watergate and his pardon of Nixon, that his ethical sense, the formalistic code by which he lived, was irreparably bent out of shape by conflicting loyalties.

Setting aside, for the moment, Ford's inability to disentangle himself from the political thicket, it becomes easy to commend Ford, as he was repeatedly, for his good-humor and his good-will. Before the universal approval of him as Nixon's vice-president, congressional investigation only reinforced the sense of his decency and lack of venal impulses. His presidency as well, divorced from the overhanging shadow of Watergate and the Nixon pardon, while singularly bland and inept (little if anything was done, or even attempted, regarding major problems of inflation, energy, and unemployment), it was at least free of scandal or war, or other major international tensions. Bold or imaginative leadership was smothered by an excess of caution and inaction, by a deference toward, and respect for the Constitution and the other branches of the Federal government, all of which only serves to emphasize the presence of a formalist in the White House. In a true sense, Ford was, all in all, a decent replacement for Nixon; it was a time for the country to heal, as Ford never tired of emphasizing, and the best medicine was to supply a 'leader' who would simply stand by benignly and, being largely incapable of tampering with it, and by not tampering with it, allow the wound to heal itself, which it proceeded to do.

Having said all this, we must come back to the sorrowful recognition that the political aspect of Ford's presidency did overshadow his entire term and even damaged him in his strength—his own sense

145

of rectitude. His pardon of Nixon a month after inauguration created the very problem he avowedly was seeking to avoid, and that was a prolonged national concentration on Nixon. A good part of Ford's dilemma in meeting criticism was that the boldness and firmness with which Ford acted upon the pardon contradicted his presumed personality traits, traits which otherwise characterized his White House tenure. This element lent credence to suspicions that a 'deal' had been worked out between Ford and Nixon, in advance of Nixon's resignation. Congresswoman Bella Abzug, a member of the House Judiciary Subcommittee on Criminal Justice observed, after the sub-committee convened on September 24, 1974, some two weeks after the pardon: "There are suspicions that Richard Nixon may have made a deal on the pardon with Gerald Ford before nominating him to the vice presidency. If Richard Nixon made Ford's elevation to Vice President conditional upon the promise of a pardon, or even if Mr. Nixon conditioned his own resignation on a promise of receiving a pardon, then conceivably Mr. Ford could be charged with accepting a bribe, which is an impeachable offense. Grim as this possibility may be, it is nonetheless the duty of this committee to investigate the facts and make a determination."

Ford subsequently tried to meet the accusations head-on by voluntarily appearing before a House Subcommittee chaired by William Hungate. According to Ford's autobiography, this decision was opposed by some of his staff members as lacking precedent: "To the best of their knowledge, not since the days of George Washington had a Chief Executive gone up to testify before Congress." However, he decided to go ahead on the advice, oddly enough, of a Democrat, Speaker of the House Carl Albert, who observed, "There's nothing more important to this country than the success of Jerry Ford as President. He has a reputation for honesty, and he ought to lay it out."

Of Ford's appearance before the sub-committee, Clark R. Mollenhoff claims that Ford left more unanswered questions than he put to rest, even though Ford announced unequivocally, "There was no deal, period, under no circumstances." But there is no strong reason to disbelieve Ford. That the possibility was aired with Ford by General Alexander M. Haig, Jr., on August 1, 1974, eight days before Nixon's resignation, is admitted, but it seems entirely probable that it went no further than simply to let it hang and gather such weight as it could.

THE LEGAL MIND AND THE PRESIDENCY

What activated Ford's uncharacteristic boldness seems to be, simply, party loyalty, or, in the jargon of his football days, 'team spirit.' Ford had to pardon Nixon, not for Nixon's sake, but for his own, and he had to do it as soon as possible. His need, given the narrow shape and dimensions of his ethical structure, was not based upon selfish or venal instincts, but upon his self-image, however unworthy and grubby it may appear from the outside, of what it meant to be an honorable and decent man. I find it difficult to believe that his motives, inviting complex implications as ingenuousness can so often do (Billy Budd comes to mind as the ultimate example of this), were designedly devious. Reminiscent of Charles Wilson (what was good for General Motors was good for the country), Ford persuades me that he genuinely believed his act of pardon, good for the Republican party in putting Watergate to bed, had to be equally good for the country. But, 'good' or 'bad,' after a life-long construct of ethics, it was impossible for Gerald Ford, at this late stage of his career, to 'let down the team.' This would have required that, in a twinkling, he restructure a lifetime of thinking in formalistic terms and consider a refusal to pardon Nixon in the self-righteous, solipsistic terms of a lawyer-moralist—like Jefferson, for example, in his vendetta against Aaron Burr, or Wilson, outraged by the Mexican leader, Carranza, for his refusal to appreciate Wilson's killing 'kindnesses' toward Mexico.

18

Anti-Intellectualism and the Popular Distaste for Lawyers

IN *THE GROWTH of American Law*, James Willard Hurst succinctly observes: "From colonial days, popular attitudes conceded to the bar a marked measure of honorable distinction. Yet this was always matched in popular lore by a character for sharpness, pettifogging, and greedy manipulation of technicality to oppress the weak and ignorant... Whether mistaken, unjust, or hypocritical, the unfavorable popular image of the lawyer was a reality throughout our social history. It contrasted oddly with the people's readiness to make a place at the bar an object of public honor and private ambition. Both faces of the image combined to make the bar a distinctive functional group in the community."

The faces of the image are familiar enough, but not what fashioned them. If, as de Tocqueville suggests, lawyers were, with warts and all, the American aristocrats, there is nothing very odd about aristocrats inviting hostility and reverence from Americans at the same time. The dilemma of the American of 1835, which has renewed itself for succeeding generations, was that he was plagued by the two opposing metaphors of 'equality' and 'making it'—that is, becoming superior. The deification of one meant the defilement of the other. The American's confusion was compounded as well by the dubious equation of 'freedom' with 'democracy'. Democracy, evolving as majority rule, is no respecter of 'liberty and justice for all'. The legal umbrella under which individual rights have been protected from the hailstones of democracy does not safeguard, even theoretically, a limitless exercise of those rights.

The early American deeply distrusted his common law courts, his judges and lawyers, precisely because, despite his ability to shoot accurately at the heart from the hip, it was finally to be they, not he, who would protect his 'rights,' his power to speak his mind, move his body freely, hold his property in 'fee simple'— to be as superior as his talents permitted. The cleavage between intellect and instinct, between superior and common sense, between the duty to exercise reason and the right to be unreasonable, shaped the terrifying fault upon which the American psyche is grounded. The mixture of arrogance and awe long distinguishing the American abroad in Europe is the mark of a human being struggling to pull himself together.

The form of fiction most unique to America is the 'western,' which perpetuates the vision of a naturally good and fearless, rather simple-minded man resisting the law's indifference to moral imperatives, to a more psychologically congenial image of the hero defending against the forces of evil that have rendered the law impotent. The most enduring American fantasy, from John Brown to John Wayne, is that of the 'Lone Ranger' taking the law into his own hands under the banner of right. While the virtue of an English Robin Hood or a French D'Artagnan consists of replacing evil rulers with good ones, only in the 'riches American dream' is the law itself the evil, especially its common law base, the Johnny-come-lately, and the more necessary, the more evil. As Alan Ryan points out, the dream refuses to vaporize: "A Pew report showed that self-delusion is alive and well: Americans believe that the US is uniquely open to talent and hard work and that social mobility is greater in the US than anywhere in the world. The truth is that the US and the UK have lower social mobility than almost all other advanced industrial societies. Yet almost 40 per cent of the population also believe that they are, or within a year will be, part of the top 1 per cent. Like any other religious conviction, faith in the great American myth is impervious to mere facts."

The common law was considered both immoral and undemocratic. A New Hampshire judge put it in the early nineteenth century, "It is my duty to do justice between parties, not by any quirk out of Coke and Blackstone—books that I never read and never will."

Exaggerated frontier legends, collected by Anton-Herman Chroust, consigning lawyers to the devil, contain a desperate longing of the westerner to stand with them at the head of the educated 'upper class': "Lawyers were never buried in the city where they lived. They were simply laid out at night in a room with the window open and the door locked, and next morning they were always gone ... (and) there was always a strong smell of brimstone in the room... On the other hand, there was also a popular saying on the frontier that if a family had several sons, they guided the dullest toward preaching and sent the brightest to study law."

The post-Revolutionary attempts to 'democratize' the legal profession out of existence were not merely a western phenomenon: "During Shays Rebellion in 1786 people...demanded that all inferior courts and all lawyers be entirely eliminated... In Vermont and New Hampshire vociferous demands were made to suppress the legal profession completely... In Vermont...courthouses were set afire...In New Hampshire... people even advanced the...proposition that all courts be abolished... In New Jersey debtors nailed up the doors of the courthouses, and irate mobs attacked lawyers on the streets."

There is, in all this, the irresistible implication that if lawyers could not be joined, they could be destroyed. That they were not—that, instead, they went on to dominate America's public business, once again says a great deal about the insatiable craving, taboo, and inexpressible of Americans for an indigenous aristocracy to which they might aspire. The significant extension of the intellectual class beyond lawyers, fostered by the vast network of American colleges and universities only exacerbated, rather than satisfied, this craving. Not even the creation of families of enormous hereditary wealth, the traditional springboard for eventual rise into the aristocratic class, could dislodge the intellectual from his pre-eminent position. Americans have consistently refused to recognize their wealthy as superior, only luckier, unless they have been involved in something more, such as public service or a broader intellectual sphere. Intellectuals, more than billionaires, have made them feel ill-at-ease. As readily happens in anti-intellectual movements, strange bed-fellows emerged, a commingling of romanticizers of the 'common man,' such as Thomas Jefferson, and commoner lawyers defending their ignorance of the common law. Jefferson spearheaded that strain of radicalism in American life that regards the rule of reason (and, consequently, the rule of law) as the Satanus rather than the *Deus ex machina* of American politics. Jefferson's radicalism, as his presidency made clear, was largely rhetorical but, much like Marx's, was eagerly embraced by others to justify less metaphysical attacks on the 'system.' Idealizing democracy in its purest form, Jefferson opposed the common law as the exercise of judicial power not granted by 'the people': "Of all the doctrines which have ever been broached by the federal government, the novel one of the common law being in force and cognizable as an existing law in their courts, is to me the most formidable…it is the will of the nation which makes the law obligatory."

Tormented and confused by the tension between liberty (freedom to be unreasonable) and rights (duty to be rational), fragmented by his devotion to both concepts, the nineteenth century American permitted the common law to build its American nest. The attacks, at the same time that ultimately victorious efforts were being made to create rigorous and exacting standards for admission to legal practice and to base American law on the judge-driven common law, make it abundantly clear that the lives, liberties, and properties of the general post-Revolutionary population, largely a debtor class, were in terrible shape despite their 'inalienable' rights. What this group demanded of the judiciary, a tender regard for its under-privileged class condition, the judges could not, and would not, give. As the judges were so often to say, such moral decisions lay with the legislature, not with the courts. This distinction between legal and social justice, between what Americans know and what they felt they had a right to expect, illumines the bloodier episodes in Supreme Court history, and marks one of the bases for the dubious assertions that the philosophy of the American judiciary has changed significantly in the twentieth century and the beginning of the twenty-first.

The twentieth century exhibits, along with the enormous increase in industrial production, the expansion of political power in organized groups devoted exclusively to the satisfaction of their members' special cravings. At the same time, the number of those genuflecting to the life of reason has correspondingly proliferated in the extensive network of American universities, and the law, not without considerable difficulties, has preserved much of its original mandate to govern. It is questionable whether, without the weight of the intellectual community behind it, the American judiciary could have so stubbornly refused to relinquish its traditional role of protecting the individual's bill of rights. Striking examples of this support occurred during the onslaughts on the Supreme Court (portrayed as the public enemy) by Thomas Jefferson and Franklin Roosevelt. Roosevelt's court-packing scheme failed, as did Jefferson's court emasculating projects, not essentially because of any popular resistance, but because of the massed opposition of the intellectual community in general, and the legal fraternity of lawyer formalists in particular.

A significant consequence of the concentration in American law schools on the case method was the pressure toward the French oriented, logic-concentrated codification, precisely defined by Roscoe Pound: "Men thought it possible to discover a body of fixed and immutable principles, from which a complete system, perfect in every detail, might be deduced by purely logical operations, and held it the duty of the jurist to find them and of the legislator to promulgate the deductions in the form of a code."

Of course, the serious push of the codifiers began almost from the moment that the common law was introduced in a more theatrical and flamboyant fashion in the post-Civil War years when selective codes became legally fashionable. In earlier days, demands for codification generated much smoke but little fire, and its primary justification was another form of the hostility to the anti-democratic nature of their common law. The pressure was for simple statements that anyone could understand to order the law, at least in areas like civil and criminal procedure, probate, negotiable instruments, and taxation, that seemed to lend themselves readily to such order. These specialized codes, however, far from simplifying the law and making it accessible, as envisaged by the 'democratic' codifiers, merely emphasized, in the complex maze of qualifications and distinctions that characterize legal definition, the need for lawyers intensively trained in the location of given premises applicable to given situations.

Specialized codes created specialized lawyers, and legal simplicity was further away than ever. It is evident that with intellect (whether or not we worry 'intellectualism' into a separate category) particularly on its way to dominance through law, the American society assigned to itself a special kind of virtue, characterized by Aristotle as 'practical wisdom' The intellectual division for Aristotle is between contemplation of ideas for their own sake (truth) and contemplation of ideas for man's sake (virtue). Too often, the modern intellectual's concept of intellectuality, self-congratulatory and, to a large degree, self-deceiving, concentrates on Aristotle's divine category of pure reason to the exclusion of his merely human 'practical wisdom.'

The American intellectual, particularly as we have come to know him from his publications, is hardly an Aristotelian divinity. He lends himself much more readily to Aristotle's lesser, merely human, intellectual category of practical wisdom, which is hardly an insult if it is understood, as it should be, to involve thought directed toward producing the 'best' rather than the 'truest' in and for man. Yet his reluctance to abandon his claim of a special and idealized reference to ideas has created very special problems in the life of the American mind. It has been a major contributor to that cluster of hostile attitudes, loosely lumped together under the label of anti-intellectualism.

The scientific spirit—logical method removed from moral purpose—nurturing an ill-concealed contempt for the imprecision and confusion of human nature and humanistic inquiry, has done much to shape the modern world. Its influence, of course, has been derived largely from its phenomenal success with technology, an almost casual by-product that has occasioned that most startling and menacing of freedoms—man's escape from dependence on his physical skills. Fortunately the scientist has nurtured a contempt for politics, for its pandering to wobbly impulses. The scientific intelligence, combining with its cabalistic mathematical language an insistence upon value-free conclusions, both terrifies and humiliates the rest of society. While it is conceivable, as exemplified in science fiction, for a physical scientist to 'take over the world', the best defense lies in the scientists themselves—the unreasoned part of the world bores them.

In recent times, crystallizing with reason's most devastating creation, nuclear devices, and concurrent demonstrations that the power of logic is the power to destroy, not only human, animal and plant life, but such crucial areas as ecology, conservation of natural resources, and printed books read in a hammock on spring days. American radicalism has once again become nakedly revealed, as in post-Revolutionary days, to be a revolt, not against social or economic inequality coloring European, Middle Eastern, Asian, African, and South American uprisings, but directly against reason itself and its prime ministers, the law and its Federal government. In these terms, the seemingly inexplicable radicalization exhibited during the 1960's by middle-class college students—their turning to gratuitous bombing and transcendental meditation, their hostility equally toward police sergeants and college professors, their reverence for Zen masters, their typically American oscillation between absolute hatred and absolute love—becomes clear. Just as the end of reason is its own tail, so the lack of reason becomes the rationale for its exercise. That it cannot survive and prosper as a political movement is implicit in premises committed to its guiding principle that it is against law and government.

19

The Ivy Leaguers: Bill Clinton and Barack Obama

ALL OF WHICH brings us to a consideration of very much alive William Jefferson Clinton and Barack Hussein Obama, not to mention, in passing, non-lawyers George H. W. Bush and George W. Bush. Apart from their first names, George H.W. Bush and George W. Bush had little in common other than to burden their successors in office with a staggering public debt, budget deficiencies, and Saddam Hussein. On the other hand, their successors, Bill Clinton and Barack Obama, lacking a common pedigree, might well have been brothers. Arresting similarities appear beyond their Ivy League law school diplomas: their certified intellectuality, with Clinton a Rhodes Scholar, Obama President of the *Harvard Law Review*, and both Constitutional law professors—their wives also graduating Ivy League law schools and practicing law. That they find themselves among the more vilified American presidents is only partly attributable, in Obama's case, to his African Americanism and Clinton to his sexual escapades. Ultimately we are dealing with camouflaging rationalizations of a deeper, persistent historical American hostility toward being governed by law and lawyers. Each was presented with the devastating possibility of a government shutdown occasioned not by the inability of the United States of America to pay its bills, but by irreconcilable ideological inflexibility, on the one hand by Republican party leaders, supported by Republican mid-term victories occasioning the relentless pressure of the far-right Tea Party's newly elected, sixty-four Republican Congressmen, and, on the other hand, the determined legal mindedness of Clinton and Obama, with its 'playing by the rules,' entailing bi-partisanship, negotiation, and compromise.

The coupling of Bill Clinton and Barack Obama has evoked unprecedented hatred and suspicion of Ivy League lawyers presuming to act as American presidents. Clinton and Obama epitomize the lawyer- formalist class of presidents. They highlight the strain throughout American history of the legal-minded element de Tocqueville tabbed as indispensable. Clinton and Barack Obama might easily be linked with two of our generally regarded greatest presidents, Franklin Delano Roosevelt, a lawyer-moralist, and Abraham Lincoln, a lawyer-rule-skeptic, as among the most vilified of American presidents. Actually they couldn't be farther apart. The accusation against Franklin Roosevelt and Abraham Lincoln is that they were dictatorial in their violations of the Constitution, while the diatribes against Clinton and Obama castigate a lack of leadership, weakness on defense, indecision, procrastination, tax-and-spend liberalism, too much Federal government, poor stewardship of the armed forces, too smart for their own good—too lawyer-like. They were, in other words, charged with being lawyer-formalists.

20

The Comeback Kid: Bill Clinton

THE EXCESSIVE FROTHING at the mouth of some Americans during Clinton's presidency is largely symptomatic of the sense of betrayal of the original 'sin' of the eighteenth-century, rank and file American, firmly lodged in the American psyche ever since—the 'sin' of embracing the elusive will of the wisp of 'rags to riches.' Clinton's audacity is his more modest dream of one having a good job, of owning one's home free from the threat of foreclosure, of children doing better than their parents. Above all, Clinton's dream fosters a strong, bitter sense of alienation and hostility toward the law and its prime enforcers, the lawyers. Clinton's accession to the presidency, armed with his mantra: "The main idea is still the old idea of the American dream, that if you work hard and play by the rules, you ought to have a decent life and a chance for your children to have a better one."—his personal 'rags to the middle class' appropriation of 'the American Dream' through education and embrace of the law—represents an unforgivable 'slap in the face' to the generally unrealized passion of many Americans, personally, to enhance the hallowed memory of the fabled, 'fast on the draw,' rugged individualists who scorned the law and lawyers as they 'tamed the west' and made the 'new world' safe for the National Rifle Association. The most remarkable element in this most flamboyant American president since Teddy Roosevelt is Bill Clinton's resilience, highlighted by his ability to 'come back,' not only from the relentless onslaughts of his adversaries, but even more, from his self-inflicted wounds.

Loren Lorensky offers an interesting analysis of the source of Clinton's refusal to buckle under a series of body blows culminating in his impeachment: "The philosopher Baruch Spinoza held that common to all entities, from chunks of matter to chief executives, was conatus, an inherent drive to maintain their integrity. Absent this urge, things would disintegrate. But although everything possesses this drive, Clinton is unique as an instance of pure conation. He will do whatever is required to hold himself together. No principles or ideals or moral scruples are allowed to get in the way of this self-protective impulse."

While conceding that Clinton 'will do whatever is required to hold himself together' and that 'no principles or ideals or moral scruples are allowed to get in the way,' it remains clear that what is required for Clinton is steadfastly to 'live by the rules,' as so many lawyer-formalists do. George Stephanopoulos, a former devoted admirer of Clinton, felt betrayed by his not 'playing by the rules' in his personal sex life, but rules are a concern of ethics rather than morality—a lawyer's ever-present problem when the two collide.

Richard A. Matasar, in an article entitled, "The Pain of Moral Lawyering" puts it this way: "For many lawyers, professionalism becomes an end in itself allowing them to avoid the need to reconcile personal morals and professional ethics. Professionalism is a commitment to producing the highest quality of legal work consistent with a client's needs. By practicing law as a master of the craft a lawyer can take pride in the resulting product. By focusing on the product and divorcing it from the ends ultimately sought, the lawyer is freed from doubt. The profession itself is the answer to the dilemma. The individual is a lawyer. The law has its own rules. Our society has adopted those rules and requested legal practitioners to follow them for their clients."

In the midst of his woes, Clinton's presidential life—his client— had to be served and here he acquitted himself admirably.

I

Of Birth and Death—Bill and Daddy

This is a story—a story with overtones of sadness, disappointments, and, miraculously, happy endings. This is the story of William Jefferson Blythe III, also known as Bill Clinton, and his tangled relationship with his stepfather, Roger Clinton.

THE LEGAL MIND AND THE PRESIDENCY

It begins with the death of a father in a car accident occurring three months before his son's birth on August 19, 1946, leaving behind a twenty-three-year-old widow, Virginia Cassidy Blythe, with a baby boy, little money, and no visible means of support. Even before he exists, the baby has misery and misadventure written all over him. Still, after staying a year with her god-sent parents in Hope, Arkansas, the widow who, like her son, is to demonstrate, time and again, the courage to beat back against Shakespearean 'slings and arrows of outrageous fortune,' decides to become a nurse anesthetist—even though it means going for her training to a hospital in Atlanta, Georgia—even though it means leaving her baby behind with her parents. This she manages to do, at least confident her parents will love the 'orphaned' child, and returns proudly to them in a year, a full-fledged nurse anesthetist. They will live together 'happily ever after' for two more years until June, 1950, when Virginia Blythe becomes Mrs. Virginia Blythe Clinton; Virginia and four-year-old Bill leave the cocoon of Bill's grandparents for a home with Roger Clinton.

For a time, but clearly not 'for ever after,' the new family does well; Roger, hard-drinking but a good, generous, loving man when sober—when drunk, which becomes alarmingly frequent, he is seriously bad. Nevertheless baby Bill, having grown into a chunky, clumsy, accident-prone boy, having inherited the father he never had and, riding the turbulent waves, lovingly calls him 'Daddy', and means it with all his heart, through two succeeding stepfathers for the rest of his life; he begins to display a sunny, half-filled glass temperament that will characterize him the rest of his life.

Bill, at the tender age of four, ushers in the mishaps that plague his boyhood; he breaks a leg by being the only kindergarten child at Miss Marie Purkins' School for Little Folks, unable to jump a rope tied between a tree and a swing set because, as he describes it, "I was a little chunky anyway, and slow, so slow that I was once the only kid at an Easter egg hunt who didn't get a single egg…because I couldn't get to them fast enough. On the day I tried to jump rope I was wearing cowboy boots to school. Like a fool, I didn't take the boots off before the jump. My heel caught on the rope. I turned, fell and heard my leg snap. I lay in agony on the ground for several minutes while Daddy raced over from (work) to get me."

Bill kept a place in his heart for Daddy despite the pile-up of abuses he committed. He recites that at five, "his drunken self-destructiveness came to a head in a fight with my mother I can't ever forget... They were screaming at each other...Daddy pulled a gun from behind his back and fired in Mother's direction. The bullet went into the wall between where she and I were standing... Mother grabbed me and ran across the street to the neighbors. The police were called... I'm sure Daddy didn't mean to hurt her and he would have died if the bullet had accidently hit either of us."

When Bill was six, Daddy moved the family to a farm outside Hot Springs, Arkansas, where he promptly got in trouble. He took Daddy's niece, Karla, out to where sheep were grazing, including a mean ram Bill should have known better than to fool with. The ram saw them and charged. They ran for the fence and Karla made it. Clumsy, slow-footed Bill of course didn't. He stumbled over a big rock and fell. The rest of the anecdote I leave to Bill to describe with his self-deprecating, sheepish humor: "I retreated to a small tree a few feet away in the hope I could keep away from him by running around the tree until help came. Another big mistake. Soon he caught me and knocked my legs out from under me. Before I could get up he butted me in the head. Then I was stunned and hurt and couldn't get up. So he backed up, got a good head start, and rammed me again as hard as he could. He did the same thing over and over and over again, alternating his targets between my head and my gut. Soon I was pouring blood and hurting like the devil... I recovered, left with only a scar on my forehead, which gradually grew into my scalp."

After a year or so on the farm, Daddy once again decided to move the family, this time to a large house in Hot Springs proper where they lived until Bill was fifteen. There he was besieged by a swarm of bumblebees who lived in a three-story bird house for martins, put up by Daddy in the back yard, only, unbeknownst to Bill, taken over by the bumblebees. He happened to be mowing the lawn when, as he recounts, "...they swarmed me, flying all over my body, my arms, my face. Amazingly, not one of them stung me. I ran off to catch my breath and consider my options. Mistakenly, I assumed they had decided I meant them no harm, so after a few minutes I went back to my mowing. I hadn't gone ten yards before they swarmed me again, this time stinging me all over my body. One got caught between my belly and my belt, stinging me over and over, something bumblebees can do that honeybees can't. I was delirious and had to be rushed to the doctor, but I recovered soon enough..."

In 1960, with Bill a boy of 14, the well-publicized incident of his rising to defend his mother against Daddy occurred: "I had secrets of my own, rooted in Daddy's alcoholism and abuse ... One night Daddy ...started screaming at Mother, then began to hit her... Finally...I grabbed a golf club...and threw open their (bedroom) door. Mother was on the floor and Daddy was standing over her, beating on her. I told him to stop and said that if he didn't I was going to beat the hell out of him ... He just caved, sitting down in a chair ... and hanging his head. It made me sick ... I suppose I was proud of myself for standing up for Mother, but afterward I was sad about it, too. I just couldn't accept the fact that a basically good person would try to make his own pain go away by hurting someone else..."

At eighteen Bill graduated high school and was starting at Georgetown University, but he hadn't finished his skirmishes with *Fortuna,* He had two accidents that might have happened to anyone, even somebody speedy and agile: one an auto accident that shattered the steering wheel instead of his jaw, and the other when he nearly drowned vacationing at Cape Cod, but was saved by a sandbar and the help of a friend.

Throughout his misadventures Bill's reaction at the age of four to Daddy's swift dropping of everything to rescue him and his broken leg presaged a lifetime of his patient forgiveness of Daddy's unforgivable abuse of Bill's mother: "I was grateful to Daddy for coming to rescue me... He also came home from work a time or two to try to talk Mother out of spanking me when I did something wrong. At the beginning of their marriage he really tried to be there for me. I remember once he even took me on the train to St. Louis to see the Cardinals... Sadly, it was the only trip the two of us ever took together. Like the only time we went fishing together. The only time we ever went out into the woods to cut our own Christmas tree together. There were so many things that meant a lot to me, but were never to occur again. Roger Clinton really loved me and he loved Mother, but he couldn't ever quite break free of the shadows of self-doubt, the phony security of binge drinking."

The view of Daddy as a Jekyll and Hyde character evoked Bill's lasting pity and forgiveness, while his half-brother, Roger, would unqualifiedly hate Daddy for the rest of his life. Just a year later, Daddy again erupted, and at long last Virginia rebelled—with Bill and young Roger, she left Daddy and proceeded to file for divorce. Daddy was distraught and begged and pleaded for their return. In familiar alcoholic fashion, he swore that he would never hit or scream at her again. Also, a familiar pattern for abused wives, his entreaties were getting to her; still, she obtained the divorce, and only then entertained such persuasive second thoughts that, disregarding the odds against his redemption, she consented to a remarriage.

Bill was not about to modify his 'Daddy' tune, then or throughout his life—except to extend it to other people, other circumstances: "Roger Clinton was fundamentally a good person. He loved Mother and me, and little Roger. He had helped Mother to see me when she was finishing school in New Orleans. He was generous to family and friends. He was smart and funny. But he had that combustible mix of fears, insecurities, and psychological vulnerabilities ..."

For four years, it did seem that Daddy had finally come to his senses. Then in 1965, when Bill was a nineteen-year-old, attending Georgetown University, during a summer vacation there occurred what Bill describes as "one last terrible incident with Daddy. One day he came home early from work, drunk and mad. I was over at the Yeldells', but luckily, Roger was home. Daddy went after Mother with a pair of scissors and pushed her into the laundry room... Roger ran out ...and over to the Yeldells' screaming, 'Bubba, help! Daddy's killing Dado!'... I ran back to the house, pulled Daddy off Mother, and grabbed the scissors from him. I took Mother and Roger to the living room, then went back and reamed Daddy out. When I looked into his eyes I saw more fear than rage. Not long before, he had been diagnosed with cancer of the mouth and throat... This incident took place early in the two-year period leading to his death... (It) would be his last bad outburst."

In the spring of 1967, some six months before Daddy died, while Bill was still at Georgetown, the relationship between Bill and Daddy reached its climax in displaying Bill's ability to be able to forgive and forget that for fifteen years, from the ages of four to nineteen, he had witnessed Daddy's beating and terrifying a mother he dearly loved, and who dearly deserved his love. It was occasioned by Daddy's hospitalization at the Duke Medical Center in Durham, North Carolina, for several weeks of cancer treatment. As Bill recounts it, "Every weekend I would drive the 266 miles from Georgetown to see him, leaving Friday afternoon, returning late Sunday night... It was one of the most exhausting but important times of my young life … On those weekends, Daddy talked to me in a way he never had before… On those long, languid weekends, we came to terms with each other, and he accepted the fact that I loved and forgave him. If he could only have faced life with the same courage and sense of honor with which he faced death he would have been quite a guy."

What finally emerges from the history of Bill Clinton's accident-ridden childhood —beginning, before Bill's birth, with the auto-accidental death of his father and ending with the miserable excuse of a drunken wife-abusing stepfather — is the resilient life-long shaping of his character highlighted by abandonment of any ideas of hatred or revenge in favor of empathic forgiveness and embrace of people in general, friend or foe.

II

The Economy, Stupid

George H.W. Bush, in the middle of his term as president, had conducted himself admirably in his handling of the Persian Gulf War—initiating it only after getting the collaboration of the UN Security Council, the Arab League, military forces from 34 countries, and some 16 billion dollars from Japan and Germany—concluding it by not pushing to finish off Saddam Hussein after the job he came to do—removal of Iraq's army from Kuwait— was completed. His reward was a stunning Gallup poll approval rating of 89% on February 28, 1991. He appeared to be unbeatable in going after a second term, particularly since the most favored Democrats—Mario Cuomo and Al Gore—decided not to run, leaving 'lesser' candidates to fight it out—Tom Harkin, Bob Kerry, Paul Tsongas, Doug Wilder, Jerry Brown— and Bill Clinton.

Fortuna, the tough-minded Goddess of Chance, sometimes chooses to play a defining role in the success of a human being courageous enough, ambitious enough, foolish enough, to gain the American presidency. Bill Clinton was one of those favored few and George H.W. suffered the consequence.

After luxuriating in his remarkable post-Gulf War Gallup poll approval ratings, George H.W. was rudely treated to a downward turning of the economy. By the end of 1991, his third year in office, his approval rating had dropped to 50%, and less than a month before the election, on October 12, 1992, the rating was a dismal 34%. Clinton won the election with 43% of the votes and George H.W. lost with 37.4%.

Political campaigns bind themselves to words or phrases that sometimes become long-lasting—like 'Obamacare', 'pro-life', 'pro-choice', 'Give me liberty or give me death,' 'Tippecanoe and Tyler too,' —and, of course, 'Read my lips—no new taxes,' conceived by Peggy Noonan for George H.W. Bush, and 'The economy, stupid,' conceived by James Carville for Bill Clinton—shibboleths that proceeded to dominate and define the 1992 presidential campaign war of words.

Bill Clinton's presidency, the crowning event of his life, began with everything in his favor. The Democrats were in control of the House and Senate, and the White House was his castle. It was time for him to dream great American dreams and metamorphose them into fungible realities. Unfortunately for him, and George H.W. as well, *Fortuna*, in her capricious, heartless way, was busy giving and taking during the critical year 1992. A report surfaced immediately after the election indicating a slight recovery in the George H.W. economy that had lost him the election. This afforded small comfort to either Bush or Clinton. For George H.W. it was sour grapes. For Bill it tarnished, however slightly, his remarkable success with the economy. From *Fortuna*'s spoilsport point of view she'd done a good job monitoring the 'can do' of chance.

After two relatively predictable years, *Fortuna* relished the highly dramatic turns of chance that began with the 1994 election leading to GOP Speaker Gingrich's control of the House of Representatives and ironically culminated in Bill Clinton's election to a second term as president. She (*Fortuna*) made use of Clinton's greatest political weapon—his strength of character which refused to display anything other than equanimity and conciliatory efforts—that, as Bill Clinton details in his 2000 State of the Union Address, produced a plethora of pluses: "...over 20 million new jobs, the fastest economic growth in more than 30 years, the lowest unemployment rates in 30 years, the lowest poverty rates in 20 years, the lowest African-American and Hispanic unemployment rates on record, the first back to back budget surpluses in 42 years, the longest peacetime economic expansion, the highest rate of home ownership in American history, the lowest unemployment rate in 30 years, the lowest poverty rate in twenty

164

THE LEGAL MIND AND THE PRESIDENCY

years, a record twenty-two million new jobs, balancing of the federal budget, and the first budget surpluses in a generation."

It is difficult tidily to pigeonhole Newt Gingrich as Speaker of the House, but it is safe to say that he was never wallpaper—that he was to be reckoned with. *Economist* does a masterful job of summing up his character: "There is a lot to like about Newt Gingrich... He is a ferociously intelligent, one-man ideas factory, gushing forth an endless stream of new policies and arguments. As Speaker of the House of Representatives after he led his party to victory in the 1994 mid-term elections, his clever "Contract With America" made him a tea-partier before there was ever a tea party. He fought against excessive spending, to the point of being prepared to see the federal government shut down. But he also has serious problems... He is erratic...he has been dead against curbing carbon emissions, and dead against the healthcare 'mandate' he once supported. He was for the war in Libya and against it, all in the space of a week or so. His ideas for tackling almost any weakness in government (waste, border security, terrorist threats, to name but three) tend to involve demolishing whole departments and starting all over again... His arrogance, meanwhile, verges on monomania. He once wrote of himself as the 'definer of the forces of civilization'... Most worrying is a populist streak that is at best nasty, and at worst downright dangerous... After four years as Speaker, he was forced out by his own colleagues, who found him unbearably capricious and disorganised."

Clinton offers a clear understanding of what made Gingrich tick when he sizes up his relentless and self-congratulatory pleasure in refusing to settle the budget controversy on anything other than his 'Contract with America' version: "Gingrich had been threatening since April to shut the government down and put America in default if I didn't accept his budget. I couldn't tell whether he really wanted to do it or whether he simply believed all the press coverage during my first two years that, in the face of ample evidence to the contrary, had portrayed me as too weak, too willing to abandon commitments, too eager to compromise."

What it all comes down to, for Bill Clinton, being born without a living father, being brought up by a drunken, wife-beating stepfather, *Fortuna*, the unpredictable phantom Goddess of chance, smiled upon him and endowed him with a lifetime strength of character, exemplified by his shaking hands with each misfortune and making it his own, forgiving it although he couldn't forget, bearing no ill-will toward even the most intransigent, or giving in to a desire to get even. He could forgive, unlike his step-brother Roger, the man Bill called Daddy, whose name he eventually legally adopted. His strength of character did not desert him under almost unimaginably dismal circumstances during his presidency—Gingrich and the governmental shut down, Hillary and Monica Lewinsky, Starr and the impreachment proceedings.

III

Foreign Affairs

The peaceful settlement of the Bosnian/Serbian war and Clinton's significant role in accomplishing it is marked, in view of the political risks involved and the barrage of criticisms along the way for his alleged early vacillation, by the characteristic steadfastness, patience, and finally boldness exhibited by Clinton. The war, beginning in earnest on April 6, 1992 by the Serbs with the Siege of Bosnian Sarajevo, was to be epitomized by bitter fighting, indiscriminate shelling of towns, ethnic cleansing, systematic mass rape, and genocide.

On January 20, 1993, Bill Clinton was inaugurated as the United States president. Several months later, on May 6, 1993, following its doctrines of 'peacekeeping' and 'humanitarian intervention', the United Nations, by resolution, designated the territories of Bosnia and Herzegovina as 'safe areas.' under its protection. Sadly the resolution was toothless, since the member states that voted in favor of it, including the United States, were initially unwilling to give it bite until April, 1994, over a year later. In the meantime, in October, 1993, one of Clinton's first presidential efforts to practice 'humanitarian intervention' resulted in a disaster in Somalia.

Kenneth T. Walsh and Gloria Borger's report highlights both the hazards implicit in 'humanitarian intervention' and the idealistic instincts irresistibly prodding Clinton on: "When President got the first intelligence reports of new American casualties in Somalia, he thought it was just another confrontation with the local thugs. But within hours, it became clear that the bungled raid against warlord

Mohammed Farah Aidid was his worst foreign policy crisis yet. It had left at least 15 U.S. soldiers dead, scores wounded, several missing, three Army helicopters down, and American policy in Somalia in shambles. Aides say Clinton has great difficulty reconciling his altruistic instincts with the realities of human hatred and brutality that are so evident in places like Somalia and Bosnia."

The Somalian debacle weighed heavily on Clinton and tempered his desire to do something about the dreadful havoc, including genocide, the Serbs were busily inflicting on the Bosnians; in April, 1994, after some six months elapsed, he could hold back no longer and pressured his NATO colleagues into approving an airstrike, employing American planes, against the Serbian troops attacking Gorazde, a Bosnian town in one of the UN's 'safe areas.' With Somalia still on his mind, the bombing was minimal, but Clinton hoped it would be enough to subdue the Serbs. It wasn't, and invited grist for Clinton's critics grinding out charges of ineptitude and lack of leadership. The major accusation shared by his military advisers was that airstrikes without ground support was futile. Nevertheless, Clinton, despite increasing pressure, resisted any suggestion to allow the use of American troops on the ground, with its inevitable fatalities.

Even with the traditional American self-confidence tarnished by the Vietnamese misadventure, Clinton remained captivated by the United Nations notion of peace-keeping, however ineffectual the organization might be in the face of a ruthless Serbian leaders, obsessed with obliterating non-Serbians from any area that used to be part of Yugoslavia. "In August, 1995, the situation took a dramatic turn," Clinton noted. "The Croatians launched an offensive to retake the Krajina, a part of Croatia that the local Serbs had proclaimed their territory... Because we knew Bosnia's survival was at stake, we had not tightly enforced the arms embargo. As a result, both the Croatians and The Bosnians were able to get some arms, which helped them survive... Croatian forces took Krajine with little resistance. It was the first defeat for the Serbs in four years and it changed both the balance of power on the ground and the psychology of all the parties."

This, combined with the Srebrenica massacre in July, 1995, involving the Serbian killing of more than 8,000 Bosnians, mainly men and boys, and the pressure imposed by Clinton, triggered massive NATO airstrikes. His patience and stubbornness had finally prevailed. A ceasefire was instituted and the Dayton Peace Agreement shortly followed in December, 1995.

The war in Bosnia was finally terminated, but the genocidal treatment of non-Serbs in Kosovo was not to be resolved until 1999. Clinton remarks, "...we were moving toward another Balkan war in Kosovo. The Serbs had launched an offensive against rebellious Kosovar Albanians a year earlier, killing many innocent people; some women and children were burned in their own homes... The killings were all too reminiscent of the early days of Bosnia, which, like Kosovo, bridged the divide between European Muslims and Serb Orthodox Christians, a dividing along which there had been conflict from time to time for six hundred years."

Finally, on March 24, 1999, after exhaustive diplomatic efforts had failed to get anywhere with the Serbs, other than several, tentative, short-lived occasions, Clinton brought matters to a head: "After Holbrooke left Belgrade, NATO General Javier Solana, with my full support, directed General Wes Clark to begin air strikes... The bombing campaign had three objectives: to show Milosevic we were serious about stopping another round of ethnic cleansing, to deter an ever bloodier offensive against innocent civilians in Kosovo, and if Milosevic didn't throw in the towel soon, to seriously damage the Serbs' military capacity... In June, the punishing bombing raids on the Serbs finally broke Milosevic's will to resist... on the ninth (of June, 1999, NATO and Serbian military officials agreed to them... I announced to the American people that after seventy-nine days, the bombing campaign was over, the Serb forces were withdrawing, and the one million men and children driven from their land would be able to go home."

Clinton's successes in Bosnia and Kosovo were very comforting to him, not only for their own sake, but because it rounded out and completed his sustaining sense of the best in him, evident, as well, in the 1994 peace dealings in Ireland. Edward Gaffney, Jr. reports it nicely: "One should not exaggerate the American contribution to the resolution of the Irish question. The heavy lifting is being done by the Irish and the English. But it remains true that at each turning of a very complicated path over the past year, President Bill Clinton has nudged the process of reconciliation along with subtle and appropriate external pressure. In February 1994, over the objections of Prime Minister John Major and Secretary of State Warren Christopher, the president granted a visa to Gerry Adams, president of Sinn Fein, when

168

Adams was still viewed as a terrorist pariah by the British government. As the Irish Taoiseach, John Bruton, remarked at the Shamrock Ceremony in the White House this past March 17, 'The willingness to take risks, to do things that many of us might have thought foolhardy at the time—like granting a visa to Gerry Adams—has been proven to be right. You made the right decision."

21

The Spirit of 1787: Barack Obama

I

The Year is 1787

A joke surfaces early in the records of the Constitutional Convention of 1787, offered by that irrepressible gentleman too old to know better, and recorded by scrivener Madison, unable for once to resist a comic irrelevancy. On the question of whether Congress or the president should appoint 'national' judges, Benjamin Franklin suggested instead fellow lawyers "who always selected the ablest of the profession in order to get rid of him, and share his practice among themselves."

A modest joke, but there it is—a gentle ribbing of the lawyers surrounding Franklin on all sides. Perhaps, he felt, a little humor inserted in the game before the rules hardened might relax the players a little, alert them to the merely human possibilities of their high endeavors. But the lawyers, thirty-three of the fifty-five men who attended the convention at one time or another, were not to be jollied out of setting the tone even by clever Gouverneur Morris. Nor were the legal scholars, James Madison and George Mason. One is in awe at their unrelenting gravity, and so it has generally gone in American politics. In a grim typical cartoon of his day, the Pagliacci of presidents, Abraham Lincoln, is portrayed as standing surrounded by the Union dead at Antietam and buttonholing a bystander with "sing us 'Picayune Butler' or something else that's funny."

Of course, humor is a self-deprecation that only long established societies can afford, because only they have sufficient history for the required confidence. A mere six years before, these fifty-five men, particularly the well-educated among them, had forfeited their historical heritage by 'winning' the war against the British. It must have been a chilling experience. The war had not, after all, been for keeps and they were Englishmen too, merely asserting their right to be respected. Yet off they went, their English siblings, back across the sea, taking with them Milton and Shakespeare, Cromwell and Edmund Burke, Bacon, Hogarth and Reynolds, Christopher Wren, even Robin Hood, maliciously leaving behind that fictionalized, murky version of Brittania—Blackstone's Commentaries. They were otherwise endowed, fifty-five beached British subjects, with a vast expanse of raw, eccentric land seeded with bittersweet English namesakes: New York, New Bedford, New Hampshire, New Britain, New Jersey, Charleston, Jamestown, Richmond—and a spotty classical education (modeled, most of them, after the English public schools) of Aristotle, Plato, Polybius, Cicero, and Theognis.

The Constitutional Convention of 1787 imposed upon the United States, with no little success, a 'rule of reason' secured by establishing the supremacy of a capitalized law: *Non sub Deo et homine sed sub Lege*. It is important to realize that for reason, like God, to exist for man, it must be premised upon belief in unprovable premises, with the consequence that the legal mind, conventionally regarded as realistic and tough, has at its soft and fluid center the world of make-believe.

Meanwhile, to the farmers, wheelwrights, blacksmiths, stonemasons, and the rest of some three and a half million citizens, equality and liberty were not rhetorical asides, but spiritual absolutes, endowments from their Creator, wrested from 'monarchical, aristocratical, rotten-boroughed' British law. Thomas Jefferson, the moralist dressed in legal-minded clothing, was to preach to them what became their gospel; their natural right was to be as free as can be of the law of the land. The government that governed least governed best.

But Jefferson was absent during the Convention in 1787. He was in Paris scoffing at the stupidity of kings. Not that his presence would have made much difference. Liberty or death, or the pursuit of happiness, were not choices in Philadelphia that long, hot summer.

The law was reason's exercise and absolute equality, absolute liberty, absolute anything but reason itself, violated reason absolutely. Reason's great distinction as a faith was in the concentration on process rather than ends. No end is wrong if it resulted from reason. Moral absolutes, on the other hand, were committed to the attainment of the 'right end' whatever the means. With the political establishment of the rule of reason at the convention, the subsequent clashes between it and other faiths became inevitable.

An unusual situation surfaced in regard to the presidency. Most of the delegates seemed to suffer from the same intellectual nervous breakdown. They were confronted, not so much with each other, as with a moral imperative, 'Thou shalt not have an American king,' that shrugged off argument, however reasoned. Classical definition upon which they relied so heavily served only to confuse them. Starting with the premise that the executive element, the presidency, was to check the 'will of the people' embodied in the legislative branch, they were faced with the fearful prospect, unqualifiedly repugnant to an America which had mounted its revolution by symbolizing a limited English monarch as an absolute tyrant, of fashioning a king of their own. Balancing of 'monarchical,' 'aristocratic,' and 'democratic' forces, the classical methodology, the logical springboard for consequent reasoning, was a precarious base since monarchy, however diluted, could not be presumed to exist as an American possibility. Each time logic tentatively led the delegates to outfitting the president with 'monarchical' trappings, they recoiled and flailed about, lifeguards, diving in to rescue drowning concepts that unaccountably had forgotten how to swim.

Yet if the president was to play a role consonant with the rule of reason, he simply had to be given certain 'royal' prerogatives. Whatever the psychological hang-ups, there was no getting around this recognition. If the law was to be paramount, logically the other two governmental arms must balance each other. America lacked monarchical and aristocratic traditions by which to control the dreaded mob rule (legislative supremacy?). It followed that the Constitution, a self-generating force, must provide these traditions, especially the monarchical (after the loss of aristocratic prospects in the Senate), with the curious, transvaluating result, that, instead of traditions forming the law, the law would form the traditions.

The aristocratic element, posited in the classical mode by Madison to reside in the Senate, found its American home, instead, in the chambers of the judiciary. A kingship, however, had to function through executive channels if it was to function at all. There was no other avenue open to it, and from this recognition evolved the extraordinary rhetorical agonies of the delegates over the presidency. How to provide for a king who was, nevertheless, nothing at all like a king?

This was the logic-defying paradox the delegates were compelled somehow to resolve. Their solution, ultimately, was simple. Reason would concentrate on its necessity of a limited monarchy while rhetoric, that dramatic, distracting smoke-screen, would deny the king's existence.

Unquestionably the monarchy would be limited if only because this was its classical and eighteenth-century British form, but a monarchy it would be. For the period of his reign, no one could without enormous difficulty remove him. He would be commander-in-chief of the military forces. He could, on the merest whim, veto Congressional legislation. He would be in charge of foreign affairs, the 'federative' element in Locke's governmental triad. He would be the ceremonial and diplomatic head of state. Through him the purple-mountained majesty of America would be revealed to the rest of the world.

The convention's king-makers, not to be shamed out of their limited monarchy, ended up by moralizing their guilt. Not only did the rule of reason demand a division of power between the legislature and the executive to insure the supreme authority to be the law that, defining that division, could maintain its control, but a royal president satisfied an emotional craving as well—a craving for a man who, not permitted to shoot from the hip, could at least shout from the housetops in the name of goodness and let the law, in its patient, deliberative, after-the-fact wisdom, decide whether he ultimately made sense. The delegates, wedded to reason, lusted for a morality arising out of kingship that could rationalize their doing 'wrong' in creating a monarch at all. In the end, they were romanticizing intellectuals erecting an Aristotelian structure of the mind and dreaming Platonic virtue into it. The dream has never left us. If a president such as Jackson infects us with a sense of the genuineness of his moral passion, the devil takes his inadequacies. We will ride even unto Hell under his banner.

Our most revered presidents, whatever their intellectual qualifications, or lack of them, have emerged as symbols, certainly not of reason and its handmaiden, legal-mindedness, but of the moral impulse, ostensibly relentless in pursuit of the 'right,' defined, of course, as 'the American way'—the Washingtons, Lincolns, and Franklin Roosevelts who have appeared at American ' high noons.' Still, the superstructure of reason has never left us. While we will shout defiance at its inattention to conventional moral passions, we will tremble with fear that it will take us seriously and abandon us to our clamorous desires.

Pressured and made timid by Jefferson's moral fervor, Madison offered weak excuses and summoned up a singular lack of enthusiasm for a Bill of Rights after the fact of a Constitution; he, a man not only of reason but common law origins, suspected that rights were better enforced when not codified; that, yoked to codified rights (after all a faith at best), reason might chew itself up in efforts to accommodate resulting irrationalities. To prohibit the legislation of faith was to suggest the unthinkable, that faith *could* be legislated. Nevertheless, he went ahead to compose the Bill of Rights and have it approved by Congress as the first ten amendments.

All in all, the Convention of 1787 was a phenomenon in the political story of mankind, not because it adapted classical theory to daily practices, but because it did the reverse. It compelled a society to adjust to Aristotle's demand that the 'wild beast' of 'human passions' be ruled by reason and to Plato's insistence that rulers of men could, and must, be educated to serve reason rather than themselves.

The constitutional delegates chose to be blind to man's self-hatred that leads him to curse the most reasonable part of himself, the part that bit into the apple and informed him that he was mortal. If awareness of the certainty of death is the distinction of man from other animals, the devil, delighting in tormenting man, may well have invented reason. Man theoretically then would be better served by the instincts of an absolute monarch or a politburo than ruled by reason. One result has been the devastating humbuggery of the American system of government. Denied by the law of the privilege of making instinctual and faith-guided decisions, of acting upon its sense of what is right instead of what is rational, it has been forced to hide behind the rhetoric of virtue to justify the intelligence of its performance. European mockery of American diplomacy that must moralize even the very fact of its existence springs from this deceit.

More ominous is the frustration of Americans at their inability to compel virtuous action from any of the visible parts of their government. Scurrying back and forth between the president, Congress, and the Supreme Court, they are met with the shell game played by reason. Wherever they look for the moral pea, it seems to be hidden elsewhere. In desperation, lifting all of the shells at once, they realize there is no pea. What, finally are we to make of the rule of reason, frozen and codified in a Constitution born of an Enlightenment period that has been shredded and recycled by history, taking its physical shape as the American system of government. It is much too easy to say that it is a mockery for abstracted intelligence to order a society composed of human beings and let it go at that. Certainly, morality, in its search for the one true, unimpeachable absolute , with its Hitlers, Lenins, bin Ladens, Inquisitions, its First French Republic, has the poorest of political track records. Whatever may be said of the rule of reason, and much can be made of its scorn of human frailty, the conclusion remains that, in the long run and it has had a long run, it has been a more benevolent governor of man than his shifting, intuitive sense of 'right' and 'wrong.'

Having made this concession, we should not be dazzled into ignoring its painfully apparent inadequacies, particularly its paralyzing slowness in accommodating moral imperatives. In the American system, whichever party is in power, that power is split between a Congressional party and a presidential party, each of which is determined to rule at the expense of the other. Only rarely, even during extreme crises, have the president and Congress, even if of the same party, fused as a unity in moral purpose.

A larger consideration remains beyond that of the tension between reason and virtue, as if that were not large enough, and that is the gulf between the Aristotelian conception of law as reason, adopted by Madison and his colleagues at the Convention of 1787, and the law as applied in practice. The Constitutional delegates posited a perfect equation between the rule of reason and the rule of law but, of course, this was an idealized impossibility. Men are, after all, neither gods nor programmed machines; they bite of the apple and learn to be unreasonable. They inevitably clutter any immaculate conception of the legal mind with the domestic detail of daily human emotions, instincts and desires, and it is in this complicated mix of human nature that the American legal mind and its Galetea, American political history, fashion their ultimate shapes. It is alluring, but ultimately too easy, to find the American 'fault' in a clean break between the head and the heart. For the legal mind has moved in more than one direction in attempting to come to terms with the unaccountable heart, and the heart, in turn, has its own reasons, one of which has often been a provocative embrace of the head.

II

The Year is 2012

Startling as it may initially seem, it doesn't take too much a stretch of the imagination to visualize a Barack Obama, in terms of personality, temperament and intelligence, as an ally and confidante at the Constitutional Convention and during Madison's presidency, or to fast forward Madison as Obama's Chief of Staff in the twenty-first century. As the American Heritage Company points out in its pictorial history of the United States Presidents: "But although Madison was probably the most effective advocate of a powerful federal government, it was his willingness to compromise that made him the 'Father of the Constitution.' Most of the great compromises that made ratification of the Constitution possible—the two legislative branches, the 'federal ration' (slaves were counted as three-fifths of a man although Madison was emphatically anti-slavery) that helped maintain a balance in representation of Northern and Southern states— were suggested by Madison, as were many of the checks and balances."

This section involving Obama is being written while his second term in office is *in medias res,* but it has become abundantly clear, even though it has hardly been recognized, that he personifies the formalist-lawyer president who resists controversy and especially war, who prefers, as long as it seems feasible, a settlement of disputes through compromise, bargaining, diplomacy, verbal skills, and reasoning powers. Only after considering all the evidence available, will he proceed without vacillation, firmly and and stubbornly to act, despite being highly vulnerable to attack as being too little too late..

He is denigrated as lacking in leadership and being too timid, for vacillating, for not immediately displaying that aggressiveness in the presidential personality, the burning drive for greatness in the Roosevelts, Wilson, Kennedy, and Lincoln, which strikes a responsive chord, not only in historians, but in each American who would be aristocratic if it were not forbidden. His compulsion to compromise is regarded as the major evidence of his lack of leadership capability not only by, predictably, conservative Republicans— particularly the far-right Tea Party faction—but by far-left Progressives in his own Democratic Party.

The Tea Party's opposition is lodged in a profound belief in the total catastrophe of a Democrat, any Democrat, being President of the United States and, as such, being possessed of a Satanic desire to expand endlessly the Federal government rather than reducing, or even eliminating it, to tax the rich and spend on the needy poor— in short, to convert the American way of life from capitalism to Socialism.

John Bolton displays the contempt for President Obama expressed by far-right Republicans: "… the explanation for his policy's failure, and its well-deserved collapse now unfolding before us, lies in a jumbled mix of philosophy, political priorities, and personal inadequacy. Like Obama's presidency generally, his national-security flaws combine ideology, naïveté, weakness, lack of leadership, intellectual laziness, and a near-religious faith in negotiation for its own sake."

Shelby Steele, echoing Ayn Rand, in the name of exceptionalism, accuses Obama of fostering American mediocrity: "Anti-exceptionalism has clearly shaped his 'leading from behind' profile abroad—an offer of self-effacement to offset the presumed American evil of swaggering cowboyism … As a president, Barack Obama has been a force for mediocrity. He has banked more on the hopeless interventions of government than on the exceptionalism of the people. His great weakness as a president is a limp confidence in his countrymen. He is afraid to ask difficult things of them."

"President Obama flinched," the National Review charges. "Last night he announced his decision to begin rapidly unwinding his Afghan surge. Of the 30,000 additional troops committed, Obama wants 10,000 out by the end of this year and the rest out by the end of next summer. This risks giving back to the Taliban all that's been won over the last year with blood, sweat, and tears."

In what appears to be an inopportune moment, James Taranto launches an effort to minimize a generally regarded triumph of Obama's: "It was early May (2011) and the President was riding high. Politico reported: 'Killing Obama bin Laden isn't just an important moment in Barack Obama's presidency—it's the moment of his presidency...' Three months later, Obama looked as weak as any president since Jimmy Carter, or maybe in living memory. Like a leaky balloon he kept getting smaller... It is a safe bet that Barack Obama's reelection campaign will be every bit as vacuous, negative, and whiny as Jimmy Carter's was."— Of course, Taranto lost his 'safe' bet after Obama's victorious reelection campaign effectively proved to be the reverse of 'vacuous, negative, and whiny.'

The disillusionment of Progressives in Obama's performance as president is more complicated in expressing a desire at the same time, both to chastise and to extenuate Obama's conduct of his presidency. What emerges from their disappointment is a testimonial to the values inherent in lawyer formalism as it reveals its vulnerability to criticism. Drew Westen draws an arresting picture of what he views as a puzzlement begging to be reconciled: "The President is fond of referring to 'the arc of history'...with his deep-seated aversion to conflict and his profound failure to understand bully dynamics—in which conciliation is always the wrong course of action, because bullies perceive it as weakness and just punch harder the next time—he has broken that arc... The real conundrum is why the president seems so compelled to take both sides of every issue, encouraging voters to project whatever they want on him... A final explanation is that he ran for president on two contradictory platforms: as a reformer, and as a unity candidate. He has pursued the one with which he is most comfortable given the constraints of his character. He and his political team have consistently chosen the message of bipartisanship over the message of confrontation."

Romano and Kurtz gather quotations that reflect the frustration of liberal leaning critics: "Paul Krugman dismisses the president as a 'bland, timid guy who doesn't seem to stand for anything in particular.' *The Daily Beast*'s Eric Alterman likened the leader of the free world to 'a boxer who ... (spends) the entire fight taking punch after punch on the ropes.' And Jonathan Chait of *The New Republic* declares

Obama 'a horrendously weak negotiator on the brink of becoming a uniquely powerless president.' The quotations are a prelude to Romano and Kurtz's intention vigorously to defend him: "Whatever your opinion of Obama, 'weakness' is not a particularly illuminating description of his leadership style. It makes more sense to see him as a hard-nosed pragmatist determined to maximize results ... When Democrats controlled both houses of Congress, the White House's top priority was simple: getting legislation passed ... Obama's initial leadership strategy was tailored to a time when Republicans couldn't torpedo his agenda. In policy terms, the approach paid off, helping him put more points on the board during his first two years—the stimulus package, health-care reform, financial reregulation, and so on—than any president since L. B. J... But now that the GOP controls the House, no laws can pass without Republican support, and no Republicans will support anything the president proposes because they're afraid it will help him get reelected."

Charles M. Blow reiterates Obama's character deficiencies most troubling to the Progressives: "It's not that people don't believe him, it's that an increasing number don't believe in him ... Americans want to clearly identify his core beliefs. It's simple: They want to fully understand his values and how they apply to us as individuals and as a country ... The vacillation between hot and cold, stern and pliable, resolute and accommodating hasn't inspired that confidence ... Obama has a list of accomplishments as long as your arm. But a less-than-masterly use of the bully pulpit has allowed both opponents and supposed allies to minimize them. A very vocal part of the progressive base had painted many of his successes as capitulations while many on the far right have painted them as a threat to the security and solvency of the republic."

While he chastises him, Thomas L. Friedman finds room for praise: "Obama is smart, decent and tough, with exactly the right instincts about where the country needs to go. He has accomplished a lot more than he's gotten credit for—with an opposition dedicated to making him fail. But lately he is seriously off his game. He's not Jimmy Carter. He's Tiger Woods—a natural who's lost his swing ... He needs to get back to basics."

Paul Krugman surfaces with a guarded appreciation of the 'new' Obama: "First things first. I was favorably surprised by the new Obama jobs plan, which is significantly bolder and better than I expected. It's not nearly as bold as the plan I'd want in an ideal world. But if it actually became law, it would probably make a significant dent in unemployment. Of course, it isn't likely to become law, thanks to G.O.P. opposition."

Positive views of Obama's presidential performance have emerged, particularly from his successes in foreign affairs, an area where he was originally regarded as too inexperienced and naïve. James M. Lindsay offers a summary, exhaustive but illuminating: "Obama's embrace of diplomacy made him popular abroad and revived America's image around the globe. Expectations of what he would accomplish soared... Obama's first 28 months in office did produce some notable accomplishments. In June 2010, the UN Security Council imposed new sanctions on Iran in a bid to curtail its budding nuclear programme. The move was significant, not just because it intensified pressure on Tehran, but because it won the support of the two Security Council members that had previously resisted sanctions, Russia and China... In September 2009, he revamped US missile defence, scrapping the long-range missile defence system that Bush had begun and the Russians opposed in favor of a system that relied on shorter-range interceptors that caused Moscow less alarm. That policy change enabled the signing and eventual ratification of the 'New START' treaty as well as facilitating Moscow's cooperation in the passage of materiel through Central Asia to Afghanistan. In March 2011, Obama worked with Britain and France to secure Chinese and Russian cooperation at the Security Council once again, this time to pass a resolution authorizing action to protect Libyan civilians against attacks by Muammar Qadhafi's forces. Obama succeeded on several core national security objectives as well. US combat troops left Iraq in August 2010 as promised, and the withdrawal of the remaining 50,000 non-combat troops was on schedule to be completed by the December 2011 deadline. He quintupled the number of strikes by armed drones against suspected terrorist hideouts in Pakistan and elsewhere. And most notably, in May 2011, US Navy SEALS killed Osama bin Laden in a high stakes raid in Abbottabad, Pakistan."

Obama's 'leading from behind' support for the operation in Libya, led by NATO to protect civilians from being slaughtered by dictator Muammar Qaddafi, has on the whole been approved for sidestepping the risk of putting more troops on the ground along with those in Iraq and Afghanistan. Predictably, at the same time, he invited a barrage of criticism from conservative Republicans that David Remnick, after quoting a goodly number of them, strenuously disputes: "Obama was daily pilloried as a timorous pretender who, out of a misbegotten sense of liberal guilt, unearned self-regard, and downright unpatriotic acceptance of fading national glory, had handed over the steering wheel of global leadership to the Elysee Palace. Many of Obama's critics still view a President who rid the world of Osama bin Laden (something that George W. Bush failed to do) and helped bring down Muammar Qaddafi (something that Ronald Reagan failed to do) as supinely selling out American power… The trouble with so much of the conservative critique of Obama's foreign policy is that it cares less about outcomes than about the assertion of America's power and the affirmation of its glory. In the case of Libya, Obama led from a place of no glory, and, in the eyes of his critics, no results could ever vindicate such a strategy. Yet a calculated modesty can augment a nation's true influence. Obama would not be the first statesman to realize that it can be easier to win if you don't need to trumpet your victory."

A telling and detailed account that mounts a defense of Obama's presidency is offered by Andrew Sullivan: "The attacks from both the right and the left on the man and his policies aren't out of bounds. They're simply—empirically—wrong … When Obama took office … Obama did several things at once: he continued the bank bailout begun by George W. Bush, he initiated a bailout of the auto industry, and he worked to pass a huge stimulus package of $787 billion… in retrospect, they were far more successful than anyone has yet fully given Obama the credit for. On foreign policy, the right wing has been the most unhinged… Obama reversed Bush's policy of ignoring Obama bin Laden, immediately setting a course that eventually led to his capture and death…by 'leading from behind' in Libya and elsewhere, Obama has made other countries actively seek America's help and reappreciate our role. As an antidote to the bad feelings of the Iraq War, it has worked close to perfectly… The Iraq War… has been ended on time and, vitally, with no troops left behind… Gays now openly serve in the military … Fuel-emission standards have been drastically increased. Torture was ended… nearly universal health care has been set into law… he practices a show-don't-tell, long-game form of domestic politics. What matters to him is what he can get done, not what he can immediately take credit for… I am biased toward the actual record, not the spin: biased toward a president who has conducted himself with grace and calm under incredible pressure, who has had to manage crises not seen since the Second World War and the Depression, and who as yet has not had a single significant scandal to his name."

It's not easy to be President of the United States; the First Amendment to the Constitution guarantees that—freedom of speech in an electronic age in which charges and countercharges, accusations and death-wishes can be conveyed instantly all over the world by its merest citizen. Vilifying shots in the dark flood the internet—and the favorite target is the president. Every word, every action, every movement even of an upraised eyebrow or curled lip, is savaged. It makes one marvel that anyone, no matter how ambitious, greedy for power, hungry to make and win wars, or morally impelled at least to try to save the world from tornados, hurricanes, floods, famine, nuclear war, global warming—even chickenpox or shoplifting— would take the relentless, hate-filled mercilessness the American president must suffer simply for being insolent enough to bring it on. As if it weren't enough, the vitriol is magnified when the Oval Office is occupied by an intellectual lawyer, constitutional law teacher, graduate of an Ivy League law school— in short, the apotheosis of a lawyer-formalist president who, whether he might succeed or not in eliminating wars and doctoring the ailing economy, whether, after his successful election in 2012 to a second term, he can overcome the historical denigration of being such a president.

NOTES

INTRODUCTION

Page

1 legal counselors: Alexis de Tocqueville, Democracy in America, The Henry Reeve Text as revised by Francis Bowen, further corrected and edited by Phillips Bradley, (New York: Vintage Books, a Division of Random House, 1945), 1:289.

3 power to destroy: Richard Nixon, The Memoirs of Richard Nixon (New York: Grosset & Dunlop, 1978), 129.

3 judge and jury: Nixon, Memoirs, ibid, 202.

6 can be any rules: H.L A. Hart, The Concept of Law (London: Oxford University Press, 1961), 126-27,135.

7 and 'legalisms': Victor Lasky, Jimmy Carter—The Man & The Myth (New York: Hill & Wang, 1968), 383.

9 religion of the nation: Abraham Lincoln, The Collected Works of Abraham Lincoln, ed. Roy D. Basler, 9 vols. (New Brunswick, N.J.: Rutgers University Press, 1953), v.1, 112.

PART ONE—
LAWYER RULE-SKEPTICISM IN THE PRESIDENCY

1

A Birds Eye View of Rule-Skepticism Presidents

13 but of historians: See R. Murray and T. Blessing, The Presidential Performance Study: A Progress Report (70 Journal of American History 535 (Dec. 1983). See also, Historical Rankings of Presidents of the United States-Wikipedia, the free encyclopedia.

13   criticism of it: D. Fehrenbacher, Lincoln In Text and Context: Collected Essays (Palo Alto: Stanford University Press (1987), 15, 23, 125.

2

Father and Son: John and Quincy Adams

14   antagonism and scorn: John Quincy Adams, Memoirs of John Quincy Adams, Comprising Portions of his Diary from 1795 to 1848, ed. Charles Francis Adams (12 vols.; Philadelphia: J. B. Lippincott & Co., 1876), 1:521.

14   course of reasoning: Quoted in John R. Howe, Jr., The Changing Political Thought of John Adams (Princeton, N. J.: Princeton University Press, 1966), 21..

14   the memory of them: Adams Family correspondence, eds. L. H. Butterfield and Marc Friedlander 4 vols., Cambridge, Mass: Harvard University Press, 1963-73), 4:224.

13   dejection of spirits: Mary W.M. Hargreaves, The Presidency of John Quincy Adams (Lawrence, Kansas: University Press of Kansas, 1985), 252-3.

15   and desperately wicked: John Adams, The Works of John Adams, ed. Charles Francis Adams, 10 vols. (Boston: Little Brown, 1851), 6:61.

15   particularly the Jews: Gilbert Chinard, Honest John Adams (Boston: Little Brown & Co., 1933), 15-16.

15   in close relations: Reported in H. N. Hirsch, The Enigma of Felix Frankfurter (New York: Basic Books, 81), 201-3.

16   for every purpose of justice: John Adams and John Quincy Adams, The Selected Writings of John and John Quincy Adams, ed. and intro. Adrienne Koch and William Peden (New York: Alfred A. Knopf, 1946), 288. (John Quincy Adams to John Adams, 8/1/1816).

16   pattern to the rest of the world: John Adams, Works, ed. C. F. Adams, supra p.15, 10:393 (John Adams to Henry Channing, 11/3/1820).

16   sometimes self-righteous: Liva Baker, Felix Frankfurter (New York: Coward-McCann, 1969), 236.

16   old and wealthy families: Felix Frankfurter, From the Diaries of Felix Frankfurter, with biographical essay and notes by Joseph P. Lash (New York: W.W. Norton & Co., 1975), 35.

16   the most charming people: Hirsch, Frankfurter, supra p .15, 90.

16   Dean G. Acheson: Baker, Frankfurter, supra p. 16, 36.

17   morals of the people: Adams is quoted in Chinard, John Adams, supra p. 15, 58.

15   overturn them partially: John Adams, Works, ed. C .F, Adams, (To Benjamin Hichborn, January 27, 1787), 9:551.

18   this period is read: ibid, 2:231.

THE LEGAL MIND AND THE PRESIDENCY

18   merchants of the town: Chinard, John Adams, p..21, 62-3.

18   Virtue and Talents: John Adams and Thomas Jefferson, The Adams-Jefferson Letters: The Complete Correspondence Between Thomas Jefferson and Abigail and John Adams, ed. Lester J. Cappon (2 vols, Chapel Hill, N.C.: The University of North Carolina Press, 1959), 2:423 (Jefferson to Adams, Jan. 24, 1814).

19   Rotundity to him: William Maclay, The Journal of William Maclay: United States Senator from Pennsylvania, 1789-1791 (New York: Albert & Charles Boni, 1927), 21-2, 29. See also Peter Shaw, The Character of John Adams (Chapel Hill, N.C.: The University of Carolina Press, 1976), 227-9.

19   Science and learning: Adams-Jefferson Letters, supra p. 18, 2:298.

19   for further advancement: J.Q Adams, Memoirs, supra p. 14, 4:64. alone must I stand: ibid, 2:64, 9:305-6.

20   rather than himself: ibid, 8: 307.

20   friendly society with him: ibid, 8:307, 5:59, 5:325, 6:258.

21   much the same course: M. Hargreaves, John Quincy Adams, supra p.13, 253.

21   current of human thought: Daniel Webster, The Writings and Speeches of Daniel Webster (18 vols., Boston: Little, Brown & Co., 1903), 1:292.

22   and only 49 for Jefferson: Adams-Jefferson Letters, p. 18, xxxi.

23   authority upon society: See J. Howe, John Adams, supra p.14,149,176.

24   under the guise of law: "In a period of fifteen months (from around April, 1793 to July, 1794), it has been calculated, about 17,000 persons had been executed in France under form of law." Encyclopedia Britannica (11th Ed.) 11:165.

24   Aristotle instructs us: "Therefore he who bids the law rule may be deemed to bid God and Reason alone rule, but he who bids man rule adds an element of the beast; for desire is a wild beast, and passion perverts the minds of rulers, even when they are the best of men. The law is reason unaffected by desire." Aristotle, The Works of Aristotle, ed. W. D. Ross, tr. Benj. Jowett and others (Oxford: Oxford U. Princeton University Press, 1957) 1:286.

24   ever man was engaged in: Thomas Jefferson, The Works of Thomas Jefferson, ed. Paul Leicester Ford (12 vols. New York and London: G. P. Putnam's Sons, 1904), 6-311.

24   and look at the result: See: Howe, John Adams, supra p. 14, 158-9.

24   from Shay's Rebellion: Shays' Rebellion was an armed uprising in Massachusetts from 1786 to 1787 that produced fears the Revolution's democratic impulse had gotten out of hand.

3

Self-Inflicted War With Mexico: James K. Polk

26   believe it his nature: The statement is attributed to Charles Jared Ingersoll in William M. Meigs, The Life of Charles Jared Ingersoll (Philadelphia: J.B. Lippincott Co., 1897), 274.

27   minds of most historians: Richard Nixon, Leaders (New York: Warner Books, 1982), 30.

27   one of the boys: See: Charles Grier Sellers, Jr., James K. Polk, 2v. (Princeton, N.J.: Princeton University Press, 1957-66) 1:39; Nixon, Leaders, supra p. 27, 30.

27   what the cost in effort: See: Sellers, Polk, ibid, 1:40-1; Richard Nixon, Six Crises (Garden City, N.Y.: Doubleday, 1962), 34.

28   his controlling intentions: James K. Polk, The Diary Of James K. Polk, 4 vols. ed. Milo M. Quaife (Chicago: A .C. McClurg, 1910), 1: xiii-xiv.

29   heaven against him: Lincoln, Collected Works, ed. Basler, supra p. 9, 1:439.

29   invasion by Mexico: Polk, Diary, supra p. 28, 1:1.

30   to be sacrificed: Sellers, Polk, supra p. 27, 2:223. Polk to Houston, 6 June, 1845.

30   upon American soil: See Samuel Eliot Morison, The Oxford History of The American People (New York: New American Library, 1972), 325.

30   on the subject: Polk, Diary, supra p. 28, 1: 396ff.

30   but wicked: Polk, Diary, supra p .28, 2:308.

31   a human being: See: Meigs, Ingersoll, supra p. 26, 272; Sellers, Polk, supra p. 27, 2-4; Garry Wills, Nixon Agonistes (Boston: Houghton Mifflin, 1970), 370-80; Eli S. Chesen, President Nixon's Psychiatric Profile (New York: Peter H. Wyden/Publisher, 1973), 82,112,116.

31   without regret: Sellers, Polk, p. 27, 1:286, citing Nashville Union, Nov. 19, 1835

32   personal fortunes of James K. Polk: Sellers, Polk, supra p. 27, 1:112-3.

32   permanently corrupted: ibid, 2-6.

32   president of the U. S.: Polk, Diary, supra p. 28, 2:278-9.

32   revered Democratic party: See: Polk, Diary, p. 28, 20, 296, 329ff, 458ff.

4

A Great Life and Death: Abraham Lincoln

34   Frustrated dramatists: David Donald, Lincoln Reconsidered (New York: Alfred A. Knopf, 1966), 103-4.

34   lack of money: Actually, while the Lincolns were far from affluent, they were not as abysmally poor as myth would have it. See: Benjamin P. Thomas, Abraham Lincoln, A Biography (New York: Alfred A. Knopf, 1952), 5ff

34   near illiteracy: Stephen B. Oates, With Malice Toward None (New York: MacMillan, 1972), 5, 7; Lincoln, Collected Works, supra p. 9, 1:456.

34   when he was eight: William H. Herndon, The Hidden Lincoln: From the Letters and Papers of William H. Herndon, ed. Emanuel Hertz (New York: The Viking Press, 1938), 73-4.

34   painful than pleasant: Lincoln, Collected Works, , ed. Basler, supra p .9, 1:96-7.

35   loveable anyway: Historians have found the combination in Lincoln of intense shame and desire difficult to explain. See: Albert J. Beveridge, Abraham Lincoln, 1809-1858, 2 vols. (Boston: Houghton Mifflin, 1928), 1:144; Lord Charnwood, Abraham Lincoln (New York: Henry Holt, 1917), 81; Reinhard Luthin, The Real Abraham Lincoln (Englewood Cliffs, N.J: PrenticeHall,1960),82;. Thomas, Lincoln, supra p. 34,70;

35   Charles B. Strozier, "The Search for Identity and Love," in the Public and Private Lincoln, Contemporary Perspectives, ed. Cullom Davis, Charles B. Strozier, Rebecca Monroe Veach and Geoffry C. Ward (Carbondale, Ill.: Southern Illinois University Press, 1979),8,10-11.

35   well-educated and witty: Beveridge , Lincoln, supra p. 35, 1:145.

35   beyond reason: Lincoln, Collected Works, ed. Basler, supra p .9, 94-5.

36   bear that patiently: ibid, 1:78.

36   betrayed by his youthfulness: See: The Living Lincoln, The Man, His Mind, His Times and the War He Fought, Reconstructed From His Own Writings. ed. Paul M. Angle and Earl Schenck Miers. (New Brunswick, N.J.: Rutgers University Press, 1955),4,27

37   still unanswered: Donald, Lincoln Reconsidered, supra p. 34, 68.

37   family background: Beveridge, Lincoln, supra p 35, 1:145; Donald, Lincoln Reconsidered, supra p. 34, 68.

37   enervating depression See: Oates, Malice, supra p .34, 55ff.

37   all eyes and ears: Donald, Lincoln Reconsidered, supra p .34,49.

38   too well, proliferated: See: Herndon, Hidden Lincoln, supra p. 34, 364-5, 103, 382, 363, 316.

38	expect to see: William H. Herndon and Jesse W. Weik, Life of Lincoln, (New York: Albert & Charles Boni, 1930), 356. See also, Fehrenbacher, Lincoln Essays, supra p. 13, 96.
38	lived and moved: Herndon, Hidden Lincoln, supra p .34, 119
38	ambitious soul: Ibid, 119,124. Cf. Rowland Evans and Robert Novak, Nixon in the White House: The Frustration of Power (New York: Random House, 1971), 351, 437; Nixon, Memoirs, supra p.3, 513,628; Bruce Mazlish, In Search of Nixon (New York and London: Basic Books, Inc., 1972), 56-57.
38	feel flabby and undone: Herndon, Hidden Lincoln, supra p. 34, 165. Cf. John Ehrlichman, Witness to Power (New York: Simon and Schuster, c.1982), 21-22.
38	Society of intellectuals: Thomas, Lincoln, supra p.34, 14.
39	the game of checkers: Ruth P. Randall, Mary Lincoln: Biography of a Marriage (Boston: Little, Brown & Company, 1953), 163.
39	quick as a flash: Herndon, Hidden Lincoln, supra p. 34, 123-4.
39	whistling down sadness: See: S. Oates, Malice, supra p. 34, 55.
39	so disturbed John Adams: See Howe, John Adams, supra p. 14,112,115.
39	religion of the nation: Abraham Lincoln, Life and Works of Abraham Lincoln, ed. Marion Mills Miller, 9 ls (New York, The Current Literature Publishing Co..), 2:20, 25-6.
40	fighting faiths: Abrams v. United States, 250 U.S.616, 630 (1920) Holmes, J., dissenting).
40	the Mexican War: Lincoln, Collected Works, ed. Basler, supra p. 9, 1:437-8, 440-2.
40	which you would do: ibid, 2, 1:446-7 (Letter to William H. Herndon, 2/1/48).
41	and internal improvements: Oates, Malice, supra p. 34, 79
41	his presidential performance: e.g. James G. Randall, Constitutional Problems Under Lincoln (New York: D. Appleton & Co., l926), l57, 514-520.
41	his sense of superiority: Edmund Wilson, Patriotic Gore: Studies In The Literature Of The American Civil War (New York: Oxford University Press, l962),107-8.
41	and absent–mindedness: Herndon, Hidden Lincoln, supra p, 34, *120-3; S.* Oates, Malice, supra p. 34, 99-101.
41	democracy and the law: Randall, Constitutional Problems, supra p. 41, 1-2,34-47, 519-22.
41	respect for the Constitution: ibid, 45-6, 519ff.; Richard Hofstadter, The American Political Tradition and The Men Who Made It (New York: Alfred A. Knopf, 1948),102; John J. Duff, A. Lincoln: Prairie Lawyer (New York: Rinehart & Co., 1960), 367.
41	his flouting of it: Donald, Lincoln Reconsidered, supra p. 34, 188-91; Fehrenbacher, Lincoln & the Constitution, in The Public and

Private Lincoln, 89-90; cf. J .Randall, Constitutional Problems, supra p. 41, 157, 183-85, 513-19.

41   jokes and anecdotes: Reinhard H. Luthin, The Real Abraham Lincoln (Englewood Cliffs, N. J: Prentice-Hall, 1960), 394-96; S. Oates, Malice, supra p. 34, 100.

41   passion for secrecy: Ibid, 99; Donald, Lincoln Reconsidered, supra p. 34, 240. 50.

41   by Herndon himself: Strozier, Lincoln's Search, supra p.35, xiv-xviii.

42   spring up among us: Lincoln, Works, ed. Basler, supra p.9, 1:114.

42   *in an heroic role: E. Wilson, Patriotic Gore, supra p. 41, l07-8. See also, Herndon, Lincoln, Life, supra p. 38, 163,162, 304; Herndon, Hidden Lincoln, supra p. 34, 15; Strozier, Lincoln's Search, supra p.35, 15. Nixon, Six Crises, supra p. 27, xiv; Mazlish, Nixon, supra p. 38, 110; Fawn Brodie, Thomas Jefferson: An Intimate History (New York: W. W. Norton & Co., 1974), 246-7; Fehrenbacher, Lincoln Essays, supra p. 13, 216.

42   never could forgive: See: E. Wilson, Patriotic Gore, supra p .41, 118-19.

42   a great lawyer: See, e.g. Duff, Prairie Lawyer, supra p. 41, 366-7; Herndon and Weik, Lincoln, Life, supra p. 38 ,270-71; S. Oates, Malice, supra p. 34, 100-5.

42   prized being a lawyer: C. Strozier, Lincoln's Search, supra p. 42, 139 S. Oates, Malice, supra p. 34, 104.

42   before they reach you: Donald R. McCoy, Calvin Coolidge: The Quiet President (New York: MacMillan, 1967), 193.

42   first shot at Sumter: Donald, Lincoln Reconsidered, supra p. 34, 69. Cf. Nixon's reverse spin of fear of passivity in Mazlish, Nixon, supra p. 38, 115,119; cf. Wills, Nixon Agonistes, supra p. 31, 28; Nixon, Memoirs, supra p. 3, 513.

43   the American experience: Fehrenbacher, Lincoln Essays, supra p. 13, 128.

43   constitutional law: See Samuel Eliot Morison, The Oxford History of the American People (New York: New American Library, 1972), 2:441. Cf. J. Randall's more temperate view: J. Randall, Constitutional Problems, supra p. 41, 45.

43   during World War 1: See J. Randall, 524-5; John H. Blum, Woodrow Wilson and the Politics of Morality (Boston: Little, Brown, 1956), 689,134,136-8,140,143.

43   passive, calm manner: Donald, Lincoln Reconsidered, supra p. 34, 68-69,191

43   for his client: See S. Oates, Malice, supra p.41, 101; Perry Miller, The Life of the Mind in America(Harcourt, Brace & World, 1965) 116; Herndon and Weik, Life of Lincoln, supra p. 38, 140; J. Frank , Lincoln as a Lawyer (Urbana , IL, University of Illnois Press, 1961),147); Cf. Frost/Nixon, behind the scenes of the Nixon interviews/Sir

David Frost with Bob Zeinick (New York: Harper Perennial, c2007), 270.

43   issue of all—slavery: R. Hofstadter, Political Tradition, supra p. 41, 25 6.

43   must be kept: A. Lincoln, Works, supra p. 9, 7:500.

44   Supreme Court as well: Herndon and Weik, Life of Lincoln, supra p .38, 478.

44   in the race of life: A. Lincoln, Works, supra p. 9, 7:12 (Speech to 166th Ohio Regiment, 8/22/1864.

44   as Wendell Phillips: J. Randall, Constitutional Problems, 66, 1; R Hofstadter, Political Tradition, supra p. 41, 108; S. Oates, Malice, supra p. 34, 302.

44   and Frederick Douglass: Lincoln, Works, ed. Basler, supra p9, 1:260.

44   Douglass be explained: ibid, 7:500.

44   better than tolerable: ibid, 1:260.

45   let it rest in peace: ibid, 2:255,276.

45   for white Americans: See: ibid, 5:388.

45   and better their condition: ibid, 2:172.

46   its further extension: R. Hofstadter, Political Tradition, supra p.41, 111-2.

46   rebel side to ours: A. Lincoln, Works, ed. Basler, supra p.9, 7:499-500. See Fehrenbacher, Lincoln Essays, supra p. 13, 98.

5

An American Tragedy: Richard Milhaus Nixon

47   paths of expediency: Donald, Lincoln Reconsidered, supra p. 34, 3.

47   America's worst presidents: Murray and T. Blessing, supra p. 13, 535 555.

47   standing among historians: See e.g. Brodie's reference to Theodore White's pre-Watergate evaluation: Brodie, Jefferson, supra. p .42, 22.

48   country, ambition, industry: Mazlish, Nixon, supra p.38, 125; Wills, Nixon Agonistes, supra p.31, 6, 144; 65. David Abrahamsen, Nixon v. Nixon, an Emotional Tragedy (New York: Farrar Straus and Giroux, 1977), 115.

48   deficiencies in Richard Nixon: Wills, Nixon Agonistes, supra p. 31, ix.

48   within the character itself: Dictionary World Literary Terms 423 (J. T. Shipley ed. 1955).

48   sense of tragic flaw: Allan H. Gilbert, Literary Criticism: Plato To Dryden (New York: American Book Company, 1940), 86.; Master-pieces of World Philosophy In Summary Form (F. Magill ed. 1961), 176.

48	reverse the decree: Herndon, Hidden Lincoln, supra p. 34, 122.
48	the man makes history: Nixon, Memoirs, supra p. 3, 291.
48	and destroys us: George Steiner, The Death of Tragedy, (New York: Alfred A. Knopf, 1961), 8ff.
49	doing too little: Wills, Nixon Agonistes, supra p. 31, 321-3.
49	and Robert Ablanalp: See: R. Evans & R. Novak, Nixon, supra p.38, 4.
49	not even invited to apply: Earl Mazo and Stephen Hess, Nixon: A Political Portrait (New York: Harper &, Row, 1968), 22.
49	with Zhou-Enlai: Nixon, Leaders, supra p. 27, 217-48 (1982).
49	and Brezhnev: Nixon, Leaders, ibid, 204-10.
49	Family Assistance Plan: R. Evans & R. Novak, Nixon, supra p. 38, 223-232.
51	not lose our birthright: A. Lincoln, Works, ed. Basler, supra p. 9, 7:512.
51	affinity for Wilson: See: Wills, Nixon Agonistes, supra p. 31, 496-7.
51	over his bed as a child: Mazlish, Nixon, supra p. 38 133; F. Brodie, Jefferson, supra p. 42, 118.
51	presidential cabinet room: Nixon, Memoirs, supra p.3, 368.
51	debilitating depressions: Mazlish, supra p. 38, 55 (1972);, Nixon Ago nistes, supra p .31, 38, 39; Stephen E. Ambrose, Nixon: The Education Of A Politician 1913-1962 (New York: Simon and Schuster, 1987), 12. As to Lincoln, see Oates, Malice, supra p .34 ,55ff.; Herndon, Hidden Lincoln, supra p .34, 120-3.
51	grew up in poverty: Roger Morris, Richard Milhous Nixon: the rise of an American politician (New York: Henry Holt, c 1990), 55; E .Mazo and S. Hess, supra p. 49, 16.
51	sixth-grade 'learning': See Brodie, Jefferson, supra p. 42, 51; Mazlish, Nixon, supra p. 38, 29,142; R. Nixon, Six Crises, supra p. 27, 318.
52	life and death: As to Lincoln: and Weik, Life of Lincoln, supra p.38, 163,172,304; W. Herndon, Hidden Lincoln, supra p. 34, 15. C. Strozier, Lincoln's Search, supra p. 35, 18. As to Nixon: Nixon, Six Crises, 27, 295; R. Morris, Nixon, supra p. 51, 164; S .Ambrose, Nixon, supra p. 51, 139.
52	his political being: R. Hofstadter, Political Tradition, supra p .41, 94.
52	Nixon stated simply: Nixon, Memoirs, supra p .3, 294.
52	'moral'solutions: See Mazlish, Nixon, supra p. 38, 146; Wills, Nixon Agonistes, supra p. 31, 143; D. Frost, Nixon Interviews, supra p.43, 184, 294.
52	figures to analyze: Mazlish, Nixon, supra p.38, 146.
53	his verbal facility: Consider Mazlish, Nixon, ibid., 55, 76-77,128; cf. Lincoln: W. Herndon, Hidden Lincoln, supra p.41, 120-23; S. Oates, Malice, supra p. 34, 101.
53	along with Polk: Charles Grier Sellers, James K. Polk, Continentalist (Princeton, N.J.: Princeton University Press, 1957).

53	frustrated by charmlessness: R. Evans & R. Novak, Nixon, supra p. 38, 4; Nixon Agonistes, supra p. 31, 24-25.
53	at all costs, continue to be: Nixon, Memoirs, supra p. 3, 454-5.
53	in the Gobitis case: Minersville School District v. Gobitis, 310 U.S. 586 (1940).
53	a paradigmatic Justice: William Safire, Before the Fall, an inside view of the pre-Watergate White House (Garden City, N.Y.: Doubleday, 1975), 564,572.
53	meant so little: Mazlish, Nixon, supra p. 38, 128; International Herald Tribune, 5/17/71, 7ff; R. Evans & R .Novak, Nixon, supra p. 38, 366.
53	last note died away: Nixon, Memoirs, supra p. 5, 454-5.
54	and short on facts: R. Evans & R. Novak, Nixon, supra p .38, 52
54	sense of nation: R. Evans & R. Novak, Nixon, supra p. 38, 53.
54	any of his friends: Nixon, Six Crises, supra p. 27, 295.
55	what might yet be: Wills, Nixon Agonistes, supra p. 31, 42,163.
55	bought by crooks: Nixon, Six Crises, supra p. 27, 295.
55	nationally prominent: Nixon, Six Crises, ibid., 71
55	checkers speech: Public Papers, Presidents: Richard Nixon (1971), 2; Nixon, Six Crises, supra p. 27, 129.
55	'farewell address' to reporters: See E. Mazo and S. Hess, supra p. 49, 264-82.
55	simple trappings: Public Papers, Presidents: Richard Nixon (1971), 2.
55	Zhou Enlai: R. Nixon, Leaders, supra p.27, 211-48.
55	talk to Brezhnev: R. Nixon, Leaders, ibid, 204-10.
56	ex-master politician: See J. Ehrlichman, Witness To Power, supra p. 38, 308
57	American greatness: See R. Evans & R. Novak, Nixon, supra p. 38, 405.
57	to make him win: Nixon, Memoirs, supra p. 3, 226, 357. Cf. Nixon, Six Crises, supra p. 27, 402: Mazlish, Nixon, supra p. 38, 138; S. Ambrose, supra p. 51, 139.
58	defy the law: See Bob Woodward & Carl Bernstein, The Final Days (New York: Simon and Schuster, 1976), 74.
58	presidential actions: R. Max, A Judicial Interpretation of the Nixon Presidency 6 Cumberland Law Review 213 (1975).
58	a great president: See Brodie,Jefferson, supra p.42, 247.
58	Henry A.. Kissinger, Nixon's Secretary of State; Melvin Laird, Nixon's Secretary of Defense; George Shultz, Nixon's Secretary of Labor.
58	a hound's tooth: Nixon, Six Crises, supra p. 27, 93; Wills, Nixon Agonistes, supra p. 31, 100.
58	truth and lying: M. Miller, Plain Speaking (New York: Berkley Publishing Corporation, 1974), 135.
58	full of pussy-footers: E. Mazo & S .Hess, supra p. 49, 121.

THE LEGAL MIND AND THE PRESIDENCY

58   dirty for you: See: Nixon, Memoirs, supra p. 3, 849.

59   about the Democrats: ibid. 357. dirty tricks team: See B .Woodward & C .Bernstein, supra p. 58, 51-52.

59   Tricky Dick: Brodie, Jefferson, supra p. 42, 244.

59   No coordination at all: Mazlish, Nixon, supra p. 38, 49

59   better than that: R. Nixon, in the Arena: A Memoir of Victory, Defeat, And Renewal (1990), 172, 161.

59   or you resign: Nixon, Six Crises, supra p. 27,424, 175.

59   loyal Republican: See: Clark R. Mollerhoff, The Man Who Pardoned Nixon (New York: St. Martin's Press, 1976), 1, 5.

59   the best educated: Wills, Nixon Agonistes, supra p. 31, 30-31.

59   with Leonid Brezhnev: Nixon, Leaders, supra p. 27, 217-48, 204-10.

59   to do right: Blum, Wilson supra p.43, 65.

60   Man and Nature: R. Randall, Mary Lincoln, supra p. 39, 163; W. Herndon, Hidden Lincoln, supra p .34, 104-5.

60   it's unbeknownest to me: See: Donald, Lincoln Reconsidered, supra p. 34, 70.

60   wait for his return: R. Randall, Mary Lincoln, supra p. 39, 163; W. Herndon, Hidden Lincoln.

60   quip and misdirection: supra p. 41, 103-4.

61   enforcing the draft: Donald, Lincoln Reconsidered, ibid., 70.

61   presidential tradition: Fehrenbacher, Lincoln Essays, supra p. 13, 122.

61   my paid informers: ibid, 128.

61   a well one: Nixon, Memoirs, supra p. 3, 646.

61   'kill' the bank: Herndon and Weik, Life of Lincoln, supra p. 38, 244.

62   or 'ineffective' one: Nixon, Memoirs, supra p. 3, 646.

63   good day: Herndon and Weik, Life of Lincoln, supra p. 38, 6, 244

63   than he seemed: See Wills, Nixon, supra p. 31, 39-43

63   kick around: Nixon, Memoirs, supra p.3, 245; E. Mazo & Hess, supra p. 49, 282; Brodie, Jefferson, supra p. 42, 463.

PART TWO—
LAWYER MORALISM IN THE PRESIDENCY

6

A Bird's Eye View of Moralist Presidents

66   in this moral climate: Alexis de Tocqueville, Democracy in America, The Henry Reeve Text as revised by Francis Bowen, further corrected and edited by Phillips Bradley, (New York: Vintage Books, A Division of Random House, 1945), 1:285-286; 2:42.

ALBERT LEBOWITZ

67   after fact and reason: John Keats, Poems and Selected Letters.

7

Words Speak Louder Than Actions: Thomas Jefferson

68   American Enlightenment: Adrienne Koch, ed. The American Enlightenment—The Shaping of the American Experiment and a Free Society (New York: George Braziller, 1963), 278.

68   only through reason: Garry Wills, Inventing America: Jefferson's Declaration of Independence (New York: Doubleday & Co., 1978), 168 180. See also: J. Boorstin, The Lost World of Thomas Jefferson (Boston: Beacon Press, 1948), 200.

69   by artificial rules: Thomas Jefferson, The Papers of Thomas Jefferson, ed. Julian P. Boyd (21 vols, Princeton, N. J.: Princeton University Press, l958), 12:14-15.

69   controlled by his ambition: John Quincy Adams, Memoirs of John Quincy Adams, Comprising Portions of his Diary from l795 to l848, ed. Charles Francis Adams (12 vols, Philadelphia: J. B. Lippincott & Co., l876), 9:305-6.

70   as fourth best: See: Wikipedia, the free encyclopedia, Historical rankings of Presidents of the United States.

70   ignore its existence: See: Adrienne Koch, American Enlightenment, supra p. 68, 278; Adrienne Koch, Jefferson And Madison: The Great Collaboration (New York: Alfred A. Knopf, 1950), 168, 177, 189,199; Dumas Malone, Jefferson and His Time (2 vols.; Boston: Little Brown & Co., l951), 1:304; Forrest McDonald, The Presidency of Thomas Jefferson (Lawrence, Kan.: The University Press of Kansas, l976), 132-3; Leonard W. Levy, Jefferson and Civil Liberties (Cambridge, Mass.: Harvard University Press, 1963),48, 166-7; Daniel J. Boorstin, The Lost World of Thomas Jefferson (Boston: Beacon Press, 1948), 20002; James Morton Smith, Freedom's Fetters: The Alien and Sedition Laws and American Civil Liberties (Ithaca, N.Y.: Cornell University Press, l956), 231ff.

71   manacles of the Law: Jefferson, Works, ed. Ford (TJ to Dr. James Brown, 10/27/1808), supra p, 34, 11:53.

71   act of critical charity: Adrienne Koch, Jefferson And Madison: supra p. 68, 168.

71   Wythe, Blair & Pendleton: Jefferson, Works, (Letter of Thomas Jefferson to James Madison, 3/15/1789). supra p. 24, 7:309.

71   burdens grievous to bear: John Adams and Thomas Jefferson, The Adams-Jefferson Letters: The Complete Correspondence Between Thomas Jefferson and Abigail and John Adams, ed. Lester J. Cappon (2 vols, Chapel Hill, N.C.: The University of North Carolina Press, 1959), (Jefferson to Adams, Jan. 24, 1814). 2:423.

THE LEGAL MIND AND THE PRESIDENCY

72   which feeds them: Jefferson, Works, ed. Ford, (TJ to Judge Spencer Roane, 9/6/1819), (TR to Thomas Ritchie, 12/25/1820) ,(TJ to Judge Spencer Roane, 3/9/1821), supra p.24, 12:137, 177, 201-02.

72   and separate power: Jefferson, Works, ed. Ford (TJ to William Short, January 3, 1793), supra p..24, 6:153-4.

8

The Bank Is Trying To Kill Me, But I Will Kill It: Andrew Jackson

75   he is a dangerous man : Daniel Webster, The Papers of Daniel Webster, ed. Charles M. Wiltse (5 vols., New Hampshire: Dartmouth College by University Press of New England, 1974), 1:375-6.

75   outrage on the Republic: See: Marquis James, The Life Of Andrew Jackson (New York: Bobbs Merrill, 1938), 130. James cites an "excerpt from a version published in 1824 by Thomas Ritchie, the distinguished Richmond editor. Once asked concerning its accuracy, Jackson said it was not strong enough."

75   I've ever seen: Quoted in Burke Davis, Old Hickory: A Life Of Andrew Jackson (New York: The Dial Press, 1977), 47.

76   start on my premises: Amos Kendall, Autobiography of Amos Kendall, ed. William Stickney (Boston: Lee and Shepard, 1872), 634.

76   bush for the game: James K. Paulding, Literary Life of James K. Paulding, ed. William I. Paulding (New York: Charles Scribner and Co., 1867), 288.

77   statesman and soldier : See: John William Ward, Andrew Jackson, Symbol For An Age (New York: Oxford University Press, 1962), 44.

77   the decision stood: Burke Davis, Old Hickory, supra p. 75 33.

78   untechnical, unlearned: Burke Davis, Old Hickory, supra p. 75, 32,

78   Adams quoted it: Henry A. Wise, Seven Decades of the Union (Philadelphia: Lippincott, 1881), 151-2.

78   an eminent degree : John William Ward, Andrew Jackson, supra p. 65.

78   same time as Jackson: Natty Bummpo is James Fenimore Cooper's hero in The Pathfinder, published in 1840, and The Deerslayer in 1841. Jackson was resident from 1829-1837.

78   and bad debts: See: James C. Curtis, Andrew Jackson and the Search For Vindication (Boston: Little Brown & Co., 976), 24.

78   assault and battery: Reported in Malone, Jefferson, supra p__, 1:122.

79   demagogues of the day: Andrew Jackson, Correspondence of Andrew Jackson, ed. John Spencer Bassett (7 vols., Washington, D.C., Carnegie Institute of Washington, 1926-1935), 3:167.

79   Roosevelt after him: See: Charles Gayarre, Louisiana History (New York: William J. Middleton, 1866), 622-625.

79	prevalent at the time: See: Robert V. Remini, Andrew Jackson and the Course Of American Democracy, 1833-1845 (New York: Harper & Row, 1984), 23-26, 316-17, 337-39. See also, Major L. Wilson, "What Whigs And Democrats Meant By Freedom," in Edward Pessen, ed., The many-faceted Jacksonian era: New Interpretations (West-port, Conn. Greenwood Press, 1977),195-96.
80	ruins of the General government: Joseph Story, Life And Letters Of Joseph Story, ed. and commentary, William W. Story (2 vols., Boston: Charles C. Little and James Brown, 1851), 2:47-8 (JS to Mrs. Joseph Story, 2/26/1832).
80	he will do nothing : Story, ibid., (JS to Mr. Professor Ashmun, 3/8/1832), 2:83..
80	such an occurrence: Story, ibid. (JS to Mrs. Joseph Story, 2/6/2833), 2:119.
80	but I will kill it: Martin Van Buren, The Autobiography of Martin Van Buren, ed. John C. Fitzpatrick (New York: Augustus M. Kelly, 1920), 625.

9

The Man Who Would Save The World: Woodrow Wilson

82	occupied the presidency: Forrest McDonald, Jefferson, supra p. 70, 139
83	but no principles: Woodrow Wilson, The Papers of Woodrow Wilson, ed. Arthur S. Link (55 vols, Princeton, N.J.: Princeton University Press, 1966-86), 2:119.
84	of all human morality: Reported in Peter Schwab and J. Lee Shneidman, John F. Kennedy (Boston: Twayne, 1974). 79.
84	backed up by deeds: Theodore Roosevelt, Theodore Roosevelt And His Time: Shown In His Own Letters, ed. and commentary, Joseph Bucklin Bishop (24 vols. New York: Charles Scribner's Sons, 1923-6), 24:459 (TR to Owen Wister, 7/7/1915).
84	was perpetually right: Reported in: Robert E. Quirk, An Affair Of Honor: Woodrow Wilson And The Occupation Of Vera Cruz (Lexington, Ky.: University of Kentucky Press, 1962), 29
84	characters in history: Wilson, Papers, supra p. 83,12:263-4.
84	parallel to Jefferson's: Reported in: Wikipedia, the free Encyclopedia, Biography of George Wythe.
85	his greatest teacher: Wilson, Papers, supra p. 83, 1:370 (J. Hemphill to W.H.Taft, 1/18/1912).
85	haggling practices: ibid, 2:343. 2:356 (letters to Robert Bridges, 4/29/1883 and 5/13/1883)
85	law that was meant: ibid, 37:385 in Worcester, Massachusetts, Jan.30, 1902.

THE LEGAL MIND AND THE PRESIDENCY

86	bombast that can breed...war: Blum , Wilson. supra p .43, 86.
86	stand by that belief: Wilson, Papers, supra p. 83, 37:386. Address to Businessmen, July 10, 1916.
87	I believe in justice: T. Roosevelt, Letters, ed. Bishop, supra p. 84, 24:454 (TR to Owen Wister, 6/23/1915, 24:458-9) (TR to Owen Wister, 7/5/1915).
87	New York American: New York American, Jan. 18, 1912, quoted in Woodrow Wilson Papers, ed. Link, 1:370.
87	as a presidential candidate: J.C. Hemphill to W. H. Taft, Jan. 18, 1912, quoted in Woodrow Wilson, Papers, supra p. 83, 1:370.
87	corrupt political machine: New York World, 1/19/1912, quoted in ibid, 1:170.
88	induced to change his mind: W. H. Taft to C. Cobb, 7/19/1916, quoted in ibid, 5:141
89	a temporary dictatorship: Thomas Jefferson, Works (TJ to James Brown, 10/27/1808) , supra p. 24, 11:53.
89	Treasury, Albert Gallatin: ibid, (TJ to Albert Gallatin, 8/11/1808), 11:41.
89	the end to the means: ibid, 1:146(TJ to John B. Colvin, 9/20/1810.
89	that of self-preservation: : Charles Gayarre, History of Louisiana (New York: William J. Middleton, 1866), 613.
89	will be urged or felt: Jackson, Correspondence , supra p. 79, 2:389.
90	* a state issue: See Blum, Wilson, supra p. 43, 132; U.S. Statute of July 14, 1798 and U .S. Statute of May 15, 1918, 68.
91	his own salvation: Earl Latham, ed. , The Philosophy And Policies Of Woodrow Wilson (Chicago: University of Chicago Press, 1958), xiii, xv.
91	love and universal harmony: Quoted in: Wilson, Papers, supra p .83, 5:27

10

The Fox and the Lion: Franklin Delano Roosevelt

92	in exhaustive detail: Burke Davis, Old Hickory, supra p. 75, 365.
92	ever more elusive: Henry F. May, The Enlightenment in America (New York: Oxford University Press, l976), 278-279.
92	pass judgment on him: Colonel Edward M. House, The Intimate Papers of Colonel House, ed. Charles Seymour (4 vols., Boston, Houghton Mifflin Co., 1926-28), 4:479-80.
93	creature of contradictions: See James McGregor Burns, Roosevelt: The Lion and the Fox) New York: Harcourt Brace, 1956), 465.
93	keep faith with them: See Niccolo Machiavelli, The Prince and Other Works trans. Allan H. Gilbert (Chicago Packard and Company, 1941, 1946), 148
93	may justify 'amoral' means: , Burns, Roosevelt, The Lion, supra p. 93, 476.

94	the average citizen: Franklin D. Roosevelt, On Our Way (New York: DeCapo Press, 1973) 24 8, 252.
95	under the United Nations: The American Heritage Pictorial History Of The Presidents Of The United States (2 vols.; New York: American Heritage Publishing Co., Inc., 19 68), 2:787
96	he said in 1932: Burns, Roosevelt, The Lion supra p .93, 475.
96	Herbert Spencer's Social Statics: See Lochner v. New York, 98 U.S. 45 1905)
98	only be called liberalism: Wills, Nixon Agonistes, supra p. 31, ix.
98	first two years in office: Burns, Roosevelt, The Lion, supra p. 93, 238.
98	**in general circulation:** Lionel Trilling, The Liberal Imagination: Essays on Literature and Society (New York: Doubleday & Company, Inc., 1957), vii.
99	variousness and possibility: ibid, viii, xl, xl.
99	shared sense of community: See Alasdair MacIntyre, After Virtue: a study in moral theory (Notre Dame, Indiana: University of Notre Dame Press, 1981).
100	by office ideology: Burns, Roosevelt, The Lion, supra p. 93, 28-9.
101	that is the way I feel: Frances Perkins, The Roosevelt I Knew (New York: The Viking Press, 1946), 153-4.
103	to use Machiavellian means: Burns, Roosevelt, The Lion, supra p. 93, 473-75.
104	he was on our side: Isaiah Berlin is quoted in John Major, The New Deal (London: Longmans, Green & Co., 1968); William E. Leuchtenberg, ed., Franklin D. Roosevelt: A Profile (New York: Hill & Wang, 1968), 219-220.
104	leadership principle: G. W. Johnson is quoted in Major, 182-3.
104	concentrated responsibility: Perkins, Roosevelt, , supra p.101, 156.
106	regimentation of men: See: Herbert Hoover, The Memoirs of Herbert
106	Hoover: The Great Depression 1929-1941 (New York: The Macmillan Company, 1952), 336-42.
106	generations of inheritance: Ibid, 340.
107	beyond 'minist' ring reason.': Keats, Poems, ed. Carlos Baker (New York: Bantam Books, 1962), 30.
108	as interpreted by Endicott Peabody: See James McGregor Burns, Roosevelt: The Lion and the Fox (New York: Harcourt Brace, 1956), 475.
108	instincts and passions: A. J. Schlesinger, Jr., The Politics of Upheaval (Boston: Houghton Mifflin, 1960), 385-6.
108	coruscations of the souls: See D. H. Lawrence, Preface to "Maestrodon Gescualdo," Verga, in Phoenix (Hammonsworth, Middlesex, England and New York: Penguin, 1978), 227,
109	on the skin of things: Comment, according, by the Nation's Washington correspondent. Burns, Roosevelt, The Lion, supra p. 93,243.
109	on any permanent basis: Quoting in Perkins, Roosevelt, supra p. 101, 252-3.

THE LEGAL MIND AND THE PRESIDENCY

110   done under the Constitution: Perkins, Roosevelt, ibid., 330.

111   quite aware of the distinction: Burns, Roosevelt, The Soldier of Freedom (New York: Harcourt Brace Jovanovich, Inc., 1960) 213-17.

111   any new problem of democracy: Attributed to FDR by Rosenman, in Samuel Irving Rosenman, Working With Roosevelt (New York: Harper & Brothers, 1952), 144.

111   into a lawyer's contract: Franklin D. Roosevelt, The Public Papers and Addresses of Franklin D. Roosevelt,. 13 vols. (New York: The Macmillan Company, 1938-50), 6:362-3.

111   is the Supreme Court: Hoover, Memoirs, supra p. 106, 332.

PART THREE—
LAWYER FORMALISM IN THE PRESIDENCY

11

A Birdseye View of Lawyer Formalist Presidents

115   vested in him: Gallatin, Albert. The Writings of Albert Gallatin, Henry Adams, ed., Philadelphia: J .B. Lippincott & Co., 1879, V.II, 291 (Gallatin to Walter Lowrie, 5/22/1824).

115   to the formalists: Consider, for example, the following views from the 'dough faces': "Next in importance to the maintenance of the Constitution and the Union is the duty of preserving the Government from the taint or even the suspicion of corruption. Public virtue is the vital spirit of republics ..." James Buchanan, in a Compilation of the Messages and Papers of the Presidents, ed. James D. Richardson, 11 vols (New York: Bureau of National Literature and Art, 1908, c1897), Inaugural Address, 3/14/1857, 5:433. "I acknowledge my obligations to the masses of my countrymen, and to them alone... They require at my hands diligence, integrity, and capacity wherever there are duties to be performed. Without these qualities in their public servants, more stringent laws for the prevention or punishment of fraud, negligence, and peculation will be vain." Franklin Pierce, Messages, ed. Richardson, ibid.,Inaugural Address, 3/4/1858, 5:201. "It shall be my effort to elevate the standard of official employment by selecting for places of importance individuals fitted for the posts to which they are assigned by their known integrity, talents, and virtues ... neglect of duty or malfeasance in office will be no more tolerated in individuals appointed by myself than in those appointed by others." Millard Fillmore, Messages, ed. Richardson, ibid. First Annual Message, 2 /2/ 1850, 5:80. .

116   long be maintained: Tocqueville, supra n. 66, 1:286. Consider, for example, John Quincy Adam's comment that "Madison moderated

some of his (Jefferson's) excesses, and refrained from following others. He was in truth a greater and a far more estimable man." John Quincy Adams, Memoirs, supra p.14, 9:306.

12

Founding Fathers: James Madison and James Monroe

119   point of stupidity: Samuel Eliot Morison, Henry Steele Commager and William E. Leuchtenburg, The Growth of the American Republic. 2 vols. 6th ed. New York: Oxford University Press, 1969, 2:104.

120   the same results: Gaillard Hunt, ed. The First Forty Years of Washington Society: Portrayed by the Family Letters of Mrs. Samuel Harrison Smith from the Collection of her grandson J. Henley Smith, ed. Gaillard Hunt (New York: Charles Scribner's Sons, 1906), 299-300 (letter of Mrs. Samuel Harrison Smith (Margaret Bayard) to J. Henley Smith, 3/12/1819).

121   hastily given: James Madison, The Writings of James Madison, ed., Guillard Hunt. 9 vols (New York & London: G. P. Putnam's Sons, l906), 8: 404-5 letter to Monroe of 12/27/18l7).

122   into civil war: Irving Brant, The Fourth President: A Life of James Madison (New York: Bobbs-Merrill, l970), 644-45.

122   when the storm arises: Cf. comments about other formalists: of Cleveland, in Horace Samuel Merrill, Bourbon Leader: Grover Cleveland and the Democratic Party (Boston: Little Brown & Co., l957), 765: "he would display the utmost caution in making up his mind. But once he reached a conclusion, no force could compel him to quit it." of Benjamin Harrison, in Harry J. Sievers , Hoosier Statesman (New York: Bobbs Merrill, l959), 63: "his temperament became more and more judicial. When he reached a conclusion after thoroughly examining a question, it was generally irrevocable." ...and of McKinley, in H. Wayne Morgan, William McKinley and His America (Syracuse, N.Y.: Syracuse University Press, 1963), 319: "Once decisions were made, he seldom reflected on them; he did not rehash what might have been. \His basic problem was making up his mind, and he often moved with maddening slowness, his ingrained caution impeding his way. Once his course was clear, however, he was inflexible."

122   so unerring: John C. Calhoun, The Papers of John C. Calhoun, ed. Robert Meriwether and others.15 vol (Columbia, S. C.: University of South Carolina Press, l959-l983), 11:453 (letter to S. L. Gouverneur dated 8/8/l831).

13

The Little Magician: Martin Van Buren

123   direction in every action:. James D. Richardson, ed. Messages, Presidents, , supra p. 115, 3:319.` (Van Buren, Inaugural Address, 3/4/1837), 3:319. cf. this constitutional grounding of 'rugged individualism' with the moral philosophical base exemplified by Hoover in supra pp. 105-6.

124   general prosperity: Messages, ed. Richardson, ibid, 3:344-5 (Van Buren, Special Session Message).

124   where it exists: Richardson, Messages, Presidents, ibid, 3:318 (Van Buren, Inaugural Address, 4/1837).

124   constitutional restraints: Van Buren, Autobiography, supra p. 80, 315.

124   will of the people: Holmes M. Alexander, The American Talleyrand (New York: Harper & Brothers, 1935), 229.

125   or self-interest: Van Buren, Autobiography, supra p. 80, 253, material resources,

125   the consequences: Holmes M. Alexander, The American Talleyrand, supra p. 124, 342.

14

The Dough-Faces: Fillmore, Pierce, Buchanan

127   in yourself: Buchanan and Pierce had personal tragedies as well. With the death of his fiancée, Buchanan remained a bachelor the rest of his life. Pierce's twelve-year-old son died in an accident on the train taking Pierce to his presidency.

128   whole family of man: Staughton Lynd, Intellectual Origins of American Radicalism New York: Vintage Books, 1968), vi, 3-156. (New ed. Cambridge; New York: Cambridge University Press, 2009).

128   nullify its commands: Richardson, ed. Messages, Presidents, supra, p. 115, (Second Annual Message, Millard Fillmore, 12/2/18510), Vol.5).

129   our action to it: ibid, (Inaugural Address, Franklin Pierce, 3/4/1853), Vol.5.

129   indeed be hopeless: James Buchanan, The Works of James Buchanan, ed. John Bassett Moore, 12 vols. (Philadelphia & London: J.B. Lippincott Company, 1911), 12:25.

ALBERT LEBOWITZ

129   so called Higher Law: Richardson, ed., Messages, Presidents, supra p. 115 (Inaugural Address, Franklin Pierce, 3/4/1853), Vol. 5.

129   over the edge: Don E. Fehrenbacher, The Dred Scott Case: Its Significance n American Law & Politics (New York: Oxford University Press, 1978), 118.

129   other doughfaces: During the pre-Civil War period the expression 'the doughfaces', defined disparagingly as Northern politicians with Southern sympathies, was applied collectively to Fillmore, Pierce and Buchanan.

130   requirement of the Constitution: Richardson, ed Messages, Presidents, supra p. 115, 1, Presidents (Second Annual Message, Millard Fillmore, 12/2/1851), Vol.5. Govt. Print. Off, 1896-1899), First Annual Message, Millard Fillmore,12/2/1850),Vol.5.

130   `of the United States: Each president recites the following oath, in accordance with Article II, Section 1 of the U.S. Constitution: "I do solemnly swear (or affirm) that I will faithfully execute the office of President of the United States and will to the best of my ability, preserve, protect and defend the Constitution of the United States."

131   darkness and light: Van Wyck Brooks, The Flowering of New England (New York: E. P. Dutton Co., 1936), 393-4.

15

The Golden Age: Hayes, Arthur, Cleveland, B. Harrison, McKinley

132   ill-advised action: Kenneth E. Davison, The Presidency of Rutherford B. Hayes (Westport, Conn.: Greenwood Press, Inc. 1972), xvi-xvii.

132   final decision: George Frederick Howe, Chester A. Arthur, A Quarter Century of Machine Politics (New York: Dodd Mead & Company, 1934), 173.

132   him to quit it: Merrill, Cleveland, supra p. 122, 765.

133   to make up their minds: B. Harrison): Harry J. Sievers, Benjamin Harrison, 3 vols (Chicago: H. Regnery Co., 1952), 2:63, 3:4).

133   he was inflexible: Morgan, McKinley, supra p. _122, 319.

133   process of education: Harry Barnard, Rutherford B. Hayes and his America (New York: Bobbs-Merrill Company, 1954), 409.

133   civil war: Roy F. Nichols, Franklin Pierce: Young Hickory of the Granite Hills (Philadelphia: University of Pennsylvania Press, 1958), 522.

133   healer of strife: Barnard, Hayes, supra p. 133, 432.

133   reform as President: Howe, Arthur, supra p. 132, 205.

134   within the law: For a summary of the rise of unionism, see: Samuel Eliot Morison, The Oxford History of the American People, 3 vols. (New York: New American Library, 1972), 3:80ff. 1966), 4.

THE LEGAL MIND AND THE PRESIDENCY

16

The Golden Age's MVP: Grover Cleveland

135 to do wrong: Allan Nevins, Grover Cleveland: A Study in Courage (New York: Dodd Mead & Co., 1966), 4.

136 he floundered: Nichols, Pierce, supra p. 133, 382.

137 attorney general: Nevins, Cleveland, supra p. 135, 627.

137 constant fire: Samuel Eliot Morison, Henry Steele Commager, and William E., Leuchtenburg, The Growth the American Republic, 2 vols, 6th ed. (New York: Oxford University Press, 1969), 3:113.

137 common sense and integrity Merrill, Cleveland, supra p. 122, 70.

17

Twentieth Century Formalists: Taft, Coolidge, Ford

139 mawkishness: Spring Rice, Sir Cecil. The Letters and Friendships of Sir Cecil Spring Rice: a Record, Stephen Gwynn, ed. 2 vols (London: Constable & Co. Ltd, 1929), 1:443-4.

140 not stop it: Roosevelt to Marcus Alonzo Hanna, 5 October 1903, The Letters of Theodore Roosevelt, ed. Elting E. Morison. 8 vols (Cambridge, Mass.: Harvard University Press, 1951), 3:625.

140 actually done: ibid., T. Roosevelt to Frederick Wollingford Whitridge, 28 May 1904, 4:808.

140 inheritance of centuries: Donald F. Anderson, William Howard Taft (Ithaca, N.Y.: Cornell University Press, 1968), ft note 104, Ch. 6, ft note 194: Taft's Acceptance Speech, 8/1/1912.

141 true of Taft: Anderson, Taft, ibid, 229.

141 and 'fathead': Paolo E. Coletta, The Presidency of William Howard Taft (Lawrence, Kan., University Press of Kansas, 1973), 233.

141 presidential terms: ibid, 233, citing "President Taft's Denunciation of Mr. Roosevelt," Literary Digest, 44 (May 4, 1912), 922-33.

141 prior to acting: Coletta, Taft supra p. 141, 259, 263.

141 and did nothing: Coletta, Taft ibid, 262.

141 with only one of them: McCoy, Coolidge: supra p. 42, 193.

142 character of the American people: Congressional Record, Vol. 67, Part 4, 4373 (February 23, 1926).

142 the highest ideal: McCoy, Coolidge: supra p. 42, 294.

142 long meditation: See: Claude M. Fuess, Calvin Coolidge: The Man From Vermont (Boston: Little Brown & Co., 1940), 386, 395.

142 interpretation of it: See: McCoy, Coolidge: supra p .42, 177 .to maintain progress: See: Fuess, Coolidge, supra p. 142, 98.

144	expected to do so: John J. Casserly, The Ford White House: The Diary of a Speechwriter (Boulder, Colorado: Colorado Associated University Press, 1977), 81 (Casserly's diary comment of April 25, 1975)
144	calculated, blindness: ibid, 236-7.
144	and falsehoods: Richard Reeves, A Ford, not a Lincoln (New York: Harcourt, Brace, Jovanovich, 1975), pp.12, 52.
144	Harry S. Truman: Clark R. Mollenhoff, The Man Who Pardoned Nixon (New York: St. Martin's Press, 1976), 1, 5.
145	in this presidential chair: Reeves, Ford, ibid, 25.
145	White House fishbowl: Reeves, Ford, ibid., 42
146	a determination: Mollenhoff, supra p. 144, 112ff..
146	William Hungate: William Hungate, a Missouri Congressman, developed a considerable reputation as a wit during the impeachment hearings conducted by the House Judiciary Committee.
146	to lay it out: Gerald R. Ford, A Time to Heal: The Autobiography of Gerald R. Ford (New York: Harper & Row, 1979), 197.
146	no circumstances: Mollenhoff), supra p. 144, 112ff.
146	is admitted: Ford, Autobiography, supra p. 14, 3ff.

Anti-Intellectualism and the Popular Distaste For Lawyers

147	in the community: James Willard Hurst, The Growth of American Law (Boston, Little, Brown and Company, 1950), 251-252
149	impervious to mere facts: See Alan Ryan, "Give 'em Hell, Barry"(New Statesman Ltd, Dec 19, 2011), Vol. 140 issue 5084/5085, 40-45.
149	and never will: Reported in Perry Miller, The Life of the Mind in America (Harcourt, Brace & World, 1965), 106.
150	to study law: Reported in Anton-Herman Chroust, The Rise of the Legal Profession in America, 2 vols (Norman, University of Oklahoma Press (1965), 2:100.
150	on the streets: ibid, 2:26.
151	the law obligatory: Thomas Jefferson, Works, supra p.24, 9:73-4 (Letter to Edmund Randolph, 8/18/1799); Gerald R. Ford, A Time To Heal: The Autobiography of Gerald R. Ford (New York: Harper & Row, 1979), 99.
151	the twenty-first: See: Roscoe Pound, The Formative Era of American Law (Boston: Little, Brown, 1938),104-5; Arthur E. Sutherland, The Law at Harvard: A History of Ideas and Man (Cambridge: Harvard University Press, 1967), 176.
152	of a code: Roscoe Pound, "Codification in Anglo-American Law," in Bernard Schwartz, ed., The Code Napoleon and the Common Law World (New York: New York University Press, 1956), 283.
152	practical wisdom: vol. 9, 1141a, 1141b (Aristotle, Ethica Nicomachea), Book VII, Ch.7.

THE LEGAL MIND AND THE PRESIDENCY

19

The Ivy Leaguers: Bill Clinton and Barack Obama

20

The Comeback Kid

157   to have a better one: Clinton quoted by Joe Sudbay, Americablog, 4/25/3008.

158   self-protective impulse: Loren Lomasky. "Piling on the Prez" (Reason, Dec.98, Vol. 30, Issue 7), 76).

158   for their clients: Richard A. Matasar, "The Pain of Moral Lawyering" (The Florida Bar Journal, June, 1997, Volume LI, No.6)

1

Of Birth and Death

159   to get me: Bill Clinton, My Life (Alfred A. Knopf: New York, 2004),19.

160   either of us, ibid, 20.2

160   into my scalp: ibid, 22

160   recovered soon enough: ibid, 24

161   hurting someone else: ibid, 45-6.

161   binge drinking: ibid, 20.

162   to a remarriage: ibid, 52.

162   psychological vulnerabilities: ibid, 51.

162   last bad outburst: ibid, 79.

163   quite a guy: ibid, 105.

II

The Economy Stupid

165   in a generation: Bill Clinton, 2000 State of Union Address, Jan. 27, 2000.

165   and disorganized: Economist, "Not So Fast, Newt,"Jan.28, 2012.

165   too eager to compromise: Bill Clinton, Life, supra p.159, 682.

III

Foreign Affairs

167   like Somalia and Bosnia: Kenneth T. Walsh an d Gloria Borger, "The Unmaking of Foreign Policy"(U.S. News and World Report, 10/18/1993, Vol. 115, issue 15), 30.

167   of all the parties: Bill Clinton, My Life (supra p.159, 604-09.

168   for six hundred years: Bill Clinton, My Life, ibid, 848-9

168   able to go home: Bill Clinton, My Life, ibid, pp.850-1.

168   the right decision: Edward Gaffney, Jr., "Clinton's Green Thumb" (Commonweal, 5/5/1995, Vol. 122 issue 9).

19

The Spirit of 1787

I

The Year is 1787

170   practice among themselves: reported in Debates in the Federal Convention of 1787 by James Madison, June 5.

179   something else that's funny: reported in Wikipedia sing us 'Picayune Butler', ref. Harp Week/Elections/1864002E.

II

The Year Is 2012

176   checks and balances: The American Heritage Pictorial History of the Presidents of the United States, 1968, Vol.1, 137.

177   for its own sake: John Bolton, "The Innocents Abroad," From the September 19, 2011 issue of New Republic.

177   difficult things of them: Shelby Steele, "Obama and the Burden of Exceptionalism " Wall Street Journal, September 1, 2011). Opinion.

178   blood, sweat and tears: by National Review editors, "Obama Flinches," (National Review, June 23, 2011)

178   as Jimmy Carter's was: James Taranto, "After Obama" (American Spectator, Oct. 2011 issue).

178   message of confrontation: Drew Westen, "What Happened To Obama? (New York Times, Sunday, Aug. 7, 2011).

THE LEGAL MIND AND THE PRESIDENCY

178   liberal leaning critics: Romano and Kurtz, "From Wimp to Winner," (Newsweek, 4/25/2011), vol.157, issue 17, pp 6-7.

178   anything in particular: Paul Krugman, reported in Romano and Kurtz, "From Wimp to Winner," supra p. 178.

178   on the ropes: Eric Alterman, reported in Romano and Kurtz, "From Wimp to Winner," supra p. 178.

179   powerless president: Jonathan Chait, reported in Romano and Kurtz, "From Wimp to Winner," supra p. 178.

179   help him get re-elected; Romano and Kurtz, "From Wimp to Winner," supra p. 178.

179   solvency of the republic: Charles M. Blow, "Rise of the Fallen?" (New York Times, September 9, 2011, Opinion Pages).

179   back to basics: Thomas L. Friedman, Obama, "Tiger, Golf and Politics" (New York Times, 8/23/2011), Opinion Pages.

179   G.O.P. opposition: Paul Krugman, "Setting their Hair on Fire" (New York Times, The Opinion Pages, Sept.8, 2011).

180   Abbottabad, Pakistan: James M. Lindsay, "George W. Bush, Barack Obama and the future of US global leadership," (International Affairs July 2011, Vol. 87, issue 4, 765-779).

181   to trumpet your victory: "Behind the Curtain," David Remnick, New Yorker, 0/5/2011, Vol. 87 Issue 26, 19-20.

181   scandal to his name: Andrew Sullivan, "How Obama's Long Game Will Outsmart His Critics," (Daily Beast/Newsweek, Jan. 15, 2012).

CPSIA information can be obtained
at www.ICGtesting.com
Printed in the USA
LVOW04s0212041016
507303LV00012B/265/P